"Clark tells his story with a modesty that becomes him and a brisk straightforwardness that does nothing to dim the excitement and danger—and with a sincere admiration for South Koreans that ran counter to the usual American attitude." —*Chicago Sun-Times*

"A solid work of military history by an authentic hero who illuminates the opening days of a now little-remembered conflict."
—*Kirkus Reviews*

"An authentic American hero—Commander Eugene Franklin Clark, USN—jumps out from the pages of this riveting Korean War memoir. . . . *The Secrets of Inchon* is the story of a fearless intelligence officer whose covert activities paved the way for General MacArthur's celebrated amphibious invasion. An instant American classic."
—Douglas Brinkley, director,
Eisenhower Center for American Studies at the University of New Orleans,
and the author of *The Unfinished Presidency*

"A modern classic of military history, an astonishing first-person account that fairly crackles with drama. As we have seen so recently, heroism can come at any time—but who even suspected that *this* Korean War hero could write so well."
—W.E.B. Griffin,
New York Times bestselling author of *Under Fire*

"The story of one of the most daring and important missions of the Korean War—a compelling tale of adventure, courage, and devotion to duty."
—Colonel Harry Maihafer (Ret.), West Point '49,
author of *From Hudson to the Yalu* and coauthor of *The Korean War*

continued . . .

"Eugene Clark's true story of his commando mission behind enemy lines reminds us that the essential verities of war never change. Written in 1951–1952, but never before published, his timely story is a classic first-person account of heroism, resolve, and ultimate triumph that will touch every American."

—Stephen Coonts,
New York Times bestselling author of *America*

"An amazing story. Had Clark and his handful of brave Korean men and women volunteers failed in this nearly impossible intelligence-gathering mission, it would have cost the lives of thousands of Marines and sailors. *The Secrets of Inchon* has it all—point-black firefights in the darkness on land and sea, spies and counterspies, and above all, an important tale of resourcefulness, daring, and valor."

—Charles Bracelen Flood,
author of *More Lives Than One*

THE SECRETS OF
INCHON

· · · ·

THE UNTOLD STORY
OF THE MOST DARING
COVERT MISSION
OF THE KOREAN WAR

COMMANDER
EUGENE FRANKLIN CLARK, USN

INTRODUCTION AND EPILOGUE BY
THOMAS FLEMING

BERKLEY BOOKS
NEW YORK

A Berkley Book
Published by The Berkley Publishing Group
A division of Penguin Group (USA) Inc.
375 Hudson Street
New York, New York 10014

PRINTING HISTORY
G. P. Putnam's Sons hardcover edition / May 2002
Berkley trade paperback edition / May 2003

Berkley trade paperback ISBN: 0-425-19000-5

The Library of Congress has catalogued the G. P. Putnam's Sons
hardcover edition as follows:

Clark, Eugene Franklin.
The secrets of Inchon : the untold story
of the most daring covert mission of the Korean War /
Eugene Franklin Clark; introduction and epilogue by Thomas Fleming.
p.   cm.
ISBN 0-399-14871-X
1. Clark, Eugene Franklin.   2. Korean War, 1950–1953—Personal narratives, American.
3. Korean War, 1950–1953—Campaigns—Korea (South)—Inchon.   4. Korean War,
1950–1953—Reconnaissance operations, American.
DS921.6.C55   2002   2001059181
951.904'242'092—dc21

CONTENTS

NORTH KOREA

Sea of Japan
(East Sea)

Uijongbu

Chunchon

Kangnung

Kuri

Seoul

Ullung-do

Inchon

Anyang

Wonju

Suwon

Chechon

Chungju

TAEBAEK-SANMAEK

Chonan

Chongju

Yellow Sea

Songnam

Andong-si

Kum R.

Taejon

Kimchon

Pohang

Kunsan

Iri

Kumi

Taegu

Chonju

Naktong R.

Kyongju

SOUTH KOREA

Kochang

Ulsan

Ansan

Namwon

Chinjae

Kwangju

Chinju

Masan

Pusan

Sunchon

Mokpo

Yosu

*Tsushima
(Japan)*

Haenam

N

0 *Miles*   100

0 *Kilometers*   100

Cheju Strait

Korea Strait

JAPAN

Cheju

Cheju

▲ *Halla-san*

© 2001 Jeffrey L. Ward

Han R.

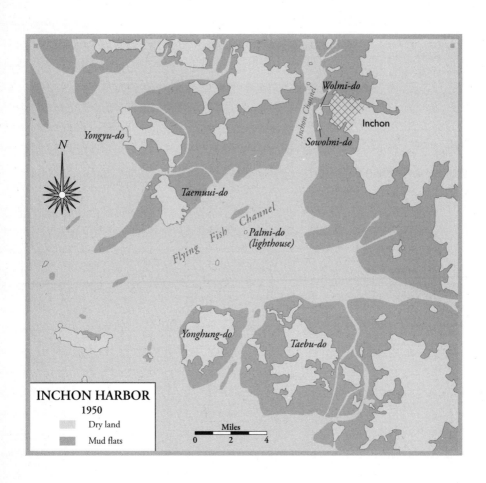

N

Yongyu-do

Taemuui-do

Inchon Channel

Wolmi-do

Inchon

Sowolmi-do

Flying Fish Channel

○ *Palmi-do*
(lighthouse)

Yonghung-do

Taebu-do

INCHON HARBOR
1950

Dry land

Mud flats

Miles

0   2   4

INTRODUCTION

YOU ARE ABOUT to meet Eugene Franklin Clark, one of the forgotten American heroes of the twentieth century. His courage was the linchpin of the first and possibly the most crucial victory won by American fighting men against the military power of Communism—the defeat of North Korea's attempt to conquer South Korea in 1950.

For two weeks, Clark and his two Korean lieutenants survived on Yonghung-do, an island within a dozen miles of Communist-held Inchon, while they gathered the information that enabled General Douglas MacArthur to stage an amphibious flank attack that demolished the stunned North Korean army. Operating on as little as two hours' sleep a day, they fought off Communist assaults by land and sea, captured enemy harbor craft, and interrogated captives who confirmed MacArthur's intuition that the North Korean high command did not suspect Inchon would be targeted. They even obtained exact information on the size of the city's garrison. Simultaneously they ventured into the heart of the city's harbor under cover of darkness to measure the height of the forbidding seawalls, determine whether troops and vehicles could advance across the ubiquitous mudflats at low tide, and pinpoint the dozens of machine-gun nests and artillery emplacements on the fortress island of Wolmi-do, at the mouth of the harbor. Without this crucial information, thousands of Americans might have died storming that heavily fortified bastion. Finally, on the climactic night of the invasion, Clark turned on the lamp in the lighthouse on the nearby island of Palmi-do to guide the United Nations armada up the narrow channel to Inchon.

Gene Clark's courage is equaled only by his modesty. He wrote this story because he felt his Korean comrades who shared the harrowing risks deserved to be remembered. He also thought it was something his wife, Enid, and his children, Genine and Roger, would enjoy reading. But he never made the slightest attempt to publish it during his lifetime.

Only when I published an account of Clark's exploits in *MHQ: The Quarterly Journal of Military History* in the summer of 2000 did the Clark family remember the narrative he had written not long after he returned from Korea in 1951. It had been lying in a safe-deposit box for decades, along with a Department of Defense clearance to tell the story as he had experienced it. They sent the manuscript to me, and I immediately recognized its importance. I believe it will become one of the classic first-person narratives of American military history.

What makes Gene Clark's story so compelling is not only the resolution, leadership, and resilience he displayed for two weeks within heart-stopping reach of one of the most murderous Communist regimes of the twentieth century. He is more than a magnificent man of action; he is a thinker who understood what was at stake in this clash between freedom and totalitarianism. He is also profoundly human, shaken more than once by doubts about his adequacy for the awesome task confronting him.

Finally, Gene Clark's story is a deeply moving account of an American discovering a sense of brotherhood with brave men and women of a different race and culture who were also ready to fight and if necessary die for freedom. I am proud to play a part in bringing this extraordinary narrative to the wide audience it deserves.

—THOMAS FLEMING

I

GROUNDWORK

1

PRELUDE TO
THE RUMBLE

ON AUGUST 26, 1950, I was summoned to the office of Captain Edward Pearce, USN, in the Dai Ichi Insurance Building in downtown Tokyo, overlooking Emperor Hirohito's imperial palace. For the past year, I had been serving under Captain Pearce on General Douglas MacArthur's staff.

"Gene," Eddie Pearce said in his gruff deadpan way, "I believe we've cooked up a little rumble you're going to like."

The twinkle in Pearce's gray eyes intrigued me. So did the eager expectation on the face of the other man in Pearce's office, Major General Holmes E. Dager. He had been one of General George S. Patton's tank commanders during World War II. Between them, these two guys had seen a lot of bullets and shells fly in that global struggle. Now a new war had exploded in Korea. I sensed they were about to invite me to sample some excitement in this fracas.

I said nothing, while Eddie Pearce shifted in his chair and leaned toward me. "We're going to make an amphibious landing at Inchon on 15 September, and General MacArthur says it's essential we obtain more timely and accurate information on everything in and around the place—at once."

"How would you like to try to get us that information?" General Dager asked.

On June 24, 1950, Communist North Korea had invaded South Korea with fourteen well-trained divisions. They quickly captured the capital, Seoul, and smashed the lightly armed Republic of Korea army with a lavish use of artillery and tanks. President Harry S. Truman had ordered General MacArthur to send American soldiers to resist this act of naked aggression.

The green GIs, mostly draftees in combat for the first time, had been driven back to a precarious perimeter around the port of Pusan, on the southern tip of the Korean peninsula. They were clinging to this enclave, under ferocious North Korean attack. Many people in General Headquarters thought it was only a matter of time before we faced an American Dunkerque. In Washington, D.C., shudders ran through the White House at the possibility that if the North Koreans succeeded in spreading Communism at the point of a gun, the Russians might try something similar in Europe. There was also a very visible threat to Japan, where President Truman had done his utmost to exclude Communist influence. The tip of Korea was only about ninety miles from Kyushu, Japan's southernmost island.

I was devoted to Captain Pearce. The white-haired Annapolis man had accepted me without the slightest hint of the condescension often displayed by some naval academy graduates toward "mustangs"—officers appointed from the enlisted ranks during World War II. That was how I had won my commission. A yeoman, I had risen from seaman to chief petty officer—the highest rank an enlisted man can achieve. But I disliked captaining what I sometimes called an "LMD"—a Large Mahogany Desk—and applied for a commission to get myself into the war zone.

I was not completely surprised by Eddie Pearce's proposition. Since the war in Korea began, I had been working in the Geographic Branch of General MacArthur's staff, gathering information about tides, terrain, and landing facilities at various ports along both coasts of South Korea. I had participated in amphibious operations during World War II, notably on Okinawa, the last big battle of the Pacific war, and knew what was needed to make a successful landing on an enemy-held shore. I and other members of my research team had scoured every possible source, from old Japanese studies to aerial photography taken during World War II—and had come up with very little that was reliable about either Korean coast. Major General Charles Willoughby, MacArthur's intelligence chief, had expressed grave dissatisfaction with our reports.

My experience as an amphibian also enabled me to grasp why a landing at Inchon required absolutely reliable information. The port was on Korea's west coast, 180 miles north of the Pusan perimeter. If anything went wrong at Inchon, the American attackers would be in serious danger of being flung back into the sea with horrendous casualties. The fighting men around Pusan were too far away to give them any support. From my preliminary research, I already knew that the approach to Inchon was complicated by tides that rose and fell twenty-nine feet in a twenty-four-hour period—leaving miles of mudflats, some extending six thousand yards from the shoreline at low water.

"I know we've gone to the limit in researching this matter," I said. "So I take it that a little personal look-see trip is in order. Is that correct, Captain?"

"That's right, Gene," Pearce said. "It's going to require a reconnaissance of the Inchon area by someone qualified to observe and transmit back to Tokyo the information we currently lack. I believe you're the man for the job."

"I'd certainly like to take a crack at it," I said—simultaneously trying to visualize what this rumble might involve. I had an uneasy feeling it was not going to be a pleasure trip. At thirty-nine, I was getting a little old for the commando game. But I preferred excitement to desk work. I had had a pretty good taste of action on Okinawa and nearby islands, dealing with Japanese troops who were inclined to stage a final banzai charge rather than surrender. After the war, I had enjoyed some highly clandestine operations along the China coast, trying to help the Nationalist Chinese in their losing struggle with the Communists.

"I told General Willoughby you'd be ready to tackle the job," Captain Pearce said, visibly pleased. "You will report to General Dager until the completion of this mission, as of now."

"Aye aye, sir!" I said.

In the elevator, General Dager told me to get him a list of what I would need for the expedition by the following morning. With it should be a target date for my departure to the vicinity of Inchon.

Back in my office, I sat down at my desk and lit my pipe. Below me spread the peaceful, exquisitely beautiful grounds of the Japanese imperial palace. It was hard to believe that men were fighting and dying around Pusan while I gazed down at this oasis of serenity. Struggling to concentrate, I called in my secretary, Florence Truitt, and told her to start pulling information from the files about Communist strength around Inchon. I began gathering data about the people on the islands neighboring the port. One of these islands would be the most likely place for me to set up this operation.

After an hour or two of note-taking and listing what I needed in the way of food, guns, and ammunition, I became dismayed at the length of the dossier I was compiling and decided to go home to think the whole thing over for twenty-four hours.

In our house on the outskirts of Tokyo, I found my wife, Enid, my daughter, Genine, twelve, and my son, Roger, nine, waiting to join me for dinner. With a pang, I realized I could not tell Enid where I was going. All I could say was that the U.S. Navy had done it again, they were shipping me to northern Japan on another confidential assignment. I loved Enid deeply. We had met in high school and married so quickly, I decided not to bother graduating. I also regarded her as one of the most patient women alive.

After the years of separation inflicted by World War II, I had hoped we would be reunited in occupied Japan. But the Navy repeatedly interfered in this happy dream by altering my orders with no warning. At first I captained LST 865, which operated out of Yokosuka, the big naval base on Tokyo Harbor, on runs up the China coast. But I was forced to surrender this, my first ship command, to the Philippine Naval Patrol, which soon beached her on an unwelcoming shore and left her there to rust.

Next I briefly captained the attack transport USS *Errol*. But I lost this ship, too, when the Navy ordered me to Guam to serve as chief interpreter in the war crimes trials of Japan's wartime leaders. Finally I was shifted back to General MacArthur's staff in Tokyo, where we endured a waiting list for decent quarters. Even when we finally got a steam-heated house in a Tokyo suburb, I was frequently away in the north of Japan, interrogating Japanese prisoners repatriated from Communist Russia. Through it all, Enid never lost her good cheer. She was a truly wonderful wife, and I tried to let her know it now and then.

It was not easy to tell Enid a white lie about my new assignment. I made it sound like some unfinished business in the repatriation centers in the north. I told myself the fib was far better than having her toss and turn all night for the next three weeks, wondering whether her husband would come back in one piece from this jaunt into Communist-held waters.

The next morning, I kissed her and the kids goodbye and returned to Tokyo to begin putting together the men and equipment we would need for our rumble. I began with the men. I flew to Taegu, Korea, another town inside the Pusan perimeter, and recruited a bilingual Korean Navy lieutenant, Youn Joung, and a former Korean counterintelligence officer, Colonel Ke In-Ju. Both had served on General MacArthur's staff before the war broke out. I had a pretty good personal estimate of their qualifications, and they had gotten gold-plated praise from several men whose opinions I respected.

While I was in the vicinity, I decided to take a look at how the Korean "police action," as President Harry Truman called it, was being fought. I found an old army buddy I knew from Okinawa, and we jeeped to the front lines. We watched while a company of infantry got ready to assault North Koreans dug into high ground just ahead of them. American artillery was plastering the enemy with phosphorus shells, a weapon we had learned they feared and detested. The North Koreans responded with mortar shells, which began kicking up a lot of dirt on the road just behind us. My friend suggested it might be a good idea to put some distance between ourselves and this firefight, since we were armed only with pistols—and the NKPA (North Korean People's Army) had an unpleasant habit of executing prisoners of war.

At my friend's quarters, I got the lowdown on Taegu. The town was being overwhelmed by a horde of civilian refugees. I had taken a concentrated course in sanitation when I trained to become part of the military government of Okinawa, and I saw at a glance the place was ripe for outbreaks of typhus, typhoid, and the other diseases that breed in filth. Later in the day, my pal took me to an area where the Americans were trying to put young Koreans through a forced-draft course in soldiering. It was located on one of the local heights, and I could see from the elevation much of the battle line of the American perimeter. I heard the rumble of artillery to the north, where the Communists were trying to cross the Naktong River, the last natural barrier before Pusan. This infantryman's-eye view of the war underscored the importance of the Inchon landing. There was little doubt that the American situation in Korea was precarious to the point of desperation.

By this time I had learned what was happening behind the scenes at the Dai Ichi Building and in the corridors of the Pentagon in Washington, D.C. It underlined the word *desperation* in my mind and put a few question marks after it. General MacArthur's decision to invade Inchon was a daring gamble in a half dozen ways. He was withdrawing badly needed troops such as the Marine brigade from the Pusan perimeter and combining them with reinforcements arriving from the United States and Europe. This strike force was supposed to drive inland from Inchon to seize South Korea's capital, Seoul, and sever the North Korean army's supply lines.

It was brilliant strategy—but the devil was in the hairy tactical details of this risky venture, code-named CHROMITE. General J. Lawton Collins, the U.S. Army's chief of staff, and Admiral Forrest Sherman, the Chief of Naval Operations, had flown to Tokyo to talk MacArthur out of it. At an historic briefing session in the Dai Ichi Building, Navy and Army planners had been more than a little pessimistic about attacking Inchon. At the end of the session, after scarcely a voice had been raised in favor of the proposal, Rear Admiral James H. Doyle, the man in command of the amphibious side of the operation, said: "General, I have not been asked nor have I volunteered my opinion about this landing. If I were asked, however, the best I can say is Inchon is not impossible."

Through this negative barrage, MacArthur sat in silence, puffing on his pipe. After the last man had spoken, the general remained silent for another full minute. Then he rose and gave a speech that for sheer eloquence has probably never been equaled in American military annals. He told the assembled admirals and generals that the very arguments they had used against Inchon were the prime reason why he wanted to execute CHROMITE. If the Americans thought it was close to impossible, so did the North Koreans, and that gave us the key element in any attack, large or small—surprise.

MacArthur ended with a peroration that was soon echoing through the Dai Ichi Building. He said the prestige of the Western world was hanging in the balance in Korea. The Orient's millions were watching the outcome. Communism had elected to launch its march to global domination here in Asia. In Europe, we were able to fight Communism with words. Here, we had no choice but to do it with deeds. Inchon was a deed that would resound throughout the civilized world—and save 100,000 American lives.

General Collins was reduced to surly silence and Admiral Sherman became a believer. They flew back to Washington, D.C., where, with great reluctance, the Joint Chiefs of Staff gave Inchon their approval. To cover their rears, they asked President Truman to give his explicit permission for the operation. The ex-artilleryman from World War I said it was a plan worthy of a great captain and gave us the green light.

Back in Tokyo from my flying trip to Korea, I told Captain Pearce we were almost ready to shove off. He handed me secret orders that introduced me to Rear Admiral Sir William Andrewes of the Royal Navy, who was in command of the naval forces blockading the west coast of Korea. Soon my two Korean lieutenants and I were in Sasebo, a port on the East China Sea in Kyushu. There Admiral Andrewes presided aboard his flagship, HMS *Ladybird*.

Before I presented my orders to the admiral, I had a final, extremely important chore to perform. I had to turn my list of weapons and supplies into reality. I had waited until the brink of departure because I had learned an old shipmate, Lieutenant Commander Russell Q. "Shorty" June, was the executive officer of the Sasebo Naval Base. I thought I had a better chance of getting everything I wanted from Shorty. Was I ever right. Laying my requirements before him, I explained that my mission was secret in nature—and urgent. Without another word, he grabbed the phone and called his supply officer, directing him to give me everything I asked for and if he didn't have it to get it from the local Army outfit.

Having placed this wheel in motion, I hopped over to the BOQ (Bachelor Officers' Quarters), took a quick shave, and called in Youn and Ke for a conference. I asked them to put their heads together and come up with an answer to how much native (Korean) food we should bring and whatever other items of gear they thought we might need. They told me rice and dried fish should be at the top of such a list—especially rice. The Reds were requisitioning every available grain of rice in South Korea to feed their invasion army. From there I headed for Admiral Andrewes's flagship, tied up alongside the wharf.

I had had the privilege of meeting Sir William and his chief of staff, Captain James, at a dinner party aboard his then flagship, HMS *Belfast*, at Yokusaka the previous May. It was at that party Enid was first introduced to the British sleeper, pink gin. In consequence, my reception by Sir William and Captain James was somewhat more than cordial. After I had broken out my secret orders and they had been thoroughly digested, the admiral queried Captain James about available transportation.

"The *Charity* is due to sail for the west coast of Korea day after tomorrow," Captain James replied.

"Will that suit your plans, Lieutenant?"

"I had planned on arriving in the Inchon area not later than the first of September, Admiral," I answered. "To do this, it will be necessary to shove off from here not later than tomorrow morning."

The admiral thought this over a moment and turned to Captain James. "Can't we set *Charity* up to leave tomorrow morning? I think the ship she is to relieve will welcome her early arrival."

"I believe that can be done, sir. Suppose we send her a signal and ask her captain to come in and discuss the matter?"

"Righto! Lieutenant, could you come back in about an hour and we'll see about getting the *Charity* set up for departure tomorrow morning?"

"Of course, Admiral."

Captain James saw me to the gangway. I thought it wise to check on how the supplies and equipment were coming along. Contacting the Sasebo supply officer, I learned that his base armory was short on Thompson submachine guns and was asked if grease guns (U.S. submachine guns) would be okay. I assured him they would and that they were preferred in view of their simplicity of operation and breakdown. Unfortunately, he could not get me any Garand semiautomatic rifles, an item I thought could come in very handy. He had obtained from the Army fifty cases of World War II C-rations containing three menus. This wasn't exactly ensuring a varied diet, but our troops in the Pusan perimeter certainly weren't better off.

Shorty had hit the officers' mess for two cases of Canadian

Club—an admirable means of placing a man at ease while conducting a friendly discussion on the relative merits of Communism. On the advice of Youn and Ke, I also obtained a million won (South Korean currency—pegged at about 1,800 to the dollar) for buying information if we needed it.

Returning to HMS *Ladybird,* I was greeted warmly by the officer of the deck, who escorted me to the wardroom, where Sir William introduced me to Lieutenant Commander P. R. G. Worth, commanding HMS *Charity.* "We've been looking into your problem, Lieutenant," said Captain James. "Could you tell us about where you would like to have your party taken off at the other end?"

"I've arranged a rendezvous with the ROK PC-703 twenty miles southwest of the island of Tokchok-do at 7:00 A.M. on the first, Captain," I replied. "However, this arrangement is subject to change at discretion."

The mess boy came in with coffee, and while the admiral's operations officer and Lieutenant Commander Worth were computing speeds and distances, the admiral was interesting himself in further support for our mission. He asked Captain James to get a signal off to the cruiser HMS *Kenya,* then patrolling the Korean west coast, informing the captain in general terms of our mission and requesting he look after us. As HMS *Jamaica* was shortly to relieve *Kenya* on station, he asked that similar instructions be sent to her. All this solicitude gave me a warm feeling for our British cousins.

Having completed their calculations, Captain Worth gave me the results, which produced an even warmer feeling—a mix of fraternity and relief from anxiety. "If *Charity* gets under way at first light in the morning, Admiral, she will make the rendezvous area nicely."

"Excellent! What time would you like Lieutenant Clark's party and cargo on board?"

"Any time at all, Admiral. The sooner we get cracking, the better. I would like to have everything on board and secured as early as possible."

"I'll have the cargo alongside the *Charity* in an LCM about 11:30 P.M. tonight," I said. "The other passengers and I will come aboard not later than 6:30 A.M. We have quarters on the beach for tonight, and I can see no reason to burden the ship unnecessarily."

"Is that satisfactory, Worth?" asked the Admiral.

"Splendid, sir."

"Very well, then, that's it," the Admiral said. "Lieutenant, will you step into my cabin a moment?"

With a quick *au revoir* to the operations officer and Lieutenant Commander Worth, I followed Sir William and Captain James to the cabin. Here I found that the Admiral had not been unaware of the heat of the day. Was it bourbon, scotch, or gin? It was scotch. Soda or water? Soda, please. As we raised our glasses, I found myself wondering, not for the first time, why the United States declined to trust its responsible officers with liquor aboard our navy's ships. I ruefully remembered how many times I had tried to explain this American anachronism to officers of other nations.

Putting this unpleasant thought out of my mind, I took this opportunity to ask the admiral to forward a dispatch to General MacArthur's headquarters, to the effect that everything was going according to plan. Then, receiving their hearty best wishes for the success of the mission, I took my leave—deeply appreciative of their friendship and support.

Ashore, I learned that the Sasebo supply officer was short only a few items, which were coming over from the Army later in the evening. At the BOQ, Youn and Ke had completed their list of native items to be procured. It was getting along toward dinnertime, so we decided to do our shopping in town after dinner.

A message was awaiting me to call Shorty at his quarters, and it turned out to be an invite for dinner. I hadn't seen Helen, Shorty's wife, since our days on Guam. Over cocktails and an excellent dinner—the last I would eat for two weeks—we discussed our old relatively carefree days in the tropics.

Later, Shorty ordered a jeep for me. Picking up Youn and Ke, we went into town and finished our business about eleven o'clock. We were able to get only two hundred pounds of rice, which distressed them somewhat. By the time we returned, all the Army items were in. Loading the LCM, we had it alongside HMS *Charity* with minutes to spare before our 11:30 deadline. The stuff was promptly taken aboard and secured for sea. Back at our quarters we awaited morning—and the start of our rumble.

2

INTO RED
INCHON HARBOR

I T WAS STILL DARK when the duty watch woke us the next morning. Looking out the window, I saw that the stars were sharply etched in deep blue velvet. Navigators everywhere in this part of the world were on the bridge, breaking out their instruments. The fortunate ones with such a sky as this would fix their position on the vast ocean expanse. The less lucky would resort to their electronic equipment or, lacking such luxury, would place before their captains an "educated guess"—a dead-reckoning position.

Washing up, Youn and Ke chatted spiritedly back and forth, seemingly without a care in the world. Although they normally spoke in Korean, they could both speak excellent Japanese and Chinese, and Youn spoke good English. Dressed, we made our way down to the pier, where Shorty June had a boat waiting. We stepped down into the cockpit, and I gave the coxswain orders to make for the *Charity,* which was well out in the stream.

The bay was crowded with warships of all types, their anchor lights gently rising and falling with the slight swells. When we passed close aboard, we could make out the sounds of reveille. These huge masses of cold steel were again coming to warm pulsating life, assuming their individual characteristics—loved by those who served in them and had come to know this secret life.

His Majesty's Ship *Charity* was riding easily as we swung around her fantail. Going alongside, we climbed up the sea ladder and were met by the executive officer. The *Charity* was a destroyer—long and lean, with two raked stacks. I could feel the awakened life in her through the thin steel deck. I knew that within a matter of minutes I would hear the familiar cry of the boatswain: "Anchors aweigh!"

After the customary formalities, the executive officer led us forward to the wardroom, where a steward appeared with some steaming coffee. Shortly, Captain Worth came in. "Ah, Lieutenant, it's good to see you again. These gentlemen are in your party, I presume?"

"Yes, Captain. May I introduce Mr. Yong Chi Ho and Mr. Kim Nam Sun, on detached duty from Republic of Korea forces. Mr. Kim Nam Sun speaks no English."

We had decided it would be best if Youn and Ke used aliases, in case they were captured by the Communists. They shook hands, giving the characteristic short, stiff bow of the Korean military.

"Your equipment has been stowed amidships," said the captain. "Is all your party on board?"

"They are, Captain."

"Fine. If you're ready, then, we can shove off immediately. Please feel free to come up on the bridge at any time. I'll be back down after we've cleared the harbor, and we'll have a bit of breakfast."

We finished our coffee and went out on deck. Beginning to pick up speed, the ship heeled gently as the rudder was put over to clear a giant aircraft carrier. The sky behind us was beginning to display a gray fan, and the stars rapidly faded as pink and red banners heralded the arrival of the sun.

A faint twinge of doubt arose in my mind as I realized that our next stop was to be in the middle of Red-held territory. Had we brought everything we'd need? Were we capable of bringing success to such a mission? I was only too well aware of the possible catastrophe for our forces if we should fail—and this knowledge weighed on me not a little.

As far as Yong and Kim (as I shall call them henceforth) knew, this was only a reconnaissance. Later, I am sure, they guessed the true purpose of our work, and could even have put their finger on the day the Inchon landing was to take place. That neither the purpose nor the day was compromised was adequate proof of their loyalty to their country, and sufficient for me, on many occasions thereafter, to place my life completely in their hands. Something along this general line of reflection must have been running through Yong's mind.

"Mr. Clark," he said, "Kim and I have been wondering about the location of our base of operations. From the information you've given us, Tokchok-do will be the island closest to Inchon in our hands which can be defended by our naval forces."

"And this island is more than twenty-five miles from Inchon," said Kim, finishing the thought.

"True," I replied. "There are many difficulties to be overcome, and this matter of time and distance is but one of the more serious. We've had no real opportunity to go into this thing. After breakfast, let's talk about it further, shall we?"

As always, the bow wake with its gracefully expanding and multiplying lines held a fascination for me. We were now passing through Sasebo's narrow channel mouth, with high green hills reaching up from it on both sides. The sudden increased tempo of throbbing engines under our feet told us that our speed was increasing to standard from the mandatory one-third speed in the harbor. With a fast mental calculation I concluded that standard would be about twenty knots for this trip—and one that would not be uncomfortable. Get these galloping tin cans above twenty-five in a seaway and there's peace for no one, I reflected.

The steward came out and announced that breakfast was ready. With a final look at the slowly receding crisp green islands and foothills lining the Sasebo channel approaches, we turned back to the wardroom. Except for the narrow passageway on each side, the room extended the full width of the main deck. Possessing in its appointments rather less formality than U.S. destroyers, it succeeded in bringing to its members a distinct "club" atmosphere. Fully one-third of the port side was taken up with a lounge outlined by wide, comfortable seats with playing (or cocktail) tables fronting the entire circuit. This section could be closed off by full-length drapes from the rest of the room. It was here that we were to spend our only night on board. The rest of the wardroom contained the usual dining tables and bookcases. Rugs completely covered the steel deck underfoot. As always, pictures of the reigning British monarchs, King George and Queen Elizabeth, were prominently displayed.

Breakfast over, Yong, Kim, and I adjourned to the lounge to talk strategy and tactics. The quartermaster came down with the large-scale chart of Inchon and its approaches, and the reprint of a Japanese chart that still retained the names and legends in Japanese, so that all three of us could read it. Studying it silently for a long while, we came to the inescapable conclusion that we could not accomplish the task set us from a base on Tokchok-do. We would have to move into Inchon Harbor proper.

This would mean carrying out our reconnaissance activity under the very noses of the Reds, who would then completely encircle us. Further, under these conditions we could not expect support from our own forces. Our job at once took on a more formidable aspect. However, I could detect no change in the faces of my lieutenants. Nor did I sense that this development was unwelcome.

The trip across the Tsushima Strait, which separates Kyushu from the southern tip of Korea, and on west through the Korean Archipelago, was made during daylight hours. The sea and weather continued ideal, and as darkness closed in, we turned north into the Yellow Sea for the leg that would see us to our rendezvous.

That evening the ship's officers not on watch gave hearty expression to their wishes for our success. We not only "spliced the mainbrace," but had a round robin of songs ranging from "Bless Them All" and "God Save the King" to rousing Korean revolutionary chants. I'm afraid I acquitted myself rather poorly at this exchange, but Yong and Kim, being excellent singers—as are all Koreans, I was to discover—very entertainingly held up our end of the soiree.

Turning in about eleven o'clock, we were awakened by the Klaxon, followed by an announcement over the loudspeaker for battle quarters. A little startled at first, I realized that we were now in potentially hostile waters and that this was the usual predawn alert. Reassuring Yong and Kim, who were sitting upright, I turned over to try and get that last soul-satisfying forty winks. However, this attempt was discouraged by the noise of the gun crews at the ready-ammo boxes, followed by commands, and guns being trained in and out, faintly heard. Folding my arms under my head,

I made a desultory effort at trying to trace my course of action for the next twenty-four hours. Failing miserably in this, I turned to an evaluation of my most valuable assets, Yong and Kim.

In making their selection, I had reasoned that the nature of the task being what it was, it would have to be my job to determine what kind of information Tokyo required, to see that it was obtained, and to ensure that it was sent back promptly. This left open the entire field of where and how the information was to be procured, in addition to its translation from Korean into English—by no means a secondary function of this job.

For this I would require Korean natives of unquestioned loyalty to the South Korean cause and personally "my men." This concurrent loyalty to their own country and to an American was not conflicting unless the American strayed from Republic of Korea objectives and interests, the exact dividing line not always as apparent as it might seem. The Republic of Korea was waging "total" war against the Reds, admitting of no compromise—utterly ruthless in her determination to expel the enemy and bring the nation together again under one flag. Korea was fighting this war under Oriental rules, with no pretense of observing the fast-becoming-outmoded "humanitarian" laws of warfare established by Western conventions. No squeamish American could hope to obtain the respect or following of such ardent Korean revolutionaries as Yong and Kim. I was thankful that my past eight years' service in the Orient in war and peace had made me a sufficiently "enlightened" leader to be acceptable to these proponents of direct action.

Yong Chi Ho was a handsome man in anybody's book. His father had been a prosperous industrialist in Seoul, the Korean capital, until the Japanese began to feel the pinch of expense on their China venture. Then came the squeeze, which ruined his father and eventually led to his death. Yong, eighteen years old and the head of the family, placed his mother with a cousin. Leaving her and his sixteen-year-old brother and what remained of the estate, Yong headed for Manchuria. There he joined the growing number of Korean patriots and revolutionaries supporting the provisional government of the Korean Republic, with headquarters in China. This was in 1938.

With the revolutionaries, Yong fought the Japanese wherever and whenever the opportunity was given, the battle ground shifting between northern Korea, Manchuria, Outer Mongolia, and southern Siberia. At the end of the war, he rushed south to his homeland ahead of the Russians. He had witnessed enough of their handiwork to know that they were the mortal enemy of his people. Arriving at Seoul, he found the Americans in occupation. Joining his fellow countrymen, he assisted in establishing the Republic under the presidency of Syngman Rhee, who had been one of the leaders of the provisional government working in Hawaii and America. Finally, he went to work organizing and building the defense forces of the young republic. Yong was now thirty, but with a lifetime of experience in guerrilla warfare and underground resistance. His quick, sharp mind, indomitable courage and will, and boundless energy made him a natural choice for the job of solving the "hows" of our task.

The second member of our triumvirate was the oldest and wisest—the steadying influence of our group. Kim Nam Sun was forty-two years old. A past master of diplomacy and intrigue, Kim could plumb the Oriental mind to its depths. He had been from his early youth a student and patriot. The dream of freedom for his country had grown in intensity with his years, though most of these years had been spent north and west of the Yalu River, which marked the northern border of Korea. Kim, like Yong, was a revolutionary. An intrepid supporter of the Korean provisional government, he had become director of counterintelligence when the Republic of South Korea was established. But Syngman Rhee had fired him for failing to predict the North Korean invasion. Kim would tell us where we would get our information, and would be in charge of interrogation. . . .

Musing thus as I lay staring at the overhead, I buttressed my confidence against the impact of the unknown ahead.

A messenger knocked lightly on the bulkhead.

"Yes?"

"Sir, we've picked up the *Kenya* and her screen, the *Athabaskan*, on radar. They're dead ahead. We should be in voice communication shortly."

"Thank you. Will you please advise the captain that we'll not require breakfast."

"Aye, aye, sir!"

"Kim! Yong! Are you awake?" Silly question. They were pulling on their clothes when I reached up and switched on the lights.

After we'd washed and I'd had what I thought would be my last shave for a "fortni't"—as my British hosts would say—we joined some other officers in the wardroom for a cup of coffee. Kim had endeared himself to these people through the simple means of talking to them in his native tongue as if they understood it. Although the resulting conversation was always rather disjointed, it certainly made for a lot of laughs and general good feeling. This morning, the boys were cutting him in on the shop talk that always prevailed in an evolution such as the one ahead. He was taking it in stride, his round face lighting up with interest when he caught a word he understood.

Listening to the banter, I chuckled to myself, recalling the story told last night about *Charity*'s name. It seems that shortly after she had been commissioned, with her name not yet dry on the Admiralty's lists, a clerk had made an error. Whether inadvertently or not was never discovered. However, the name "Chastity" was used, and this sobriquet had stuck. "'Chased' perhaps," said Captain Worth, "but certainly not 'chaste.'"

Dawn was breaking. The ROK (Republic of Korea) PC-703 had been picked up on the radarscope, heading full speed for the rendezvous. HMCS *Athabaskan* (a Canadian destroyer) and the *Charity* were in screen position off the *Kenya* to make sure some prowling Russian sub did not fire a torpedo into the cruiser's guts. All were proceeding slowly on a course that would intercept PC-703. At seven o'clock, PC-703 signaled that she was coming alongside to starboard. Now laying-to in gentle swells, the *Charity* put over her fenders, while Commander Lee Sung Ho, captain of the PC-703, eased his vessel alongside with a masterly show of ship-handling. Our gear had been uncovered, and a party standing by commenced passing it smartly to the diminutive ROK craft. Yong and Kim were immediately in animated conversation with Lee and other Korean officers.

I soon saw the *Charity*'s captain making his way down from the bridge. Walking forward to meet us, he pointed off the starboard quarter, where I saw a whaleboat headed toward us, bobbing up and down and taking spray over her canopy.

"That's Captain Brock of the *Kenya*," I was surprised to hear him say.

"Good Lord!" I murmured. "I wonder what's up."

I cudgeled my mind to find an explanation for this unusual visit. Cruiser captains don't ordinarily come aboard destroyers. It's very much the other way around. The effort was in vain, and on tenterhooks I awaited his arrival. Captain P. W. Brock, RN, had his gig brought alongside the PC. We met him as he came on board over the fantail.

"Good to have you with us again, Worth," he said briskly to the captain of the *Charity*.

Glancing at me, "Lieutenant Clark?" he queried, anticipating our introduction.

"Yes, sir."

"We received a signal from Admiral Andrewes to look after you on whatever you're up to here. Is Worth taking good care of you?"

My apprehension was relieved at once. "He certainly is, Captain. Everything is going like clockwork."

"How about communications in case you need some help? Do you have our call signs and frequencies? We can put a few planes over, you know—or, in an emergency, run in a destroyer. Worth has been in there on a few shows."

"Thank you, Captain," I replied, "but we're traveling light this trip. Our one-lung radio is only set up to talk to Tokyo. If we get in trouble, it will have to be relayed to you."

"Well, best of luck, then, Clark. We'll be ready if you need us."

After we shook hands, he stepped back into his gig, waved us a "Cheerio," and headed back to the *Kenya*. Within a week, I was to recall Captain Brock's offer.

Neither of us made any comment on this courtesy visit. I was familiar enough with British naval tradition and protocol to know that I had been honored far above my rank, and was afraid that if I attempted to express my appreciation, I would botch it.

Yong and Kim were busily supervising the stowing of our equipment in an empty gun-tub on PC-703 as we returned to the destroyer.

"The ship has something to contribute to the success of your mission, Clark," said Captain Worth. "I believe the steward has it ready in the wardroom."

Wondering what it might be at this late hour, I accompanied

him in silence. It turned out to be two bottles of excellent scotch, which, needless to say, was more than welcome. The Canadian Club we had with us would be fine for the purpose it was intended, but this was real drinking material that we could relish without thinking of the taxpayers' money. I was very grateful, and said so.

In a few minutes, the *Charity*'s first lieutenant reported the transfer of gear completed. Saying my goodbyes, I climbed over the lifelines and made my way to the bridge of PC-703, where Yong introduced me to Commander Lee.

"I have orders from Admiral Sohn to place my ship under your orders, Mr. Clark," Lee said in surprisingly good English. He followed this statement with a friendly, flashing smile. I took an immediate liking to this man Lee.

"Okay, Captain. Let's head for Tokchok."

The lines were cast off and our course set for the island of Tokchok-do, about twenty miles to the northeast. Looking back, I saw that the cruiser and destroyers had joined up and were steaming north with bones in their teeth. I hoped that we would not give them cause to return to this area.

Due to the disciplined teamwork of the United Nations' navy, our schedule had clicked all the way without a single hitch or wasted motion. This ROK PC, for instance, was normally on inshore duty, patrolling the island-studded waters south of the Ongjin Peninsula and west of Inchon. The Commander, Naval Forces, Far East, had issued orders to the Commander, ROK Naval Forces (Commander Michael J. "Mike" Luosey, USN), to have a ship available at the designated time and rendezvous. Commander Luosey had passed this along to the ROK Chief of Naval Operations, Rear Admiral Sohn Won-Il, who, in turn, had transmitted it to PC-703. Commander Lee, true to naval tradition for punctuality, had met us precisely as ordered.

Later, I learned that Commander Lee had been in southern California when the war started, having been sent there by Admiral Sohn to fit out and commission the PC-703. He worked night and day getting her ready, and then had sailed her full speed for his homeland, where she was desperately needed. Like Yong in many respects, Lee was slender, about five feet, six inches tall, and thirty-one years old.

Korea had once been a naval power of considerable consequence. In the sixteenth century, the naval architectural genius of Yi Soon Sin developed the first ironclad man-of-war, the tortoise boat. She was shaped and armored completely over the top like a common tortoise. As a figurehead she sported a dragon's neck, with a head that actually spouted fire and smoke. This ship enabled the Koreans to defeat the great "Napoleon of Japan," Hideyoshi, in Chinhae Bay. The centuries had sloughed away, and now Commander Lee and his gallant comrades were repeating history. Pouncing on every Red naval vessel that ventured out of hiding along the North Korean coast, they had speedily brought all effective enemy resistance at sea to an end.

Lee turned the conn over to his navigator. "Yong tells me you haven't had breakfast yet, Mr. Clark," he said. "Shall we go down to the wardroom and see what the cook has to offer?"

"By George, that's right! Now that you mention it, I am hungry."

The ship was spotlessly clean and a credit to any navy. Several deckhands were already busy working with chipping hammers and red lead against that constant enemy of steel ships—rust. The wardroom was small and cozy, seating about six around the single table. A ship's radio attached to the bulkhead was giving out with a Japanese program, all stations in Korea having been silenced in the Red push south. A small officer's galley was situated just aft of the wardroom, and from here came appetizing odors of coffee and bacon and eggs.

These particular fragrances surprised me no end, as I had expected to be treated to the usual Korean fare of highly spiced vegetables and steamed rice. Lee noticed the look on my face and answered my unvoiced question.

"When I was in America, I came to like your food now and then, so I laid in a small supply before we came up here on patrol. The bacon and coffee are canned, of course. I trade some with the villagers on the outlying islands for fresh eggs."

Never having expected this luxury, I settled back and enjoyed it. I guess we killed a pound of coffee at this session while we were getting acquainted.

Generally, it is not easy to break down the reserve of a Korean. The entire world had seemed against them for so many centuries that they are quite rightly suspicious of all foreigners. An intensely proud and nationalistic race, but weak in industry and the resources necessary to assert herself against formidable neighbors, her people had become frustrated and desperate. Unless they are openly and honestly treated as equals, it is hopeless to expect from them more than passive cooperation. In their recent experience, Americans personified everything Koreans (and other Oriental races) hate and despise most in foreigners. The GIs tended to look down on them; they called them "gooks." Their country had become the battleground of an experiment in international "cold war" diplomacy. The job of overcoming this natural animosity was often long and tedious.

I couldn't afford to risk our mission by going into Inchon without the full understanding and support of Commander Lee. The run up to Tokchok-do took a little more than an hour. Pulling into the small semicircular cove, Lee dropped the hook and blew his whistle for a sampan. I wanted to take a look at this island. If we were unable to maintain a base closer in, we would have to fall back here and do the best we could.

Noticing quite a few junks and sampans drawn up high on the beach fronting the small village, I asked Lee how they had come there. "The majority of them we captured up north and towed in here," he replied. "The rest were sailed in by refugees from as far north as the Yalu River."

"Where are the prisoners?"

Lee shot a quick glance at Kim.

"They're on the island," he said evenly.

Hmm. I thought it polite to make no further inquiries along this line, and ashore discreetly refrained from asking to see the prisoners.

Two sampans came sculling out to the ship. Cautiously stepping into the fragile craft, we were soon put ashore. Most of the villagers, about fifty, had come down to meet us. One, who turned out to be the village headman, immediately engaged Lee in low and intense conversation.

Yong nudged me. "This looks like the answer to our base problem, Mr. Clark. It seems that the Reds have temporarily withdrawn all but a handful of troops from Yonghung-do. That island is close to Inchon. Do you remember it?"

"I certainly do, Yong." My pulse quickened at the thought of such a break. "Where did this information come from?"

"Lee is getting that now. The ROK marines unit here will probably have all the information."

Yong and Kim required no urging from me to get in this. They were after the answers like bloodhounds. Walking on up to the village, we were met by Ensign Chang, the marine officer-in-charge.

A short verbal exchange and the news was confirmed. The school-master in Yonghung-do, a Christian, had dispatched his son by sampan to Tokchok-do the previous evening with the news, and the request that ROK marines move in and prevent the Reds from returning. The Reds were stripping the island of its food and threatening an "educational" program that meant the execution of many families and a starvation diet for the rest.

With the preliminary facts established, we went on to the head-quarters building, a small abandoned schoolhouse. A woman brought in some tea as we sat cross-legged on the straw mats in front of a low table.

"Yong, this is the break we need," I said urgently. "If Lee can as-sure us his gunboat's support, I think we can make a go of it. But first we must know about how many Reds are left on the island."

Yong didn't wait to reply. Turning on Chang and the village headman almost viciously, he demanded the exact number of re-maining Reds. The headman said ten. Chang said he thought about six. Were they armed? Some had rifles. How many? They didn't know.

We weren't getting anywhere. I suggested sending for the schoolmaster's son, and Lee dispatched one of the marines to fetch him. At a disadvantage with Korean being spoken, without thinking I asked them to speak in Japanese. Kim, hesitating momentarily, passed this on. I sensed an immediate tightening in the atmosphere. You stupid, incompetent goon, Clark, I angrily chided myself. Soon, everyone was back in Korean. I had the good sense not to re-call my blunder to their attention.

The boy came in, and Yong went after him at once. How many Reds left? Five. How many have guns? Three. Are all the Red sup-porters on the island known? The boy hesitated, then answered, "I think so." How many are known? About twenty.

Ha! This did sound good. A show of force should run any resistance into the ground—or sea.

Yong had turned to Lee. "You will take us on in to Yonghung-do?" he was asking.

"Of course! And I will send in a landing party to see that the island is secured, if you wish," he offered.

"Two platoons, about fifty Inminkyun [Red troops] are usually on the island," Kim said. "Their headquarters are on the next island to the east, Taebu-do, where a battalion is stationed. The Yonghung-do garrison is rotated about every two weeks for training purposes. Replacements are due back in the morning."

Looking at Yong and Kim, I decided that the matter was settled. Until Lee's suggestion of the landing party, I had been a little concerned. Undoubtedly the people on that island were in danger and scared. If an underestimate of the number of Red troops we would meet would guarantee our coming, they almost certainly would underestimate. However, with Lee's support I was confident we could take care of this unknown factor.

A sudden thought struck me. "How do we know this boy isn't a plant?" I put to Yong.

"A what?"

"A phony. How do we know that he isn't working for the Reds?" I clarified.

"Ah, so-o-o," he said, slowly letting the implications soak in, and then immediately went to work on the village headman. After an extended and explosive exchange, Yong's face relaxed.

"The boy's grandparents and other relatives are on this island," I was relieved to hear, berating myself for not thinking of first things first.

"We've no time to lose. Captain, can we leave for Yonghung-do now?" I asked Lee.

"It's a simple matter to get steam up with diesel engines," Lee jokingly replied, adding happily, "and we haven't seen action for quite a while."

Back on board, Yong and Kim were busily breaking out our gear and checking over the guns. Flying Fish Channel, one of the two approaches to Inchon that were navigable to large vessels, wended its way tortuously between many small islands. Turning up eighteen knots, we were soon headed up this channel for what we hoped would be our operations base. It was September 1. We had fourteen days in which to do our job.

3

AN ISLAND
OF LOYALTY

T HE RUN FROM Tokchok-do to Yonghung-do was about fifteen miles. During this time, Captain Lee and I sat in the
wardroom over a chart, making our plans. We laid it on in three
phases. First, the landing, which Lee would cover with his guns.
Second, securing the island itself. This meant killing or capturing
the Red soldiers left on the island, or driving them to cover. And
third, convincing the Red battalion headquarters on Taebu-do that
a landing in force by our troops had been made on Yonghung-do.
We hoped that a bombardment of the reported positions of the
Reds on Taebu-do by the gunboat would accomplish this strata-
gem. It was our thought that perhaps such a show of force would
keep them from counterattacking until we had an opportunity to
organize our defenses.

Our simple and forthright plan completed, we went aft to see
how Yong and Kim were coming along with the guns. The ship had
no small arms of her own, so we would be dependent on those we
had brought with us. I had not stinted in this respect, although I

now considered that my supply of "artillery" left much to be desired, considering we were to have upward of three hundred Reds for neighbors. I was unnerved when I discovered just how close these "neighbors" were.

Unnerved? Hah! It scared hell out of me.

Lee had detailed Lieutenant (junior grade) Paik and ten sailors for the landing party, and this group was now clustered around the gun tub, receiving their weapons from Yong. Five were given M-1 (automatic fire) carbines, and the other five had .45-cal. submachine guns, or "grease guns" as we called them, their appearance bearing a marked resemblance to that familiar instrument.

We loaded Lieutenant Paik down with a .45 pistol and an M-1. Having about twenty minutes to spare, they went about loading their clips and receiving instruction. Both Yong and Kim were postgraduates with these weapons, and the sailors caught on fast.

It was a clear day with scarcely a breeze, so conditions were ideal. As we neared the bay itself, we heard a few desultory shots coming from those islands nearest us, though much too far for us to see even the splashes. The tide, a factor I would always have to consider hereafter, was about half flood as we rounded the channel into the bay. We could make out the main targets of our mission, Inchon and the island of Wolmi-do, about seven miles to the north. Turning south, we passed an extended shoal area topped by huge rocks that were awash, and steered directly for the northeastern tip of Yonghung-do, now barely three miles distant.

Suddenly, the general quarters alarm began its insistent ringing, and the crew scurried to their battle stations. In less than a minute the guns had been uncovered, manned, and the ammo passers were at their ready boxes. This PC mounted a single three-inch, dual-purpose gun in the bow, two single .50-cal. machine guns on the boat deck—one each on the port and starboard sides—and one single .50-cal. machine gun aft on the fantail. The empty gun tub that had contained our gear, and was now a storage place for a small mountain of bagged rice, had mounted a twin 20mm gun. For some reason, when the ship was fitted out the gun was not installed. Two rows of empty depth charge racks on the fantail bore mute testimony to her use in World War II when she had been a subchaser in the American navy. Two large diesel engines furnished the twin screws sufficient power for twenty knots. Manned by her fearless and belligerent crew, this 173-foot ship was more than a match for any in her own weight and class.

Yong and Kim were making a last-minute check, and I followed Lee to the bridge to study the area. The officer of the deck passed his binoculars to Lee and pointed out two objects that had put out from Yonghung-do.

"Two junks," Lee informed me. "Looks like they're trying to intercept us."

He handed me the glasses. "Have a look?"

I studied the junks closely. Fairly large, rigged for sails, they were each being sculled by two men using the tandem oar arrangement peculiar to some of the junks I had seen in China. No soldier could be handling a sculling oar with such skill.

I handed the glasses back to Lee. "Must be the transportation the schoolmaster said he would have waiting for us," I commented hopefully.

Concurring in my observation, Lee slowed to one-third and made ready to take the junks in tow. His guns were trained into them as we came up; it would have been suicide for them to make a single false move. Lee ordered a tow line thrown to the first; it was dropped aft on a painter to await the second. As the second nosed in, one of her oarsmen shouted that he had a message and was taken aboard.

Both junks were dropped aft on the towline as the ship picked up speed. The islander was brought up to the bridge. "We are very happy that you have come to help our island," he said.

Lee brushed this aside impatiently. "Have the Inminkyun replacements arrived?" he asked crisply.

"No, Captain. They will not come until morning," he replied, adding quickly, "The village headman and all the villagers welcome our heroic marines."

Lee grimaced wryly at this as he interpreted. "Where are the soldiers left on the island?" he barked.

The grizzled boatman hesitated, plucking at his ragged garments. "We left the village about two hours ago," he said deliberately. "One was at their headquarters in the headman's office, and the others had gone to the beach on the side of the island facing Taebu-do."

Then, anxiously: "You are going to help us?"

Lee relented. "Yes, old boatman, we will try to help you. Go back to your boat and wait to take our marines ashore." At this, the boatman straightened up his huge hunched shoulders and permitted a sailor to lead him aft.

When ROK sailors are put ashore on an offensive or defensive mission, they automatically assume the status of marines. Returning to their ships, they resume their status as sailors: a very simple arrangement in limited actions, with many commendable administrative and operational features. Thus, Lee's landing party during this venture would be marines.

"Seems to be working out quite well, Mr. Clark," Lee said. "At least we won't have to shuttle back and forth getting everything ashore with the dinghy. With these two junks, we'll make it in one trip."

As we approached a predetermined point off the selected landing beach, the junks were hauled up alongside. By the time the anchor was let go, men and equipment had been divided as evenly as possible between the junks. A .30-cal. machine gun was mounted precariously behind the heavy timbers of the bow of each, with Kim standing by one and Yong the other. Even a Boy Scout, I thought to myself as these arrangements were in progress, is always prepared.

Legging over the lifeline and jumping into the junk, I hollered to Lee on the bridge. "Come on in for breakfast in the morning, Captain. Perhaps they have a few eggs hidden away over here."

"Good luck, Mr. Clark," he shouted back.

I noted as we pulled away that all the guns that could be brought to bear were covering the stretch of beach ahead of us, and it gave me a comforting feeling. I did not relish this "sitting duck" idea in the least. Once on the beach we could take care of ourselves, but out here we presented too slow and too good a target.

The boatmen were pulling silently and grimly, putting all their muscle and skill into each sweep. As we had planned, the tide was in our favor, giving us at least a four-knot push. I had hung my binoculars around my neck and now used them. There were many people lining the shore, and I could make out more coming up behind them. The majority of them appeared to be women and children, with a scattering of boys. No soldiers were in evidence. I thought to myself that if these people were friendly, they would certainly keep their distance from any enemy of ours. I knew that Lee, too, had his glasses on this stretch and was watching for any sign of activity that would warrant his opening up.

But this was now entirely out of the question. He could not start throwing death and destruction among those villagers. If a firefight started, we would have to take care of it ourselves.

We were still about one thousand yards off when we could see those on the beach violently waving cloths, which on closer inspection appeared to be small flags of the Republic of Korea. At least they were white-bordered and not red. The Koreans and Chinese always had at hand the appropriate flag to wave or to display from their houses. The shifting tide of battle recommended such foresight to those wishing to remain in their homes—and live. This wholesale display of ROK flags I interpreted as indicating that these islanders were not only friendly to us at the moment, but also that they were confident we could protect them from any retaliatory consequences of this act. It was a good sign.

Approaching the shore, the boatmen hauled in the rudders and dropped sails. Swinging the junks around, they beached them stern-first in the manner customary throughout the Orient. Immediately, we were swarming over the stern, with Yong and Kim struggling mightily with the light machine guns. Advancing up the fairly steep slope of the beach, we made slow progress over the loose rocky surface until we reached a low four-foot scarp. Here I called a halt to survey the situation, this scarp affording us excellent protection.

Two islanders, who immediately identified themselves as the village headman and the schoolmaster, were clamoring to gain our attention. Summoning Lieutenant Paik, Yong, and Kim, I resigned myself to the usual polite exchange of greetings and compliments. Although time was of the essence, the customs and amenities of these people were not to be denied by a mere war. If we desired the respect and cooperation of these islanders, I could not give way to Western impatience and directness. These preliminaries out of the way, we got down to business.

Once again . . . How many Inminkyun on the island? Only five. How many had rifles? All of them had rifles. Are you certain? Yes. Well, three or five rifles . . . it didn't matter much either way. Where are the soldiers now? Four are at the ferry landing across from Taebu-do, and the other is at the headquarters on the other side of the village.

Relief swelled inside of me as I realized that the island was practically ours. I suggested splitting our small force into three units. Lieutenant Paik and five men would accompany me to the ferry. Yong and three men would go to the village. Kim and two men would remain to protect the junks and equipment now being unloaded. Kim protested briefly, but acceded. Lee and his gunboat were to stand by until we had secured the island, and returned.

It was 10:30 A.M. We moved out, the schoolmaster acting as our guide and the headman as Yong's. We were to take these five alive if at all possible. It was our hope that they would supply us with information for our first report to Tokyo. In this we were doomed to disappointment. The ferry landing was about two miles to the southeast, and the guide struck off for our objective on a path that would skirt the village by some distance.

I was certain that by this time the four soldiers had been warned of our coming by one of their twenty-odd sympathizers on the island that the schoolmaster's son had mentioned. Perhaps their lone comrade was on his way to join them. Certainly, he too would have been warned. There were several courses of action open to them. It would be reasonable to assume that if they felt greatly outnumbered they would commandeer a sampan and attempt an escape to Taebu-do. Other options were to resist capture or take to the hills on the southwest side of the island. I hoped they would stand to.

While we were still a mile from our objective, Lieutenant Paik sent out his advance scouts. It would not do to fall into an ambush. Snipers were my particular concern. With my Navy billed cap and green Marine fatigues, and standing rather taller than the others, I felt I made a tempting target. However, "face" being what it was in the Orient, I could only hope that in complying with its dictates, mine would not get blown off.

One of the scouts came running back, gesticulating over his shoulder. Hardly knowing what to expect, we ran forward to meet him. "He says there's a sampan putting out from the ferry with In-minkyun in it," Paik interpreted for my benefit.

This was an unfortunate turn of events. I wanted those soldiers, intact if possible. "Let's go after them!" I said, and started running as fast as I could up the narrow path. Reaching the top of the slight rise, I stopped to take a good look at the sampan through my glasses. The scout had been all too right. All five of the soldiers were in the sampan, which was pulling out into the narrow channel, sculled frantically by what appeared to be a boy. The tidal current was sweeping them toward us.

"Lieutenant, will you please detail two of your men with carbines to throw some fire across them from here. Perhaps we can frighten them into returning."

Paik gave the orders, and we continued our dash down the path. When we reached the beach, the sampan was about two hundred yards out and rapidly moving north and away from us with the current. Carbine bullets were making splashes around the boat, and now the soldiers were returning the fire of our men on the hill. They were at a tremendous disadvantage in aiming from a rolling platform. Lieutenant Paik was shouting at them to return and surrender or be killed. This demand was pointedly answered when they turned their attention to us.

"Have the men hole the boat. Try to concentrate the fire on the waterline," I urged Paik, still hopeful that I wasn't fighting a lost cause.

The next few minutes saw a nice illustration of how a submachine gun "walks" in inexperienced hands. The men did their best to concentrate their fire, but they succeeded only in laying down paths of death with each burst. The men on the hill commenced throwing automatic fire into the boat, thinking we were out to kill the occupants. That was that.

"Well," I commented reflectively to Paik, as we started back down the trail for the ferry landing, "it's strange how this has turned out. An hour ago, I thought we would be the sitting ducks."

The rest of our work in establishing this island as a base was cut out for us. Get our tent set up under some good camouflage, put the radio in commission, then go after the problem of island defense.

We'd gone about halfway back to the beach when Yong intercepted us. He had not found his man, and hearing the firing, decided to see if any help was needed. After I explained what had happened by the ferry, Yong made his report.

"When we arrived at the village, everything was normal. So that I would not alert the Red to our presence, I sent a boy over to the headquarters to see if he was still there and to figure out how we were going to take him. In a few minutes, the boy came running back, saying that the Red was not there. The rest you know, except that they left some of their supplies that we can use."

"Any guns or mortars?" We could do with a few mortars, any size.

"No, there weren't," he replied, disappointedly, but brightened up. "There were three cases of hand grenades."

"Wonderful!" We couldn't get hold of any grenades at Sasebo and we certainly could use them. They were every bit as welcome as mortars.

"The Reds also have quite a stack of rice stored over in the old schoolhouse," Yong added as an afterthought.

The headman's ears must have been tuned in for this particular statement, for I swear he was at least twenty feet away when Yong made it. He turned and was back to us in the flash of an eye.

"The rice, *Taicho-san* [leader], it is ours. The barbaric Inminkyun have taken it from us for taxes. That rice is our winter's food." He emphasized these points by quick little hops as he kept up with us. This statement, of course, stopped just short of the rude point of directly asking for the return of the rice.

I thought it good psychology not to take the matter further at this time. It would be better to leave it uppermost in his mind so that he would debate with the other villagers the possibility of our returning the rice. Besides, I wanted to discuss the matter with Yong and Kim. Perhaps they would suggest keeping it in our control while we were here—sort of combined economic and life insurance.

"The Inminkyun will regret their evil ways," I answered the headman, noncommittally delaying decision. The headman gave me a quizzical look, dropped back a few paces, and then trotted up to his former position.

"We'll have to make up our minds soon about that rice, Mr. Clark," Yong commented.

"Right you are, Yong. Can't have them thinking we're no better than our friends across the channel."

I turned to considering what I could tell Tokyo today. We had established our base in the very middle of the Red defenses of Inchon. If we could hold it, there would be one less island for our troops to clean up. This thought gave me pause. What if we were dislodged? We had already concluded that the job couldn't be done from Tokchok-do.

Hmm . . . We'd have to secure an alternate base inside the Red perimeter from which we could operate if the necessity arose. I assigned this item a high priority in my mind for consideration. Next, the location of our command post (CP). The ferry landing? Come to think of it though, the backshore area above the scarp where we had landed had possibilities. And there were trees . . .

Yong interrupted my thoughts. "I noticed a considerable number of young men on the beach and up in the village, Mr. Clark," he said. "Evidently, the Inminkyun only took those over about eighteen."

I didn't grasp the significance of this immediately, so he expanded. "Perhaps we can get them to form our island defense guard."

Thinking this over, I recalled the extreme youth of some of the Japanese troops we had encountered in New Guinea, Hollandia, and other islands on the way back to the Philippines. Trained, and with weapons they knew how to use, they gave us as much trouble as their elders. Yes, it was certainly one solution to that problem. Better than women in any case, and that idea had tentatively crossed my mind, too.

Arriving back at the beach, Kim took the news of our little skirmish with unexpected somberness, confirming my own opinion that we had failed in our objective. Information was not to be obtained from corpses floating around Inchon Bay. Kim needed better subjects for interrogation.

"Lieutenant Paik," I called.

"Yes, Mr. Clark?"

"Will you please collect your party and return to the ship as soon as possible? The sooner the captain can commence his bombardment of Taebu-do, the better."

As Paik turned to round up his men, I looked for the schoolmaster. "*Sensei!* [learned one]," I said, finding him at hand, "what do you know of the Taebu-do defenses?" Captain Lee could use a little help in that line.

"Very little, *Taicho-san,* but there are several of the boatmen here who operated the ferry to Taebu-do. I believe they will know quite a bit about that island."

Kim was listening in and took his cue. This was his business. "*Sensei,* where are these people now?" he asked.

The schoolmaster quickly surveyed the people on the beach, and pointed. "There are two of them, Rhee and Lu," he exclaimed, starting off to fetch them.

As it turned out, between them they did have considerable knowledge of the Red defenses and bivouac areas. I dispatched them to Lee, with particular instructions to destroy every sampan and junk possible on the enemy shore. After all, without boats they could hardly threaten Yonghung-do. But this was too much to expect. Still, by reducing the number of boats available to them, any attack they mounted would be correspondingly weaker. I made a mental note to try and find out how many boats they had left after Lee's bombardment.

Yong and Kim were engaging the headman in a discussion. Seeing that I was free, they turned to me. "Mr. Clark, the headman tells us there are a little over a thousand people on this island, and he believes we can recruit about a hundred young men for the island defense force," Yong said.

That thousand figure appalled me for a moment. How the devil do you maintain security control over so many? Still, if we could be reasonably certain that the young men we recruited would be loyal, we could control most of the population through them. The close family ties of these people would play a large part.

"What do you and Kim think of the idea?" I queried.

"We believe it's the best thing we can do under the circumstances," Yong replied without hesitation. "Of course, we have nowhere near enough guns to arm them all."

"We want to be certain that we don't recruit any Reds. Remember, we were told that there were quite a few sympathizers among the villagers," I recalled. "Kim, suppose you start weeding out the Red supporters, while Yong and the headman begin recruiting. We want to establish a twenty-four-hour watch at all possible landing beaches around the island, set up a defense on the side facing Taebu-do, and mount a special guard around our camp."

As they turned to leave, I added, "Try to get an idea of how the island is fixed for food." The question of the rice had to be resolved.

Now, about our CP location. We had landed on a stretch of beach about six hundred yards in length. Above the scarp and extending the length of the beach was a fairly flat area covered with trees. At either end of the stretch was a promontory about one hundred feet high; these would make ideal lookout points for both east and west approaches. The flat area fronting the beach extended about thirty yards inland, where it dropped off abruptly into drying rice paddies. These paddies extended to the outskirts of the village about half a mile to the south. It would be a simple matter to guard this unobstructed approach away from the beach.

From a defensive viewpoint, this location was just about ideal. If we were to locate at the ferry landing, we would have none of these advantages, and in addition could receive little gunfire support from the sea, as the shallows extended well over three miles out. Here, even at low tide the gunboat could lay in as close as a thousand yards.

With the schoolmaster tagging along, I looked for a likely place to pitch our pyramidal tent, finally selecting a spot where the tent would be almost completely hidden by wide-branching trees. We had to consider the possibility of Russian Yak fighter-bombers coming over, as well as avoid temptation to our own planes. Pilots had a tendency to bomb first and ask questions later.

"*Sensei,* have all the equipment on the beach brought up here, please," I directed.

Within a very short time, the tent was up and the radio was being rigged for our first contact with Tokyo. It was 2:30 when we heard the welcome sound of Lee opening up on the Reds on Taebu-do. This was followed within a few minutes by the unwelcome deep-throated cough of a 120mm mortar. I hoped that Lee had not moved too far in. If that deadly mortar zeroed in, our gunboat was finished. Well, Lee had had plenty of experience in these waters. . . .

I tore myself away from contemplating disaster. To complete our combined CP and camp, we would need a few items that the village could furnish. Chairs and tables from the school we could put in the small clearing near the tent. Cooking utensils were undoubtedly available. I mentioned this to the schoolmaster, and he was off to the village at a trot.

Breaking out a large-scale map of the area, I spread it out on the ground and commenced studying our operations base. Yonghung-do was somewhat oval in its general contour, with an irregular coastline. Its northwestern shoreline was punctuated with small coves and headlands, while its southeastern shoreline extended five fingerlike peninsulas out into the mudflats characterizing that half of the island's approaches. The highest peak on the island was a little more than five hundred feet and was near our camp. The island itself was roughly four miles in diameter. A valley about a mile in width ran diagonally across the island from northeast to southwest, accentuating the small hills on either side, which were covered with the shrubs and low-spreading trees common to Korea.

What a devil of a place to defend, even with regular troops. With guerrilla tactics, a few unfriendlies in the hills could harass us unmercifully. We couldn't stop a few from swimming across the narrow channel between the islands at night if they had a mind to. On the other hand, that could work two ways. The big job was to keep them from coming over in force. There were a couple of low-est low tides during the month. How low would this drop the chan-nel water? The chart indicated it would be about nine feet. But the soundings were based on Japanese surveys of 1916. With all the silt and alluvium that had been washing down from the Han River delta north of Inchon for the past thirty-four years, it was likely that alluvial deposits had shoaled the channels between these is-lands considerably. It would be a matter to check on. What if the Reds could just walk across at low tide? That channel was only seven hundred yards across at most. . . .

Yong was coming across the paddies from the village, followed by a string of young men. Under different circumstances, they would not be dignified by the term, but these boys were all soon to prove their mettle as men many times over. They entered the clear-ing, and Yong introduced them. There were seven: Hyun, Paikyun, Song, Ahn, Yang, Chae, and Choi. These were to be our camp guards, bodyguards, and shock troops all rolled into one. All but two were destined to die in the next fourteen days in a valiant effort to repel the invasion of their homeland by a foreign ideology that preached class hatred and spurious tyranny.

"How many signed up, Yong?" I asked.

"Eighty-seven so far, Mr. Clark. Kim has a backlog of twenty-seven more he is checking through for security, and if they're all taken, we'll have one hundred fourteen."

Addressing the guards, I said, "I am very sorry that I cannot speak Korean, but if you all understand Japanese we shall be able to talk easily. It will be necessary that we do so." They all indicated they could understand me, and I felt better. There were very few Koreans over ten years old who could not converse in Japanese as freely as in Korean, although for understandable reasons they did not care to do so. The long-standing bitterness between these two races ran deep, and it would take generations to erase.

The guard was issued guns, instructed briefly in their use, and posted: one at the top of each promontory flanking our CP and one at our rear, facing the paddies. Hyun, the oldest of the seven, was made guard captain. The watches were four hours on and four off.

Hyun spoke a little English, having studied for two years at Seoul National University. He was twenty, and on the Reds' "wanted" list. Having exposed underground Red leaders to ROK authorities before the war, Hyun's entire family—mother, father, two sisters, and three brothers—had been slaughtered by the Reds when they raged through Inchon during their initial thrust across the thirty-eighth parallel. Hyun himself had escaped to Yonghung-do in a small sampan.

Slightly built, wearing glasses, quiet, Hyun was a typical student in appearance. But his actions belied this innocuous title. Since the Inminkyun had occupied the island in early July, among other things, Hyun had killed four of them with a stolen bayonet during unguarded moments. In league with the schoolmaster, the head-man, and others, his efforts had caused the Reds to detail over fifty troops sorely needed elsewhere to this one island.

Soon the rest of our defense force arrived for weapons and instructions. Sitting down with Yong and Kim, I pointed out on the map the spots where lookouts would be required around the island. The lookouts we could not arm, so they received instructions to leave their post and report back to the CP as fast as possible if they observed anything that seemed like a threat. They were to be given heavy clubs and one hand grenade to take care of any single enemy arrivals. This unarmed group was a pretty dejected lot until Yong suggested rotating them with the group that would be guarding the immediate approaches from Taebu-do.

Included in the force were four former revolutionaries from Manchuria. Although in their late forties, they were active and understood the problem with which we were confronted. Yong put these in charge of the four watch sections, and the first lookout watch was dispatched to their posts. They moved off with every semblance of a well-disciplined military unit. As the rest of the lookouts departed for the village, Yong instructed one of the leaders to bring back the balance of our precious stock of grenades.

Now for the ferry landing defense unit. Aside from the requirements of our CP, we could give this unit two .50-cal. machine guns, four Browning automatic rifles, and fifteen grease guns and carbines. Leaving our guard in charge, we loaded up and headed back to the ferry landing. As we approached, we could still hear Lee's gunfire, although the volume had dropped considerably.

The sun had stepped up the apparent pace of its descent and was sharpening the outline of the hills to the west when we commenced throwing up bunkers for the heavy machine guns that were to cover our exposed shore. By the time the sun had set, the guns were being test-fired, both for practice and for the information of those interested parties we could see watching our activity across the channel. I deliberately had them fired to extreme range to enhance any psychological effect they might have.

This night, Captain Lee was to lie in as close as safety permitted, covering the reach of the channel between the two islands, and now and then throwing his searchlight around where it would do the most good. For tonight at least, Yong, Kim, and I would take turns standing guard at this critical point, not only to reassure ourselves, but also to give a morale boost to these eager youngsters. I wished I had thought of bringing a field phone with a few miles of wire so that we could have instant communication between the ferry landing and our CP. Instead we would have to depend on gunfire signals and messengers.

Back at the CP, we found the schoolmaster waiting. He had brought down the tables and chairs, and not only the cooking utensils but also what were to be our cooks and maids for the duration of our stay. Two girls and one middle-aged woman were busily engaged in preparing our dinner. As women aren't introduced in the fashion of men, the schoolmaster pointed each out and gave her name.

There was Moon, Cynn, and Lim. I reckoned the ages of the latter two to be about thirteen. Later, this estimate was corrected to eighteen and seventeen, respectively. Lim, it turned out, was the schoolmaster's daughter, a Christian, and spoke good English. There was also a handyman rounding out our camp staff, whose job was apparently to fetch wood for the open fire and keep our five-gallon water cans filled from the village well.

We hadn't had time to think of eating or drinking since landing, and we now discovered we were both hungry and thirsty. They hadn't broken open our supplies, but had brought some rice down from the village, which was cooking. Yong called Moon, showed her our rice supply and how to get out the various kinds of C-rations.

"How is the island fixed for food, Kim?" I asked, recalling this important problem still to be disposed of.

"There is very little, Mr. Clark. You can see that this year's crop was poor, about half of what is normally produced." He indicated the barren paddies in back of us.

"If that's the case, then perhaps it would be inadvisable for us to mix in the matter of the rice distribution?" I suggested.

"But they are looking to us for orders in this rice thing, Mr. Clark," Yong interjected.

"Do you think that this rice must be distributed in the next two weeks to prevent hardship?" I asked.

"I do not think so," Kim replied. Yong nodded agreement.

"Then we should avoid making any decision in this touchy matter as to how the rice should be distributed," I proposed. "Let's merely tell the headman that the rice is to remain undistributed until the first of October. We'll be gone by that time, and then they'll have to make the decision themselves. We're bound to alienate some of the people if we do otherwise."

This was agreed to as the best course. Yong would inform the headman.

Lim placed small cups of Korean tea in front of us and backed away shyly. She was definitely a pretty girl. Large almond-shaped eyes, raven-black hair, and the white skin that distinguished the city from the farm girls. She had a smile delicately defined by small, white, close-set teeth. It was the kind of smile that instantly provoked an answering smile.

Cynn brought three large steaming bowls of rice, followed by meat and vegetable servings from the World War II C-rations we had brought with us. Koreans are not great meat eaters, preferring highly seasoned and pickled vegetables with their rice. The ultimate dish in this preference is *kimshi*, consisting of aged, pickled-in-brine cabbage, pickled radishes, lots of mashed raw garlic, all swimming in powdered red pepper of the hottest variety. It smells to the high heavens, and, knowing this, the polite ones, having eaten it, when speaking to you will invariably hold a hand to the mouth in such a manner as to direct the fumes to the side. Even a Korean who has eaten this dish all his life will invariably break out in perspiration.

"Kim. Did you find many Red sympathizers?" I asked.

"There are about twenty-four so far, Mr. Clark," he replied. "The village elders are still investigating facts and rumors. I imagine there will be a few more."

"Where have these people been locked up?"

"The Inminkyun had a few rooms in the schoolhouse they used for a jail. They are locked up there at present. We released seventeen people that were in the jail. That one guard at their headquarters was supposed to be the jailer."

"Do you suppose we can get any information from them?" I suggested without much conviction.

"I understand three of them have recently come here from Inchon. One other, a woman, is supposed to have been very friendly with the Inminkyun political representative on Taebu-do. I am going to talk to these four after dinner. Perhaps there will be some information."

"It might be well to spread the idea that we are after all the information we can get on this area—all the way to Seoul. Maybe some of the friendlies here can tell us a good deal. The boatmen should know something if they have been moving around at all. Unless all boat traffic was stopped, these people must have been doing some business in Inchon," I reasoned.

Kim thought this over for a while, and glanced up briefly from his rice. "The living speak," he said cryptically, and I knew he had not forgiven me those dead soldiers. Evidently, Kim had thought of these possibilities long ago and was working on them. When would I learn not to underestimate these people? I chastened myself, and let this subject drop.

"It would be good to know the types and number of boats they have on Taebu-do. Perhaps Lee has been successful in destroying some, if not all, of them," I tossed out for discussion.

They mulled this over for a while. Lim poured some more tea. "One of the boatmen who were doing the ferrying should know where to look," Yong offered.

"Two of the ferrymen are in jail," Kim said. "I think it likely that almost any of the older boatmen of the island would know where to look. Such places do not change."

A thought occurred to me. "Chae," I called to one of our off-duty guards. He rose and trotted over, anticipation lighting up his face. "Do you know where the junks and sampans are beached on Taebu-do? Where they land when they leave from Yonghung-do?" I asked, noticing out of the corner of my eye that Lim had come up almost as fast as had Chae. She stood listening intently from the background.

"Yes, *Taicho-san*," he replied expectantly.

"How do you know where those boats are?" I continued.

He looked at Yong and Kim, trying to get a clue as to what we were driving at. "Before the Inminkyun came, we all visited Taebu-do often. Many of us have relatives there, and many times our school has had athletic meets with theirs" was his straightforward answer.

"Thank you, Chae," I said, dismissing him.

Our course was obvious now. Yong would detail a couple of men from the ferry landing watch who were familiar with the target area. They would scull over at low tide in a sampan to Sonjae-do, a small rocky island connecting with Taebu-do except during periods of high tide. Then, while one stood by the boat to keep the tidal current from sweeping it away, the other would make his way to the cove over the mudflats, survey the boat situation, and return.

I referred to my astronomical data and did a little figuring. By ten o'clock, the moon, which was going into its last quarter, would be on its way up. By eleven, our men would have to be back or they would be picked off like clay pipes in a shooting gallery. Lee's searchlight would be a problem, too, but advantage could be taken of calculated intervals between flashes to get the sampan across. A piece of canvas washed with mud could serve to make our man look like one of the many rocks sprinkling the mudflats, if the light caught him on his way in or out.

It was twilight now, and it would be dark in about thirty minutes. Yong broke out one of the Marine camouflage ponchos and headed for the ferry; there was no time to waste.

Kim and I started working on the list of types of information Tokyo would require. Kim would need such a list at hand to guide him during his interrogations. While we were working this up, the four people Kim had tagged for interviews arrived under guard. They were resigned and stoical; only the woman exhibited signs of nervousness as Kim began his questioning.

To stretch my legs, I rose and walked over to the beach. The strap of my shoulder holster had rubbed some of the skin off. Hadn't worn the thing since Okinawa, I reflected, as I transferred my forty-five to my belt. I learned a good lesson in that WWII rumble. We'd run a jeep up to the Motobu area to check a report that Lieutenant Watanabe, a survivor from a Japanese cruiser, with a party of sailors had walked into one of our villages and removed the heads of the mayor and council we had appointed. As we rolled along the shore road about dusk, Watanabe's boys opened up on us from ambush. Riddled the two guys in the backseat with the first burst. The driver stomped the accelerator into the floor boards and got under the lee of an embankment on the right-hand side of the road. I had my forty-five in a holster at my hip and could no more get it out than fly. Thanks to the driver, the two of us escaped with whole skins. My combat effectiveness we rated as zero. After that, I had worn a shoulder holster.

From the beach, the view was unobstructed all the way to Inchon except for the little lighthouse island of Palmi-do, which lay about halfway between Inchon and Yonghung-do. To its right could be seen the flickering lights on the heights of Inchon—destined to be assaulted in two weeks by the combined forces of the United Nations under the directing genius of General MacArthur. Once again I was overwhelmed by the magnitude of the task ahead. A single error in judgment would wipe out our little mission, extinguishing the one hope held by the high command for lighting the dark areas of its plans. There would be no time to organize and send in a second group.

What had been bothering me about the darkened scene in front suddenly penetrated my mind. Search as I might, I could see no navigational lights. There should be three: one on the rocky island the gunboat had passed coming in, another on Palmi-do, and a third on Sowolmi-do at the entrance to Inchon's inner harbor. The Reds had put them all out of commission.

Would our fleet need them? Mines, too. Had the Reds mined the harbor or its approaches? A single ship sunk in the narrow channel would stop the invasion cold in its tracks. Guns. What size guns were on these islands and in Inchon? Mud. How deep was that mud? How soft? Would it hold a tank? An Amtrac (amphibious tractor)? A soldier? Why in the name of heaven had they put their confidence in our little group? How could we ever have hoped to accomplish this task?

I could feel myself crumbling inside again. Must get back to work—only by working could I overcome this sense of utter inadequacy. At least Yonghung-do is ours, I consoled myself, and turned back to the tent.

4

INTRIGUE

K IM WAS HARD AT IT, shooting out his questions with elec-
trifying intensity; shifting his approach to sympathetic understanding or contempt-filled sarcasm, depending upon the trend of
the interrogation. These people appeared harmless enough. Average,
typical-looking Koreans—you would not think them dangerous.
Kim had Lim at his side taking notes, which she would later trans-
late into English. She appeared frightened with her assignment
and kept her head down, avoiding a chance meeting of eyes with
Kim's subject.

Chae and the other boys representing an unvoiced threat were
standing in the background, taking in the proceedings with avid
interest. It was their first contact with one of the many facets of
war. In the flickering light of the single little Korean kerosene wick-
lamp on the table, I could detect no sign of sympathy or compassion in their youthful faces. Later, I would see these same boys kill
Reds and their sympathizers with as little compunction as we
would dispatch a snake.

Due to a condition imposed by our Korean allies, I would have no control over the disposition of captured Red troops, their civilian components, or sympathizers. Yong and Kim, as officers of the Korean military, had their directions in this regard from their Korean high command, which included instructions that my information requirements were to be satisfied as much as was possible prior to the prisoners' disposition. In a way, I was pleased with this condition; it freed me from having to plan for the detention, feeding, and other problems related to setting up and maintaining prisoner-of-war camps. I was not in sympathy with the summary manner in which these people were inclined to deal with one another, although to be truthful I could well understand their propensity in this regard.

Kim knocked off and sent the three men back to jail. Going over Lim's notes revealed a lot of information in general terms. Nothing we could put in a report unless it was confirmed by a more reliable informant. Kim's opinion was that these men were opportunists—people who had decided that for the time being it was best for them to side with the Reds. Now that we were in control, Kim felt they were not particularly dangerous, but should be checked on now and then.

The woman, about twenty-eight and not at all attractive from a Western point of view, had a reputation about the island. Her husband had been killed in the last war. She now operated a small teahouse to support herself and three children. Her occupation was not a reprehensible one in the eyes of her neighbors, but when she commenced entertaining the Red political commissar, she gained the immediate enmity of the community. She had had no information of value, and Kim let her go home—tagged, to be sure, for future use.

Lim brought us tea and stepped over to the boys with another pot. I noticed with an appraising eye that she happened to have a cup for Chae and lingered noticeably while he addressed a few soft words to her. Must be betrothed, I thought idly. A boy didn't lower himself to more than curt directions to the gentler sex in this part of the world unless they had been brought together by the ubiquitous matchmaker. Lucky boy, Chae . . .

A sharp challenge from the guard rang out, startling us all, followed almost immediately by a reply. A messenger had arrived from Yong with the news that our reconnaissance of the enemy beach had been successful. The information brought back, however, was disquieting. Lee's bombardment had failed to destroy any of the enemy boats. The information Yong had written, when translated by Lim, indicated they had three large junks of the four-sail seagoing variety, ten coasters, and about twelve sampans. Lee had been unsuccessful because his gunners had had to fire over a steep hill, under the immediate lee of which was the beach where the boats had been hauled up.

Accurate spotting could have made his fire effective, and I considered briefly whether it could have been supplied. The matter should have been considered in the first instance. Now, no matter what hindsight might prove, I had failed to anticipate the possibility. As in most matters concerning naval operations, every probable contingency had to be planned for in advance; a second opportunity rarely, if ever, occurred. This was no exception.

By the time Kim left to relieve Yong at the ferry, we had drafted a radio message, our first, to Tokyo. We told them about the absence of navigational aids in Flying Fish Channel, and about Yonghung-do and Taebu-do, two of the five major islands encircling Inchon Bay, and considered that we had done fairly well under the circumstances. Had we been less foolhardy, we would now be settling down on Tokchok-do, fifteen miles away. Moving in here was a gamble whose odds were about 10,000 to 1. As the odds General MacArthur gave for the success of the landing itself were 5,000 to 1, I felt we could afford a risk that doubled each day.

Yong returned about midnight and reported everything quiet. Taebu-do was blacked out, due to the menacing presence of Lee's gunboat. We sat down to consider our situation. The general briefing and instructions received from General Dager and Captain Pearce constituted, for the most part, the major information requirements of General Headquarters. The methods and means by which we were to obtain this information had been left entirely to our discretion. We had had neither the time nor the opportunity to do any preliminary planning as to how we were going to do our job, and, in fact, it would have been pointless for us to do so. Our *modus operandi* would have to be dictated solely by the situation and condition in which we now found ourselves.

"Yong," I said, "first thing tomorrow morning the three of us will have to sit down and do a little planning. Do you suppose we will be able to turn over the island defense to these people?"

"I think so, Mr. Clark," he replied, "but we'll have to keep an eye on them for a few days. The major threat is the Reds' ability to mount an amphibious attack. I've alerted the section chiefs to be ready to shift a fifty-caliber machine gun on a moment's notice in case they try to move in with junks. Other than that, all we have to worry about are infiltrators and turncoats."

Not exactly a happy thought to end on. But our CP guard had been handpicked and seemed as alert as could possibly be desired. I noticed that on their own initiative they had increased the guards in the immediate vicinity of our camp from two to four, voluntarily reducing their rest period by half. Our immediate danger I considered to be from nocturnal infiltrators tossing hand grenades into our tent. An effort to eliminate us at night by gunfire or hand-to-hand means would be entirely too uncertain.

As I dozed off to await my morning watch, I could not keep from wondering whether one or more of our guards might believe Communism had more to offer than democracy. What an excellent chance it would afford someone desiring to ingratiate himself with the enemy. . . .

Next morning, after a breakfast of canned eggs and ham more than five years old, we went to work on our planning. We soon evolved three major tasks, each of which had to be broken down into its component parts. These were to be tackled as far as possible in a phased order of priority, beginning with information that was needed for the landing itself; followed by information on enemy opposition that would be encountered; and, finally, a running interpretation of all information gathered to determine whether the invasion plan had become known to the enemy.

"Most important of all in the first phase," I said, "is to ensure that an invasion fleet is not stopped in its tracks by mines." Pausing a moment to lend emphasis to this point, I continued. "Our forces *are* going to make a landing, but I do not know whether it will be Inchon, Chinnampo, Wonsan, Hungnam, or half a dozen other places. It is our task to see that Inchon is ready when the time comes. To do this, we must consider that either the East Channel or Flying Fish Channel, or both, may be used by our fleet. We must consider that the Inminkyun will make an effort, if it has not already done so, to lay mines in these narrow channels. And a single ship sunk in the channel could effectively block the fleet's passage up, or retirement back down, these avenues. If we discover that mines are laid, it will be necessary for the channel to be swept before the fleet's passage. This information will require that the Navy rush in minesweepers from other Pacific areas and, therefore, the earlier we obtain an answer to this question, the more time we will give the Navy to order in the 'sweepers.'"

I paused again. "Is this matter of the mines clearly understood?" They indicated it was, but I knew that without professional experience in this form of sea warfare, they could not understand the disaster that could face our forces.

"Almost equally important is that we know whether the Inminkyun have zeroed in the channel approaches with large guns or mortars," I continued. "Any concentrations of fire from the islands lining the channels could force our ships, proceeding up the passage in single-file column, to run a gauntlet of fire. There will be insufficient room to maneuver, either to avoid the fire or to bring guns to bear. The swift tidal current will make it absolutely essential that the ships keep moving, both in order to maintain a steady helm and to avoid being set on the shoals. Further, we must consider that the initial fleet units will, in all likelihood, be making their passage up the channels in the early-morning hours while it is still dark. The navigators will have their hands full just trying to transit the passage without running aground. This darkness factor multiplies the importance of our securing accurate and timely information on the islands bordering the channels."

"You realize, *Kuraku-san*," interrupted Kim, using the Japanese pronunciation of my name, with 'san,' a term of respect, attached, "that our capability for obtaining this information is extremely limited, if not altogether lacking?"

"That is so, Kim, but it will be part of our job to build up our capability. It's not so much a question of *can* we do it at this late stage. We are the only ones here, the job has been given to us, and we *must* do it. I realize that neither you nor Yong is fully conversant with amphibious matters, and there is a not inconsiderable lack of knowledge in the field on my part. However, we are now trying to determine, by analyzing the problem with which the fleet is faced, the essential information which headquarters must have to effect a successful landing. Once we have determined what that information is to be, then we will try to get it. Our capability will be the measure of our own acumen and initiative."

I certainly wished I had a more direct and concrete answer to allay Kim's doubts, but to start with the assumption that we could do only part of the job would be like covering one eye when both were needed. For better or worse, my own attitude would be the gauge of aggressiveness in tackling the operation. I could permit no note of pessimism in my expressions.

"The matter of the fleet navigating the channels at night, and of maneuvering in the bay itself while taking up positions, brings up another important item—that of the navigational aids." Directing their attention to the chart on the table in front of us, I pointed out the various buoys, lights, and lighthouses and explained that it was by means of taking bearings on these objects that a navigator was able to fix his position while under way at night.

As a matter of interest, and to emphasize the importance of this point, I commented on the fact that under normal circumstances even the most doughty navigators in these waters never ventured into Inchon Harbor at night. Inchon Harbor pilots would pick up the ships from overnight anchorages well south of Tokchok-do and bring them in during broad daylight. Quite obviously, then, the fleet would need every bit of information we could gain on navigational aids.

As I developed this subject, I could not help comparing the coming effort of General MacArthur to that of a fly deliberately planning to invade a spider's web and take on the spider. His planners must have sat down, just as we were doing, and uncovered these factors that could spell catastrophe. The planners of the Joint Chiefs of Staff in Washington must have also gone over this thing in detail. In fact, both the Army Chief of Staff, General J. Lawton Collins, and the Chief of Naval Operations, Admiral Forrest P. Sherman, favored a landing elsewhere. Failure here could unravel support for the war in the United Nations, vastly complicating America's problems.

I was not cognizant of the many other factors that went into preparing for the invasion. Most likely, other seemingly insuperable obstacles had to be overcome in getting troops, equipment, supplies, and transportation lined up to meet the deadline now only thirteen days away. I did know, however, that there would be in the battle line two large aircraft carriers, two jeep carriers, two 8-inch (gun) cruisers, two 6-inch cruisers, and twenty-five destroyers. It was hoped to have the "Mighty Mo," the 16-inch gun battleship *Missouri,* take part. She had been conducting training operations off Cuba with a load of midshipmen on board. Putting into the East Coast, she had discharged her trainees, taken on a full load of live ammunition, and was now headed through the Panama Canal for Korea at full speed. Admiral Andrewes was committing every British and Canadian fighting ship available to him. The safety of this mighty armada, the largest since the last war, was now the immediate subject of our concern.

Having discussed the problem connected with the fleet getting into Inchon Harbor, we moved on to the next subject, that of the actual landing of troops and equipment. The enemy would literally be looking right down the throats of our troops as they come in for the assault. The landing would be very hazardous, because it necessitated an assault right into the heart of the city. An amphibious attack on a city would be especially dangerous because the enemy had splendid opportunities for defense, while the ability of our troops to fan out quickly and gain sufficient ground to secure the beachhead was restricted. There existed many obstacles in the way of the troops actually landing successfully from the ships. The most dangerous of these was the capability of the enemy to concentrate his fire on our landing craft from the many buildings that sat on the very edge of the harbor, as well as his ability to utilize any guns he may have emplaced on the heights overlooking the harbor.

I picked up our town plan map of Inchon and spread it out. This map gave a good enlarged picture of the city, its streets, railroad station, waterfront, and so on. Lines crisscrossed the entire area at frequent intervals in grid fashion, and these lines were lettered and numbered much as one of our normal city maps are laid out, so that a particular area could be found easily. By interpolating distances between the grid lines on the map, we could locate accurately even very small targets. Thus, if we were to locate a gun emplacement, we would send this information to Tokyo by grid numbers; by referring to another map, the target could be located simply and accurately. If it were not for this system, it would be necessary to locate the gun by geographical coordinates (latitude and longitude). This method, requiring extensive on-the-spot work with precision instruments, was not exactly practical with the enemy looking over your shoulder.

Another method of locating targets behind the lines, and although very difficult, nevertheless the most commonly used, was to locate the target by reference points, together with how it would appear when seen from the air. A reference point might be a prominent hill or other topographical feature of the immediate terrain—an easily distinguishable patch of brush or trees, a stream, et cetera—with the general direction and distance of each from the target. Normally, combat reconnaissance teams such as ours had to utilize both the grid and the reference point reporting systems.

"Would it not be possible for the invasion to be made at one of these points?" queried Yong, indicating beach areas both to the north and south of the Inchon headland that extended westward into the bay. "If that could be done, then the troops would avoid the concentration of fire from the town itself."

"Perfectly true," I said. "If we can locate a suitable beach, it may mean the difference in thousands of lives. However, in previous studies I have made of this area, it appears that the mudflats which extend from three to five miles out from shore along the coast at low tide would make such a landing extremely difficult, if not impossible. What we must do is determine whether the mud in these areas is of a consistency which will support troops in wheeled or tracked vehicles. We must get this information for the immediate Inchon area also, for if the landing is to be made there, it will have to be at several points at the same time. I anticipate that wherever the landing is to be made, the type of craft used to land troops and equipment will be LSTs and LCVPs, with perhaps a few LCTs."

It was necessary that the characteristics of these craft be known in order that problems connected with their use be understood. The Landing Ship Tank (LST) is a medium-size oceangoing freighter 328 feet long and of about 4,000 tons displacement. She has a rather low speed and is powered by diesel engines. She has twin screws and either single or double rudders. This ship is constructed with a large hold free of bulkheads and extending the greater part of her length, giving the appearance on the inside of a great enclosed football field. The bow section above water is formed of two doors, which can be swung back to allow the forward bulkhead of the hold—or tank deck, as it is commonly re-

ferred to—to be lowered for use as a ramp in loading and unloading operations from the beach. The tank deck will carry a great
number of the largest tanks, trucks, and artillery pieces, which can
be loaded for a voyage of any desired distance and unloaded on the
beach at the scene of operations. When used in an assault on a
beachhead, the LST may carry a deck load of tanks, trucks, jeeps,
artillery, or personnel with their equipment, in addition to the load
in the hold.

Two vital factors that influence a commander in deciding
whether or not to use an LST are the beach gradient (how steep the
slope is from shore to seaward) and the nature of the beach itself
(whether the troops and cargo can be discharged over the beach
without drowning, or in the case of Inchon, sinking over their
heads in the mud). An LST with a normal combat load must be
trimmed (leveled fore and aft) so that the slope of her keel will be
at such an angle that her bow will hit the beach first. The best loading and trim will be that which permits her bow to go up on the
beach farthest, so that her troops and cargo will have the shortest
distance to advance over an open beach area exposed to enemy fire.

However, if the rate of slope of the beach is unknown or erro-
neous, it will be impossible for the ships to trim properly, and may
well result in their getting hung up and broaching. Broaching is
that nemesis of seafaring men wherein a ship swings horizontal to
the line of the beach and then is pounded ashore and to pieces by
the surf. In this position, the ship's engines and anchors are of no
avail, and the ship is wide open to enemy fire with only the slightest chance of discharging her combat cargo. It is a rarity indeed
that a broached ship is ever salvaged. Of course, in the broader
sense, every type of landing craft is subject to these considerations.

After the last war, our naval base at Yokosuka had found on its
hands a substantial number of LCTs, the most numerous and use-

ful of the intermediate landing craft. The Landing Craft Tank is a powered barge or lighter about 100 feet long with an open hold or tank deck, and a square bow that can be lowered to form a ramp for loading and unloading troops and vehicles from the tank deck. The LCT, over long distances, is carried to the scene of operations aboard an LST, or some other large ship. As its name implies, its primary duty is to land tanks and heavy vehicles, but it is invaluable for landing large bodies of infantry, who are protected by the sides and ramp up to the instant of disembarkation. The commandant at Yokosuka, being familiar with the value of these craft, undertook a long-range program of putting these sadly beat-up and war-worn craft back into condition—something of a "mothball" project, utilizing for the most part Japanese shipyard workmen. Rear Admiral "Benny" Decker, USN (Ret.) was responsible for this program, but he returned to retirement before the result of his providential action was put to use at Inchon and other areas in Korea and Japan hard-pressed for this type of transport.

Once discharged of their original cargo, the LCTs become the fleet workhorses. Larger cargo ships unload their gear into them as rapidly as possible, and the little LCTs dash madly between ship and shore, striving desperately to maintain and increase the stockpile of arms and equipment vital to the troops attempting to break out of the beachhead and overrun the enemy before he has a chance to regroup and replenish his own troops and supplies. It's a critical fight against time, the crescendo of effort leveling off only with the breakthrough of the enemy perimeter. It is extremely difficult even for the experienced amphibious man to calculate the individual and collective effort that is expended in such an operation. Even in retrospect, it is a continuing source of utter and bewildered amazement to the amphibious planner that success was achieved.

Finally, but perhaps most important, are the Landing Craft

Vehicle or Personnel (LCVP). Thirty-six-feet long and fitted with tunnel sterns and ramp bows, they carry either troops and their equipment (about thirty-five), or a vehicle such as a light tank, a small truck, or a jeep. All these boats may carry a machine gun or two. When loaded at the transport, troops board them by means of nets over the side. A large attack troop transport carries a small fleet of them with which to discharge its troops over the beach. It is these craft that carry the initial assault troops in any landing—as they would here at Inchon.

Again referring to the map, I pointed out that seawalls lined Inchon's entire waterfront area, but noted with interest that this was not the case with the small island of Wolmi-do, a short distance to the west and connecting to Inchon by a fairly wide causeway. The significance of the seawalls was that the LCVPs could not be used in the normal way if the landing were to be made into the city. LCVPs usually rush up onto the beach bow-on, drop their ramp and discharge, then retract and head back. At Inchon, with the seawalls, it would be necessary that they slow down when approaching the wall in order not to crash their bows, ease up to the wall, and then, depending on the height of the tide, have the troops scramble up and over. It would be necessary to determine just how high these seawalls were. Perhaps scaling ladders would be necessary, I thought, thinking back to a lesson of history recounted by General MacArthur in his speech to the chiefs of staff when they visited him in Tokyo.

He recalled General Wolfe's capture of Quebec in 1759 by scaling the almost vertical cliffs behind the city. This was an operation that took the defenders by surprise and which, by its very boldness, succeeded. Yes, perhaps scaling ladders would be needed here to get over seawalls that the North Koreans considered insurmountable. But I was more concerned with the fact that the boats would have to slow down as they approached the wall and the concentration of enemy fire. Certainly, I said aloud, we must put forward a special effort to locate every possible gun site capable of covering the approaches to the seawalls, in order to avoid the outright slaughter of our troops.

Considering our problem in connection with Wolmi-do, there appeared to be both good and bad aspects. Good, in that a landing could be made without considering the seawall problem; bad, in that the little island was a logical place for the enemy to construct his major harbor fortress. Probably the biggest physical objection to landing at Inchon was the fighting potential of this island. Heavily gunned, it could command all approaches to the harbor. We must study this island thoroughly, for if it was fortified, and unless it was neutralized, D-day losses might be unacceptably high. I felt that Wolmi-do's capture must come before that of Inchon; otherwise we would have to fight the enemy front and rear simultaneously. Such being the case, we would have to place Wolmi-do high on our information priority list.

We got up to stretch our legs and walked over to the beach, where we could see Wolmi-do a scant ten miles away. Our guard on the western promontory was trotting down toward us to report that Lee's gunboat was standing up East Channel. Presumably, Lee was coming in for a belated breakfast, it being almost noon. He had done a good job in discouraging the Reds during our first night. I would have given a good deal to be able to communicate with him, but he could not come up on our radio band. Later, this would prove disastrous to us. As with the British, the only way we could communicate was by channeling our message through Tokyo, except that in Lee's case the additional step of Tokyo going through Admiral Sohn's headquarters at Pusan would be necessary. We had attempted to resolve this difficulty before leaving

Taegu, but had come up against practical objections that would involve adding heavy and complicated equipment to our supplies. A calculated risk we had to accept, along with the many others.

Now that I had an opportunity to observe the surrounding area at greater leisure in daylight, I asked Chae to bring my glasses. Starting with Taemuui-do, the next island on the bay to the north, I scanned the entire area in front of us, noting that a considerable amount of junk and sampan traffic was traveling between the various islands and Inchon. Studying Palmi-do, the lighthouse island halfway between our base and Inchon, I could detect no sign of activity. If anyone were there we should certainly see some smoke from cooking fires. I had already considered the capture of Palmi-do as an emergency base. If we were dislodged from Yonghung-do, we could not draw back, but must go closer in—even if we had to locate in the hills on the mainland south of Inchon. To move farther away would defeat our mission.

Shortly, Lee's gunboat steamed into sight and maneuvered toward an anchorage. The tide was fast ebbing, and Lee would have to drop his hook at least a mile offshore to avoid grounding on the mudflat that my chart indicated existed here. Having already fallen twelve feet, the water had reached the bottom limit of the beach, and was now rapidly uncovering the vast expanse of almost level mudflat. My tide tables indicated another twelve-foot drop before low tide in the next three hours. This fantastic phenomenon of a twenty-four-foot drop in the surface of the bay in a period of six hours I found hard to realize. It was entirely outside my experience. I could picture in my mind's eye a three-story building being completely inundated. . . .

The tidal currents set in motion by the rush of water into and out of the narrow channels between these many islands constituted a constant menace to ships negotiating these waterways or anchored in the harbor. I compared this rush of water to that in a kitchen sink when the stopper is pulled. The Japanese, during their reign in Korea, had undertaken a tremendous project to reduce the danger to their shipping at Inchon by constructing a huge tidal basin. This basin trapped the water at high tide behind massive gates, permitting the ships docked inside to remain afloat while they were loaded or discharged. If we could avoid destroying the gates to this basin during our assault, it would be a valuable prize, speeding up logistic support to our troops.

Mulling over this matter brought me to the realization that at 1700 (5:00 P.M.), the Reds could walk across from Taebu-do to our island if they chose to risk it, and a final opportunity would present itself at 0230 (2:30 A.M.) tonight. After that, we would be free from this particular menace until September 10, when low tide would be at four feet, steadily diminishing until, on the twelfth, it would be zero feet. Thereafter, until the fifteenth, the passage would be dry at low tide—an open and continuing invitation for the Reds to attack.

Yong had dispatched a sampan out to Lee to bring him in before he had a mile of mud to contend with. The boatmen were returning, sculling desperately to make the rocky shoal under the eastern promontory before stranding, and were rewarded with success. God, what an unholy mess that mudflat revealed. The islanders, mostly women, of course, were out on it in force, skirts tied to the waist, grubbing for the small shellfish that made it their home. Within a matter of minutes, it was impossible to tell where their legs left off and the mud began. Kim called my attention to the fact that they were all working in pairs, stating that this was a safety precaution; many deaths had resulted from a lone native slipping off into a hole of quickmud. With an effort, I stifled a shiver up my spine at the prospect of such an end.

We walked leisurely up the beach to meet Lee. A light cooling breeze had come up, stirring fleeting ripples over the placid surface of the bay. I had removed my marine jacket in the hope that I could rid myself of the almost sickening pallor of my skin that duty at Tokyo headquarters had forced on me. The air was invigorating, and I could feel my pores step up their effort to produce more moisture for the breeze to work on.

Lee appeared haggard. A light stubble on his face disclosed that he had not taken time to shave. Although he would not say so, I was certain that his cabin had been empty since I last saw him. His immediate request for coffee, strong and black in true modern Navy tradition, confirmed my suspicion that he had had no sleep.

Back at the CP, I complimented Lee on his bombardment, omitting mention of the failure of his shelling to destroy the enemy small craft. If he should take such news as a loss of face, I knew I could expect an effort to regain his position—with consequent risk to himself and his gunboat. We could afford neither.

Combining Lee's breakfast with our lunch, we briefly reviewed our morning's discussion for Lee's benefit, then launched into the next phase of our deliberations—that concerning information on enemy capability to impede our troops' advance once they were ashore and headed for the target area of Seoul. The capture of this strategic city would effectively pinch off the Reds' main supply arteries to their troops to the south. The resulting gangrenous effect would wither away further resistance.

Seoul being the ultimate target, we had to consider that wherever our forces might actually land, at Inchon or to the north or south, they would have to capture the harbor city before proceeding east along the main (and only) highway leading to Seoul. This analysis limited our problem. Our information coverage would include Inchon, the highway to Seoul, and insofar as we could extend ourselves, Seoul itself, including the town of Yongdungpo just west of Seoul, separated by the winding Han River.

I started enumerating the information that would be needed, while Yong rapidly made notes: defense batteries, antiaircraft batteries, machine-gun positions, trenches, barbed-wire entanglements, land mines, tanks, barracks, and supply dumps. We had to learn exact locations, gun calibers, spacing and layout, fields of fire, emplacements, observation posts, and fire-control setups. All of these were items with which both Kim and Yong were generally familiar by reason of their guerrilla training and experience.

However, I felt it necessary to expand on one point. The great majority of these targets would be attacked from the air, possibly within a matter of hours after we had reported them. It would be necessary to identify the target so that it could be recognized from the air. Therefore, if the building had a roof of a particular color, or was laid out in an unusual manner, it should be reported. Perhaps the building or other target would have another easily recognizable building or structure near it. Such a combination would be unlikely to repeat itself. Reporting the other object also could ensure recognition from the air. Gun emplacements are usually in the open and camouflaged with the surrounding area. However, unless the camouflage is changed daily, it is readily distinguishable, and paint camouflage lends itself to detection if improperly applied. Usually, a system of using two clear reference lines that have the target as their apex is the more effective. Last, but far from least, we had to learn the number of troops and their deployment throughout the general Inchon–Seoul area, together with their routine movements.

As this was being digested, a sudden gust of wind blew the maps off the table. Lim immediately retrieved them, but something disturbed me. Getting up, I walked over to the beach and tested the wind. It was odd that this gust had come from north-northeast. At this time of year, the summer monsoon prevailed. Light variable winds might blow from the south or haul to southwest. During the transitional period preceding the winter monsoon, wind might be expected to haul even farther north. Another gust confirmed the direction. The harbor no longer mirrored a calm. Walking back to the paddy side of our camp, I could see an ominous darkness extending itself over the distant hills.

"Lee," I inquired, "was your barometer down when you came ashore?"

"Nothing unusual, Mr. Clark, or I would have noticed it on the navigator's report. Why?" he rejoined.

"Don't like the look of the weather over there," I said, pointing. "Notice this gusty wind and the direction from which it's coming? North-northeast."

Lee got up and tested the wind, then gazed intently to the south at the gathering dark. "Typhoons don't get around here very often. Maybe once in two years. Never has been a real bad one," he commented uncertainly.

My own experiences with typhoons in the area that mothers them—the South Pacific—had led me to have the greatest respect for these ferocious destroyers. I had safely ridden out two of them in my last ship command, and witnessed firsthand their unbelievably destructive power in the great October 1945 typhoon on Okinawa. I was afraid of typhoons, purely and simply. This was a storm, and it centered somewhere off southern Japan. There wasn't a thing we could do about it. If the wind held and the barometer dropped steadily, we could expect the eye of the storm to pass over or near us within the next twelve to twenty-four hours. But if the wind backed to the left, we should have no worse than an uncomfortable day and night.

"I expect your officer of the deck will inform you of any unusual drop in the barometer, Lee?" I asked, recalling standard practice in my own navy.

"Yes, that's right. Any sudden drop in excess of four hundredths is to be reported at once. Although I hope my OOD will use discretion in trying to get someone ashore through that damnable mud."

"Yong, will you please see that the headman sends a detail of boatmen up to those junks?" I said. "We don't want them washed farther up on the beach when this storm hits. Have them stand by in shifts until the danger is over.

"And Kim, will you please stand by over at the ferry until this period of low tide is past? I wouldn't be surprised if the Reds didn't take Lee's departure this morning as an invitation to return here on a little crusade."

Coming up on our radio, we asked Tokyo for a weather report—not without a little atmospheric trouble due to the storm. I hoped that they could get through to us when the report was ready.

Lee was engrossed in conversation with Chae, and it soon developed that Chae was deeply interested in a career as a sailor. A quick, smart youngster, he should make an excellent hand—perhaps eventually midshipman material. Lee did nothing to quench his interest. Lim as usual was nearby, and from the stricken look on her face, I could see that she'd overheard the conversation. Little Lim was going to find her young love blighted or infinitely stronger before she came to an understanding of her inferior place in this man's world.

Calling Chae, who had seemingly attached himself to me as my aide, I set about securing everything for heavy weather. Covering up the supplies with ponchos, digging a shallow ditch around the tent, covering the vent in the tent top, we were ready for what the elements had to offer. The small stocky trees that closed in the tent

on all sides would afford an excellent windbreak. Loosening the
tent lines would keep our quarters from splitting open in the rain.

This essential work finished, I joined Lee. "Do you know how
those junks came to be here, Lee?" I asked, motioning up the beach
toward the western promontory. "There appear to be ten or fifteen
of them, and all sizes." I had noticed them for the first time this
morning and was somewhat taken aback by the possibilities they
presented.

"I should imagine that they belong to these and other islanders
in the vicinity. Probably utilized by the Reds in transporting supplies around the harbor. The rice levy they make on these islands is
high, and it would take a considerable number of junks to haul it
up the Han to Seoul. Then, too, they have used the larger junks for
carrying their guerrillas and equipment up and down the coast
during the night. I've been able to catch quite a few of them, but
there always seems to be more. I should think taking these junks
will reduce their coastal traffic considerably."

"They're maneuverable, then? Easy to handle?"

"Only in comparison with other junks. They wouldn't stand a
chance against a powered craft."

Powered craft . . . That thought gave me pause. Lee's gunboat
was excellent for blowing junks and sampans to pieces, but I knew
I'd never win Kim's respect by producing live bodies for interrogation that way. Lee carried nothing but life rafts on board his gunboat. Drawing over twelve feet, the gunboat couldn't negotiate the
narrow inlets and passages where the small craft plied, and she had
no boat to do this work for her. Further, we couldn't use the gunboat to land raiding parties, or for any other of the night reconnaissance work I had in mind. I was generally familiar with sailing,
and had handled dhows and sampans on occasion. But to handle
one in taking another by force—that was something else again.

"Do you know of any motor sampans [pompoms] around here that we can get hold of, Lee?" I asked hopefully.

"I believe I sank the only two left around here last week. They were trying to haul a string of troop-loaded barges down the coast to Kunsan, but I caught them just at dawn. Blew hell out of them. Wanted to try and save the motor sampans, but they ran toward shore, so I had to knock them out to keep them from being used again. Sorry!"

Well, at least we had a small fleet of junks with which to operate. Coupled with a group of courageous youngsters, and some wizards of sail, perhaps we wouldn't fare so badly. While this blow was on, we'd call in the best of the captains and lay down some plans that, I hoped, would give us an effective sea arm.

5

THE JUNK FLEET

THE WEATHER REPORT from Tokyo came through at last, stating that typhoon "Jane" had passed Kobe in southern Honshu, Japan, at 1520 (3:20 P.M.). Winds to 120 knots were being recorded. Further reports would be sent through as they became available.

When I imparted this information to Lee, he came to his feet with a nervous exclamation. Together we rushed over to the paddies to recheck the wind. In the last two hours, the sky had taken on a foreboding dark gray color over the entire southwestern quadrant, inexorably chasing the cirrostratus clouds deep into Manchuria. Gusts of wind were now arriving with increasing strength and frequency. We noted with consternation that they still held steady from north-northeast.

"Chae!"

"*Hai!* [Yes.]"

"Tell the headman to send two sampan men down here immediately. Commander Lee will return to his ship at once," I directed, anticipating Lee's request.

"Half the mudflat is covered again, Lee. The sampan should be afloat down at the shoal."

Kim returned from the ferry. "No sign of activity on Taebu-do," he reported. "Have you noticed the weather?"

"We have been studying it, Kim. Report from Tokyo says it's a typhoon. We may be in trouble unless it starts recurving east soon."

We could see a group of men hurriedly making their way around the hill from the village toward the beach where the junks had been hauled up. The waves generated by a storm could wash them so high on the beach it would take days to haul them back down. Fortunately, the junks were under the lee of the promontory and would escape the full force of the wind.

Yong returned with Chae and the two boatmen. We all headed for the sampan. "No reason for you to try to ride out the storm in here, Lee," I said, as he climbed into the boat. "Deep and open water is safest. Return here as soon as you consider it safe."

"Suppose it will be safe to leave? Maybe those Reds will start acting up with my ship gone," he said anxiously.

"I doubt very much if they'll risk their necks in this weather. You should be able to get back in before it's calm enough for them to do anything."

We pushed them clear of the rocks, and the scullers took over. Waves were beginning to build, with scattered whitecaps showing. The weather was making up faster now, and even though the typhoon recurved, it might come near enough to make this harbor a death trap for any small craft.

By the time we had returned to the CP, it had started to rain. The women had moved two hibachis inside the tent and were busy cleaning shellfish. Evidently, we were going to have a treat for dinner.

Sitting on our cots, we explored the unexpected situation presented by the weather. "I can't see where this storm will set us back, Mr. Clark," Yong offered. "Providing it lets up early tomorrow," he added. "As I see it, we can do nothing until we get the junks ready, and we have some of the best skippers going over them now. Once they've finished their inspection, we'll know how many can be used and what will be required to fit out the rest."

"That's true," I said. "I wonder if we can't go so far as to start organizing crews and detailing those lads in our defense force with sea experience as a marine force for the junks?"

"I'll take care of that this evening, sir," Yong replied.

"We'll need a considerable number of straw bags filled with sand in order to provide platforms for the machine guns we'll mount in the junks. Do you think you can handle that, too?"

"I'll have some women do it in the morning."

"Try to get bags smaller than these rice sacks. We want as little weight as possible."

"We have no information for tonight's report yet, *Kuraku-san*?" asked Kim.

"None as yet, Kim."

"I have made arrangements with the headman to talk to all the people on the island who have been away from it during the past month. Something should develop from such a screening."

"An excellent idea, Kim," I said. "It should afford us a good background against which to check any new information we receive. When do you start?"

Kim would begin his screening about 1730 (5:30 P.M.) and would carry it through until midnight. It was going to be a long siege, requiring intense concentration the entire period.

"I'll give you a hand with it, Kim," I said, "and we'll take Lim along with us to help catalogue the information."

"Yong, let's break out a few bottles of—" I started to say, but stopped abruptly.

The three women appeared to be frozen beside their cooking, all staring fixedly at the ground beside the hibachi. Rising slightly to see over the end of the cot, I saw a deadly little viper, a mamusha, its head pointed directly at the bare feet and legs of the women. The thing was too close to them to risk a shot with my .45. I started reaching for my bayonet-knife on the foot of the cot. I had hardly moved when an object blurred past my face and buried itself an inch behind the viper's neck, neatly severing the head completely from its body.

Kim had certainly not lost his touch with the knife; that throw had been a good eight feet—and fast. Moon recovered the knife, cleaned it off, and returned it to Kim. The two girls were still tense as Moon picked up the two parts of the snake and tossed them into the fire pit just outside.

"Many of those things around here, Moon?" I asked.

"There are not many at this time of the year, *Taicho-san*," she replied, "but the rain will bring them out."

True to form, no expression of thanks was extended by the women to Kim, although he may well have saved one of their lives by his quick action. It was not that they were ungrateful. They merely understood that the saving of a woman's life was so negligible an act on his part that an expression of gratitude would demean him.

My attention was again attracted to the floor, and close inspection revealed hundreds of little bugs that had the appearance of what are called "jiggers" back in the States. The floor was literally crawling with them. The dry ground held an attraction for more than snakes.

"You mentioned something about bottles, Mr. Clark," Yong prompted.

"Yes, I wish you would break out two bottles of the Canadian Club. We'll take them with us. Perhaps a well-placed shot or two will win us a prize." A heavy pun, but oddly enough not lost on Yong. Perhaps we could all use a drink, come to think of it.

"Let's sample that scotch, Yong. I hope there will be more auspicious occasions, but right now I can't think of a more appropriate one."

"Right sir. Coming up. Lim, set out our canteen cups. How about a can of cheese to go with it?"

"Cheese! Where the devil did you find any cheese?"

"It's in one of these C-rations. Small can. Kind of orange cheese. Not bad."

"Crackers?" Might as well go whole hog.

"There are crackers, but I'm afraid the weevils have beat us to them."

"Give a couple of packages to Moon and have her roast the weevils out. I'll not be denied my crackers at this stage."

For the next half hour, we gave ourselves over to relaxation. Looking back, none of us had averaged more than four hours' sleep a day in the past four days, and last night it had been cut to two hours. Kim's face took on a rosy hue after the first drink. Yong's face soon followed suit, and they both launched into animated conversation with Moon. They had reverted to Korean, which I couldn't follow, but it soon developed that Moon was an expert masseuse.

Kim promptly climbed out of his clothes, and Moon commenced the ritualistic kneading, pressing, and thumping. Within a matter of minutes, she was finished and working on Yong. Kim had dashed outside, and I could hear him stomping around in the cold downpour, slapping himself, and singing some outlandish Manchurian song. Shortly, Yong and I joined him. It was marvelous what a massage and cold shower could do to rejuvenate a tired body. Inside the tent again, the three women, laughing and giggling, went to work on us with towels until our skins were beet-red. Moon had thoughtfully broken out clean clothes for us, and we donned them gratefully.

"The typhoon is recurving," I announced. "The wind has backed almost to northwest in the past two hours. I shouldn't be surprised to see it calm down by noon tomorrow."

"We'll be able to proceed on schedule, then," Yong said. "Do you have any operations planned for tomorrow if we can have the junks ready?"

"I've a few things in mind. The most urgent business, however, I hope we'll be able to get a start on tonight. Kim, while we're running through the villagers, will you please try to select one or more that appear trustworthy, and with some near relatives that live on Taebu-do—preferably near the Red headquarters? We want to set up a courier run in order to learn any of their plans. You might consider using the lady friend of the political commissar. Perhaps she can be induced to follow her boyfriend and send back what she can learn."

"Use her as a courier?"

"Sorry, I didn't make myself clear. We'll still need the courier setup. She could be a means of tapping the knowledge of the commissar. She would stay there and, shall we say, comfort him after his arduous day's work."

"But how will we be able to ensure her loyalty? She has already shown a fine disregard of patriotic fervor in that respect," Yong asked, pointedly.

"The method is obvious," Kim answered. "We shall see that her children have the best of care during her absence."

"No coercion," I admonished. "She may desire to volunteer as a means of regaining the goodwill of the village."

They both gave me a quizzical and searching look at this dictum. I knew at once that I had gone too far. To them, she was nothing but a traitor. Her life and the lives of her children were forfeit. No Korean would defend their right to life. We had granted her a reprieve, and now I was suggesting that she might resume a place in society by the simple process of indulging our request. The Republic of Korea had executed thousands of people like her without the slightest compunction. Yong and Kim had been through too much, suffered too much, to see any need for compassion in such an arrant object case as this. They saw through my motive instantly. Perhaps they would heed my order, but most likely they wouldn't. I let it stand, accepting the inevitable loss of face.

Cynn served us a huge portion of rice and a side dish of the shellfish. Yong surprised us both by reaching under his cot and producing a bottle of soy sauce that he had bartered from the village. The shellfish reminded me vaguely of the huge Japanese snails I had found so delicious on Okinawa, and later on Palau, where they were busy destroying the coconut farms.

"Do they have snails in Korea, Cynn?"

"I do not know, *Taicho-san*," she replied. "I have never been to the mainland."

This reply caused Yong to interrupt the steady action of his *hashi* (chopsticks) and direct a stream of Korean at her. These people were no different than we were. Some were born, lived, and died having never ventured out of an area of a few square miles.

"She did not understand the Japanese word 'snail,' Mr. Clark," Yong said. "The Japanese did bring snails over here, but kept them under strict control. They are very dangerous to many crops. The Japanese needed all our crops," he finished bitterly.

Lim started calling in the boys from outside, where we had rigged them a shelter under a couple of ponchos. They had refused to take shelter in the village. Perhaps the large steaming bowls of rice had something to do with their decision, it being so scarce to the average family, but it was my opinion they would have remained in any case. Lim must have been disappointed when they were all fed and Chae hadn't shown up. He had the watch. Lim would have to arrange for a few minutes' privacy with him later.

"This evening I'll give these boys further instructions in how to break down and use these machine guns," Yong said. "Do you know where the cleaning equipment is, Mr. Clark?"

"There should be a set of equipment with each gun, Yong. Check the boxes carefully. There should be a couple of extra fifty-caliber barrels, too. They still have packing preservatives on them that will have to be removed. Better save that for tomorrow—it'll be a mess."

Kim and I threw on our ponchos, enveloped little Lim in another, picked up the whiskey, and headed for the village schoolhouse, where we hoped to glean material for tonight's report to Tokyo. I had felt pretty grim, but the massage, shower, and a stomach warmed and full of rice returned the edge to my spirits. I looked forward with anticipation to this evening's work, and even found cause for optimism. Surely these people must have a considerable fund of information that we could use. We could reasonably expect a number of direct leads to other profitable sources in Inchon. The Oriental system of family loyalty could be depended on to produce lines of communication into that city, and perhaps even into Seoul itself. With these comforting thoughts tracing intricate battle patterns through my mind, my pace unconsciously quickened so that I had to slow down when I heard Lim trotting behind me.

By midnight, we had finished. I had been more than justified in my optimism. We had nine items of vital information to report to Tokyo, all confirmed by two or more parties. Sending Lim home—she had stubbornly refused to go earlier, although she had fallen asleep twice—we headed back to the CP. By 0130 we had cleared our report with Tokyo, and we turned to cataloging the rest of our data while it was fresh in our minds. A veritable treasure-trove of useful leads and information, it would prove the basis for all our future planning and operations.

Outside, the wind had increased in force—I judged it to be about thirty knots—and was whipping the rain almost horizontally along its path. But the wind had again backed and was now coming in from west-northwest. The typhoon had just about passed, and this effect was like the final angry switch of its tail as it slowly receded along the conventional path to the northeast and the Aleutians.

Yong had set up cots for Moon and Cynn. When we had returned, Moon, who was sleeping with one eye open, had made us coffee—undoubtedly at Yong's prompting. She kept our canteen cups full. We needed every drop. Yong had made two trips out to the ferry to check the guard, which was no mean accomplishment. Trudging over miles of trail in this weather was something more than routine.

"Anything left in that bottle, Kim?"

"*Hai!*"

"Let's kill it, then, and turn in," I said. It was 0400, and I felt the need for a soporific. I didn't want to dream about this business.

We were up again at 0630. The wind had fallen off to a fresh breeze. The continuing rain afforded us the opportunity for another invigorating shower. After some hot black coffee, Yong and I headed for the junks to see how they had fared during the storm, while Kim went to inspect the guard at the ferry.

Except for some minor damage to rigging, the junks had weathered the storm well. Fortunately, the period of high winds had coincided with that of low tide, so that no damage had occurred as a result of the uprush of waves against the boats. We could count ourselves very lucky, and I idly wondered how the invasion fleet loading in the ports of southern Japan had come through the typhoon.

Yong introduced the chief of the local fisherman's association, who, far from looking like a businessman, had all the physical attributes and appearance of a China coast pirate. This impression was enhanced when I saw nestled against his side a beautiful *kukri*, a long, double-curved knife commonly found in Nepal, and used extensively by the Gurkhas.

Chang was his name. I would never forget it. It was Chang who would attend to the details of manning and fitting out the junks. I looked around for the women who were supposed to fill sandbags. "What time were the women coming down, Yong?"

"They should be here about eight."

"Better put it off until we can get some dry sand. This wet stuff will add too much weight."

"How many of these can we use, Chang?" I asked, indicating the boats.

"All of them will sail, *Taicho-san,* but I would not trust more than seven of them in an emergency. Those two coasters down at the end belong to [the island of] Yongyu-do. They are good sailers and handle well, but their rigging is very bad," he concluded, shaking his head.

"How about the sampans?"

"Only four of them are seaworthy. The rigging on all of them is bad."

"You say you wouldn't trust some of these in an emergency. Just what is wrong with them?" I queried.

Chang shuffled nervously and glanced several times at the junks before replying. I felt certain that he expected I would criticize his judgment and that he would lose face in front of the boatmen that surrounded us if I did so. Nevertheless, he answered my question directly—a tribute to his strong character.

"Several of the seagoers have cracked keels which have been re-inforced. The reinforcing has worked loose due to the many beach-ings the boats have made. This has sprung several of the ribs, and the caulking between the planking has come loose. At sea it would require several men to keep them bailed out. The others have poor rigs and will handle sluggishly. I know most of these boats," he concluded, with a note of challenge in his voice.

I thought this over deliberately for a short time while Chang glanced around at the others. Then I changed the subject. "Perhaps you can shift the good rigging from the bad boats and then we can use the other good boats," I suggested.

This proposal took Chang by surprise. It meant, among other things, robbing the good rigging of some Yonghung-do boats to supply boats that were owned by Yongyu-do. Most likely, the own-ers or the association officers weren't here to discuss such a mo-mentous matter. Such arrangements were normally consummated only after days and perhaps weeks of artful dissimulation, more often than not furnishing a welcome excuse for *kisaeng* (geisha) parties—the end object of which being to befuddle the other side's wits into extending an advantage in the deal.

The immediate huddle into which my radical proposition had

sent Chang was attracting the others. Although I didn't understand Korean, it was not difficult to see that the entire group had
definite opinions in the matter. Yong and I moved out of the driz-
zle under the lee of one of the seagoers.

"Do you think they'll hedge on an answer, Yong?" I asked.

"Very likely, Mr. Clark. From what I gathered, there are difficulties stemming from association rules, as well as interests of absen-
tee owners."

I still found it difficult at times to be patient with these people,
and under the stress of circumstance I had occasionally given way
to impatience. But it was never a wise thing to do if it was cooperation that was being sought. Generally, in a situation where they
wanted to oppose an order, one or more alternatives would be offered, carefully tailored to avoid any impression of resistance. Unless you were prepared to accept one of these alternatives, it was
well to look elsewhere for support. My position here was such that
I could not look elsewhere. The next move was obviously up to me.

"Chang!" I summoned.

Waiting until all of them had gathered around, I changed my
proposal to a different plane. "Chang, during the course of shifting the rigging, some gear will be broken and sails will probably
be torn. Perhaps more damage will occur when it is transferred
back again. Of course, the owners will have to be paid for such
damage."

I paused to let this take effect. "I will, therefore, turn over five
sacks of rice to the association to pay for such damage."

This brought an instant response. The work would proceed immediately, Chang assured us.

We would soon have two seagoers, three coasters, and four sampans, with rigging the best that could be had by cannibalizing the
others. Yong had given the complete picture of our plan to Chang

and had entrusted him with all the details concerning the use to which these craft were going to be put. Chang would be the commander of our small seagoing task force. Now if we wanted to run a mission, all we'd have to do would be to inform Chang, and the boat would be manned and ready.

"Yong, will you see that Chang makes his headquarters at the CP? We'll have many matters to discuss, and most of them will involve using his boats. Particularly, we'll want to discuss two operations I have in mind for tonight for which we'll need one of the coasters and a sampan. Suppose you invite him down for lunch."

When we returned to the CP, Yong dispatched Song, one of the off-duty guards, to the village to stop the women from coming down to fill the sandbags. Kim had not yet returned from the ferry, so we had a cup of coffee while waiting for his return and for breakfast.

Lim opened the tent flap and looked in with big red-rimmed eyes. Lack of sleep certainly had taken its toll. I forgot such mundane matters immediately when she rolled half a dozen eggs out on the bunk for us to feast our eyes on. Things were definitely looking up for the expedition. First an army, then a navy, and now fresh eggs! Lee hadn't given me a wrong steer when he suggested they might have eggs here.

I took off my wet shoes and trousers, which Moon hung up to dry. Sitting cross-legged on the cot, I contemplated my surroundings. The tent had taken on a distinct homey atmosphere in the last twenty-four hours. The ground was dry, although still crawling. The women had found a mirror and hung it on the center pole, with the kerosene lamp just above it. In one corner, our radio sat on a field table, with a folding chair in front. In another, the women had set up their wet-weather kitchen. I had taken a corner position for my cot—considering it a strategic spot in case I had to move rapidly. When I ran, it would be for cause and I didn't intend my way to be obstructed unnecessarily by other obstacles. Fully a quarter of the floor space, including the remaining corner, was covered by supplies, equipment, and ammunition.

Five cots were set up, including the two Yong had assigned Moon and Cynn last night, and I assumed Lim would pitch her cot in the kitchen corner when the hibachi were moved outside. I thanked the fate that, during my past eight years in the Orient, had inured me to the casual treatment afforded nakedness by these people. At least a few of my friends and acquaintances would have developed a psychotic condition under such circumstances.

It was crowded, no mistake, but far less crowded than those houses up in the village where at least fifteen people lived and slept in a room the size of this tent. This was living in luxury. Lim and Cynn were about the size of my daughter, who was twelve. I found it difficult to consider them older. Moon, in her early thirties, clucked around us like a hen looking after her chicks. As far as the girls were concerned, there was no question as to who ruled the roost.

I was cleaning my forty-five when Kim shoved back the tent flap and walked in—soaked. Everything was in order at the ferry. The boys had taken good care of the guns and ammunition. I could sense that he was very well pleased with the result of his inspection.

"The section leader reports that there was considerable firing on Taebu-do early this morning. Machine-gun tracers were seen from two different points. It lasted about thirty minutes."

"Any explanation for it?"

"*Iie. Sono koto wa chittomo wakarimasen.* [No, I don't understand it at all.]"

"Guess they must be jittery," I said, chuckling to myself at the prospect. After breakfast, we returned to our plans. "Will the woman undertake our little mission to Taebu-do, Kim?" I asked.

"*Hai*. We will send her over tonight. Accompanying her will be the two boys and the girl we screened last night. What time is low tide?"

I checked my tables to be sure. "Low water will be at 0310. Depth will be about seven and a half feet at the deepest point. They'll have to work it as we did before, except that they won't have Lee's light to contend with. Do you think it wise to send them all over at once?"

I could see that Kim was in over his head. "We have only the one sampan left at the ferry. It'll hold only five at most. Maybe it would be better to send only the woman and one of the boys tonight?"

He had missed the point. "The woman does not know our courier plan, nor the two boys and the girl we intend to use as couriers. That is so?" I led him to the crux of the matter.

"Ah, so!" he breathed audibly, as understanding overtook him. "But if they are to get the information from her, she will come to know them. Is it not so?"

"It is not such a simple thing, Kim. First we chose the couriers because they have close relatives living in Taebu-do. The woman will take a message to one of the relatives who owns a house. The message will instruct the owner to give the woman a room so that she may entertain her friend, the commissar. The owner will do this because of his near relatives on Yonghung-do."

I lit a cigar while Yong and Kim considered this procedure. "The information she obtains will be written and given to the courier at the house at a designated time. A simple system of signs and countersigns will have to be developed for each day for the next two weeks and given her. These will be used by the courier in making contact to pick up the information. Each meeting will be made in total darkness to avoid recognition of the courier. Is this understood?"

"*Hai, hai.*"

"One courier will be dispatched at a time. They will not know each other. Each will live with his relative until information has been received, when he will return. The process will be repeated by the other couriers in turn. Such is the method we will use here."

"One final caution. Secrecy is absolutely essential. We will say that the woman is being sent to Tokchok-do for punishment. Her absence then will not be a subject for gossip. The youngsters, during their absence, will be on board our boats as helpers. Only their parents will know the truth."

"The details of the signs, and arrangements to carry over the couriers and bring them back, you can work out, Kim?"

"*Hai, Kuraku-san.* I will do this thing. Will you wish to check the arrangements?"

"It will not be necessary, thank you, Kim," I replied. Detailed supervision could only lead to dependence, and would in time kill Kim's initiative. The success of this operation could mean a good deal to us, but failure would not be such a catastrophe as the loss to me of Kim's keen mind and broad experience.

Song stuck his head in and reported his errand to the village completed. The women would not come down to fill the sandbags today. He had no sooner withdrawn than Ahn, another of the guards, reported that some of the junks were afloat. Pulling on our still-wet clothes and boots, we walked out to the scarp to take a look at our incipient navy. Chang had succeeded in warping out the two seagoers and two of the coasters. The heavy lug-sails had not been hoisted. Instead, the junks were being maneuvered out to anchorage by huge sweep-oars with the advantage of the now-ebbing tide. The light sampans would be floated with little trouble.

The rain had stopped completely. A gentle breeze was calmly ironing the wrinkles from the bay. Overhead high winds were scudding jagged storm clouds over the eastern horizon. Soon I should expect to see Lee's gunboat steaming in. He'd most likely spent another sleepless night. Better plan on having him in for lunch. A good stiff shot, a massage, and a few hours' sleep would compensate for his night's vigil.

Yong called Ahn over. "Go tell all the section chiefs that I wish to see them here at eleven," he directed. Ahn was off for the village at a trot. Now that we knew we'd have boats, it was time to select their marine contingents.

"Mr. Clark, I would recommend we assign all but two of our own guard unit to accompany us in the junk you select. We will require at least two guards to remain with the CP."

"An excellent idea, Yong. Will you inform Hyun, please." I would be interested to see whether Yong selected Chae to remain behind out of consideration for Lim.

The wind blowing on our wet clothes made it chilly, and we returned to the tent. It was time to contact Tokyo. The news was bad. The typhoon had damaged quite a few ships and set back the invasion loading schedule by at least thirty-six hours. It would mean around-the-clock work from here on in to overcome this time loss—but the landing would still be made on schedule. We had no traffic for Tokyo, and signed off.

Lim had been busily combing her hair in front of the mirror. "I am a Christian, *Taicho-san*," she stated abruptly. "Today is Sunday. I wish to go to church. May I?"

Sunday the third already. Eleven days to D-day.

"Yes, yes, of course, Lim," I said. Then, thinking further, "Do you, Moon, or you, Cynn, want to go to church?"

"We are both shamanists, *Taicho-san*," Moon replied for both of them.

"Is there a shaman, then, on the island?" I asked in surprise. Actually, Confucianism is the semi-official cult of the Koreans, and ancestor worship is universal. However, the popular cult is the propitiation of demons, a modified version of the shamanism of northern Asia. The shaman is a combination of priest, medicine man, and prophet. Family worship is connected with the domestic ritual. Each family possesses one or more drums, and when these are beaten, some member tries to communicate with the spirits. Because I had not heard these drums—they are taken up at almost any hour of any day—Moon's statement surprised me.

"No, *Taicho-san*," she replied pensively. "Only our family shaman."

"Are there many Christians on the island, Lim?"

"There are about two hundred, *Taicho-san*," she said, and added proudly, "My father, the schoolteacher, is also the Christian preacher."

In spite of the unsympathetic attitude of and, at times, outright persecution by the Japanese of Christian missionaries, the religion flourished in Korea. These Christians now formed a hard core of Korean resistance to Communism, and the missionaries themselves were in no wise inactive. I thought of accompanying Lim to church, but realized I would not be able to understand the sermon. However, I would drop in later for a few minutes for the psychological effect it might have on the congregation. It could do no harm to cement our relations with this group.

"Captain Lee is coming in," Ahn announced.

Good. There was always the chance that something might have happened to him. Lee's gunboat was really all that stood between the Reds and ourselves. With him gone, they could sweep over us at any time they chose. I regretted our mission having to depend upon such a thin lifeline.

While Yong and the off-duty guard went to work again on the machine guns, Kim and I smoothed up our catalogue of information, gleaning from it two more items for Tokyo that we had overlooked.

After lunch—we had moved outside again—I laid open for discussion the two operations for this night. "It would be unrealistic for us to believe that the Inminkyun do not, by this time, know about us. We must assume that they do and plan accordingly. I am greatly surprised that there has been no attempt as yet on this CP. Undoubtedly, the weather has worked against any plans they may have had for attacking us. From now on, we must be particularly alert."

"I have instructed the section chiefs to check all the guards' hand grenades," interjected Yong.

"That's fine, Yong. Now, if the Reds know our weakness, they are certain to make a concerted attempt to dislodge us. Should they succeed, we must be ready to move to another base. We've discussed this problem at some length and concluded that moving farther away from Inchon will only serve to defeat our mission. The problem, then, is to decide on a suitable alternate base. Lee, do you have any suggestions?"

"Have you considered any of the small islands to the north of Inchon, Mr. Clark? Yui-do lies about a mile from the city. Its western tip extends into the channel. Then there is Chongna-do about a mile farther north, but not on the channel. I guess that wouldn't be suitable, though, come to think of it. It has a large fishing village. But Yui-do is rocky. Few people ever go there. Chang, you've been there. What do you think of it?"

Chang was studiously puffing away on one of the cigars I had given him. After a lengthy deliberation, he replied. "It is well-situated. Our boats can get in and out easily, both to the channel and to the mainland above Inchon. At low tide, it is easy to walk from the island to the mainland—"

"Walk?" Yong interrupted.

"*Hai, so desu.* [Yes, that is so.]"

"At every period of low tide?"

"*Hai.*"

"Ah, so! I hadn't considered the tide," Lee muttered apologetically. "The same would be true of Chongna-do."

"In order to have a bare minimum of protection on an island base," I explained, "the island should be surrounded by channel water at low tide. Yonghung-do has something less than this minimum, as the channel is fordable from Taebu-do at low tide about eight days out of fifteen. It will not be fordable again until the eleventh. If we are deprived of this minimum safety factor, it will be better to move to the mainland, where we can evade any pursuers in the hills. There, at any rate, we will not have to fight with our backs to the sea. Do you have any other suggestions, Lee?"

"The adjacent islands of Si-do and Sin-do meet your requirements, and are about ten miles due west of Inchon. However, the Inminkyun have about fifty troops stationed on them. We might be able to take them," he finished doubtfully.

"Let's take a look at the chart," I suggested.

Spreading it out on the table, we studied intently the two islands Lee had referred to. If it were a good spot, I would venture an attack on it. "You will notice that although there is channel water at low tide," Chang observed, "the channels themselves are very narrow on three sides. It would be hazardous to maneuver your gun-boat, Captain Lee, in such confined waters."

"And the Inminkyun have a row of islands spaced like stepping-stones from Inchon right up to the back door," Yong added.

This was true. In a series of very short boat hauls, the Reds could feed troops into Sin-do directly from the Inchon garrison force. They would be under the protection of their coast defense guns at all times. It did not look good.

"Kim?"

"It appears as though if operations were run from Sin-do, every boat we would send in or bring out would have to run a gauntlet past nearby islands which will be alerted and on the lookout for them. Compare such a situation with that which exists here, where we have a direct run into Inchon or any of the other islands without the possibility of the Inminkyun observing our movements. I think it would be a bad choice, *Kuraku-san.*"

This discussion was providential indeed. I had determined in my own mind that of all the islands in the gulf, there was only one alternative to Yonghung-do. That was Palmi-do. None of the objections that had been raised to Lee's proposals were applicable to this little lighthouse island situated practically in the middle of the harbor, five miles from the nearest island and from Inchon. I waited for a few minutes while they discussed the pros and cons of Sin-do, and to see if Palmi-do would be mentioned.

Cynn took the opportunity to pass around the tea. While everyone relaxed, it occurred to me that the Oriental way of approaching things had definite advantages—where time could be afforded the give-and-take of the game.

"What do you know of Palmi-do, Chang?" I asked.

He sucked air in between his teeth with a hissing sound. "Palmi-do. Ah so."

Chang weighed the question carefully. "The island has been restricted for many years, and only the lighthouse people go there. There are two or three well-built houses on the southwestern slope. These can be readily seen when passing by, although they—"

"Those houses are badly damaged, Mr. Clark," Lee interrupted to say.

"How did that happen, Lee?"

"When Inchon was being evacuated, the houses were shelled to deny their use to the Reds."

"The lighthouse?"

"Oh no, it was not touched."

"Has anyone actually been on Palmi-do?" I asked, looking at each face. There was no response. "Chang, have any of your fishermen ever visited there?"

"*Iie. Ton demo nai.* [No, they've had nothing to do with it.]"

"We don't have much to go on, then. What do you think of using Palmi-do as our alternate base?" I asked, coming directly to the point.

They turned to the chart again. "One advantage from a defense viewpoint, Mr. Clark, is that the only possible place to make a landing on the island is this narrow sand spit," Lee commented, referring to the chart. "The island is otherwise steep-to [vertical cliffs]. A single machine gun could cover the entire spit."

"Maybe the Reds have thought of that and set one up," Yong said, after a moment's thought.

"Do we know for a fact that there are any Reds on Palmi-do?" I asked.

This question met with silence, so I continued, hoping to bring the matter to a decision. "We are in agreement, then, that Palmi-do should be surveyed as a possible alternate base?"

No dissent was forthcoming, so I wrapped it up. "The first step, then, will be to determine whether Palmi-do is occupied by the Inminkyun. Yong, will you, Kim, and Chang please lay on a reconnaissance mission to Palmi-do tonight? Better write this down, Yong: High tide will be at 2117. It will be dark at 2030, and moonrise will be at 2200. However, its light will be dim. I would recommend the approach be made during the dark period and the reconnaissance be carried out after moonrise."

"Don't you think it might be well to be prepared if our reconnaissance proves there to be no Reds on Palmi-do?" Yong asked. "Perhaps we should . . ."

"Of course, Yong. Will you see that a small guard detachment is detailed to accompany us? We can only spare it one light machine gun, but I doubt that they will need it. Lee's gunboat should prove a sufficient threat to keep any Reds away."

Hyun had brought up a youngster who was impatiently trying to catch Yong's attention. "What is it?" Yong demanded crisply.

The lad let loose with a torrent of Korean.

"They have found an abandoned sampan over on the southwest shore. It was pulled up behind some big rocks," Yong interpreted, and fired some more questions.

"No footprints or drag marks leading up from the beach. It's one of the several places on the island where there is no mudflat."

"Did this lad find the boat?" I asked.

"Yes, sir. He had the eight-to-twelve watch nearby, where he discovered the sampan. He says it wasn't there yesterday."

I shrugged in resignation. It was bound to happen. Probably had happened several times before. This one had landed recently, though. Last night, undoubtedly. During the storm, too. Most likely early this morning when it had started to let up. Well, in that case, there should be footprints in the wet earth—if the rain hadn't washed them away. Then, too, he or they should be soaked to the skin. Not much to go on, but it'd have to do.

"Have the off-duty sections make a thorough search of every house on the island, Yong. Look for wet clothes—men's or women's. Any wet clothing they find, see that its condition is explained. Bring in anyone that doesn't have a good story."

I turned to Hyun. "Hyun, will you please take a couple of your men and this lad, go back to where the sampan was found, and search carefully for footprints in the wet ground covering the exits from the beach. Put yourself in the position of having landed last night. You would want to get out of the rain quickly, and dry or change your clothes. If you find no footprints, follow your own ideas of what you would have done—and do it. Consider the probability that whoever landed is familiar with the island and may even have relatives here. Any questions?"

"No, *Taicho-san*," he answered briefly, and hurried off with his charge. Yong set out to contact his section chiefs. "Should we double the guard here, *Kuraku-san?*" Kim asked with concern.

"I think not, Kim, Hyun has two men guarding the CP at night now. The off-duty guard sleeps right here. If anything comes up, they'll handle it," I answered hopefully, and turned back to the business at hand.

"Kim, let's take a look at the catalogue and review the information on the motor sampans at Inchon."

He handed the cards to me and I studied them briefly. "This information indicates that there are either three or four motor sampans in the inner harbor. One is about a hundred tons, and is probably damaged. The other three are small, condition unknown, except that they have not been seen in operation since the Reds occupied the city. I believe we all understand how important it is to secure a motor sampan in good condition. With such a craft, we could sink or capture every sailing boat in the harbor. Wind and tide could be ignored."

It was a wonderful thing to contemplate, and I did not then realize that it would have its limitations, too.

Cynn put another pot of tea on the table. I took this as an excuse to sit back and light up another cigar, offering one to Chang, who, of course, accepted happily. It was not difficult to see that Chang was used to good living. Someday I must try to uncover his background. The others had switched to Korean, probably discussing the question of the motor sampan.

It was September 3 already. It seemed like yesterday that Captain Pearce had called me in to discuss the operation. I found it hard to account for the hours that had since elapsed. Time had advanced unchecked and uninterrupted by the usual periods of eating and sleeping that serve to accentuate an awareness of its passing.

There was something basically different in handling a ship or firing a gun. It was being able to see or feel or otherwise being sensible of the work being done. Gathering information, without doing anything positive with respect to it, yet knowing full well its potential, was positively frustrating. In consequence, it seemed that I had accomplished little in furthering the mission. The bare mechanics of getting the operation started was an unexpectedly time-consuming business. I was not at all certain that the skeleton plans I had formed would be blessed with any degree of success.

Had I not been so confident in the ability of my lieutenants, I would long since have given way to the strong urge to move into the mainland hills a few miles south of Inchon. As always in a critical evolution, there is the desire to push aside the helmsman or signalman and "do it yourself." Fatal as I knew giving way to this urge to be, I nevertheless entertained it.

"*Kuraku-san!*"

"Yes, Kim?"

"Rhee, the boatman, is the best man to send in to find out about the motor sampan. Chang says this is so. Chang says Rhee has been into Inchon many times since the Inminkyun came and knows many people on the waterfront. His son and daughter live only two blocks from the harbormaster's office."

"You talked to Rhee last night, did you not, Kim?"

"*Hai, so desu.* Rhee is ready to go at any time. He has no family here. His parents live on Tokchok-do, where he has also lived since his wife died. He was supposed to have gone in to Inchon the morning we landed here. Nothing will be thought of his being in the city if he says he stopped by Yongyu-do for a few days," Kim explained further.

Rhee seemed a likely candidate for the job. He and the other boatman, Lu, had given Lee excellent assistance on the gunboat. "What is your plan, then, Kim?"

"When we go to Palmi-do tonight, we will take a small sampan in tow. We should arrive at Palmi-do about 2100. That will leave an hour of darkness for Rhee to get to Inchon. Both the wind and sea will be with him, so he should make it with ease before moonrise. He will stay at Inchon until he finds out everything about the motor sampans. If he finds a good one, he will try to bribe the owner into bringing the boat out here or will recruit some other men and steal it."

There were a lot of details unexplained, such as how they were going to move the boat away under the eyes of the Reds, but I knew they must have an answer for it. The general plan was good—I'd let it go at that.

"Okay, Kim. You know where the won [Korean currency] is. Better take about sixty thousand. Will you want any rice?"

"*Iie*. [No.] Rhee can promise rice if he wants to, but it would be dangerous to carry a sack into Inchon."

That took care of the plans for tonight. Yonghung-do was beginning to seem more like an enemy prison camp than our own operations base. The trip to Palmi-do, with its prospect of action, should relieve this feeling.

6

EXPLORATORY
OPERATIONS

I MEANT TO TELL you earlier, Mr. Clark," Captain Lee said, "that I destroyed a floating mine a little west of Tokchok-do this morning on the way in. First one I've seen that far south."

"Did you report it, Lee?"

"No, sir. We are shooting up things all the time. Do you consider it that important?"

"The single mine itself isn't so important, Lee. It's the pattern that is established when reports of many such lone mines are plotted on a chart. From such a plot, an analysis can sometimes be made which will tell us where a minefield is located or if the mines are just being dumped indiscriminately into the sea to float down into the paths of our ships. Could you show me approximately where you destroyed the mine?"

Lee pointed to a spot on the chart about thirty miles west of Tokchok-do. Breaking out my current tables, I showed Lee how it was possible to assume that the mine had floated down from the vicinity of Haeju, an important harbor on the south side of the Ongjin Peninsula in North Korea.

"Now, if Intelligence receives further reports in which the mines can be similarly traced, a general warning will be broadcast with regard to the Haeju area. It is particularly important that every mine sighted in or near Inchon be reported immediately. I'll have to contact Tokyo soon and will include this item in my report. But in the future, I wish you would report your sightings direct to Admiral Sohn at Pusan, with the request that such information be relayed at once to General Willoughby, General MacArthur's intelligence chief, at Tokyo."

"I'll certainly do that, Mr. Clark," Lee replied, visibly impressed, whether by the note of urgency in my voice or mention of Admiral Sohn I couldn't rightly tell.

"How do you suppose the Reds would lay a minefield, Lee?" I asked.

Lee considered this question carefully. "At our Naval Academy at Chinhae, we were taught this subject briefly. As I recall, there are several different types of mines. Some explode when a steel hull passes close to them. Magnetic mines, they were. Others would blow up on contact with anything. These had horns on them that, when broken, would release some chemical and activate a trigger. Influence mines, too—they were complicated. Mines would require special handling and the attention of experts in arming and laying. None of the naval officers I know, who are now in the North Korean Navy, had sufficient training to do this work. Of course, they may well have received some such training from the Russians at Vladivostok or Port Arthur. Or the Russians might do it themselves," he concluded.

Junks could do the job, I reasoned. Mines weigh thousands of pounds, but Oriental ability to improvise would easily overcome this problem. Laying the mines in a straight line, however, would prove difficult. Strong currents working against unpowered craft would be a hard thing to control. I turned my attention to Inchon and its approaches.

"Lee, you remember those junks at Tokchok-do?"

"Yes, sir?"

"It will be necessary for us to establish a constant surveillance over Flying Fish Channel, the East Channel, and Inchon's outer harbor to detect any minelaying activities. The areas in which they might lay mines is fairly restricted due to . . ."

A plane buzzed by close overhead. We upset tables and chairs getting over to the scarp for a look at it. It was a Russian Yak. It was three Russian Yaks, and they were buzzing Lee's ship, obviously taking a close look. Lee had turned pale and stood rooted to where he was standing, staring fixedly at his ship. It was a sitting duck unless she got under way in a matter of seconds. The Yaks hauled up just past Palmi-do and started winging-over to another pass, a firing pass this time. Chae shoved my glasses into my hand, and I passed them to Lee quickly.

"It's coming in! No, it's dragging. Hyun's under way," Lee exclaimed breathlessly. Lieutenant Commander Hyun Shi Hak, his executive officer, had the gunboat under way and she was dragging her anchor. I could see the ship gathering speed, kicking up a tremendous wake as the rudder was put over. The anchor chain was up and secured when the first Yak started its pass, its guns chattering fiercely. The tracers kicked up a line of splashes heading for the bow, which was slowly hauling off to port. The line of fire seemed to have passed directly over the anchor detail, laboring at the windlass. The second Yak raked a line of fire along the starboard side. The third appeared to have missed completely, as the gunboat picked up speed and heeled over into the turn, her anchor now housed.

Lee was beside himself, jumping up and down and hurling violent imprecations at the Yaks. Calming briefly, he whipped the glasses to his eyes, studying the ship's maneuver. Hyun had the gunboat headed straight for Palmi-do. Excellent. The Yaks would have to take a greater swing to get back on her on the next pass. As the lead plane began its third pass, Hyun went into a sharp turn, his guns now lacing death into the sky. The Yak had time to correct, but zoomed by well clear of the port quarter as Hyun threw the helm hard over again. The second plane raked along close aboard to port as the gunboat heeled into another turn. Hyun had her straightened true for Palmi-do again when the third plane, now thoroughly confused, passed wide to the starboard through a wall of tracer fire.

It was an amazing display of evasive action. The gunboat was now almost alongside the steep cliffs of Palmi-do, and I recognized Hyun's intention. He was going to try to use the island as a shield. Lee was again shouting unintelligibly, waving his arms as though Hyun could see and hear his captain. But the planes had continued on to the north and were shortly out of sight.

I sank down on the scarp and lighted a cigar. Lee wilted to the ground alongside me, blood on his thin lips where he had bitten them, glasses still glued to his eyes, scanning the distance where the Yaks had disappeared. What an awful situation to be in, I thought, to be away from your ship when it went into action. But Lee had nothing for which to reproach himself. Yaks had been unreported in this area. I know that he had plane lookouts posted on the ship, and unquestionably it was due to their alertness that the gunboat had been given a chance to survive the attack. He was ashore at my orders. His officers and his crew, which he had trained daily since leaving the California coast, had proven themselves equal to the challenge. Perhaps if the Yaks had made another pass his gunners might have downed one. In all probability, it was the accuracy of their fire that had caused the pilots to put discretion before valor.

As soon as Lee was satisfied the planes wouldn't return, I would undertake the delicate task of convincing him that, far from losing face, he should be proud of himself and of his crew. Failure would mean I would have to request Tokyo to send in another gunboat. Lee must be observed carefully in the next few hours.

The brief flurry of action had attracted a crowd of villagers and more were arriving momentarily. My initial concern had been for our camp when the Yaks first buzzed over, thinking that it had been reported to the Russians, forgetting completely the gunboat and its vulnerability. The PC-703 had slowed to one-third speed and was making lazy turns around Palmi-do, shy at returning to the restricted maneuvering area from which she had so recently escaped. Hyun would probably remain out there until dark unless he had some seriously wounded men. Without radar, there could be no substitute for the advantage of being under way if the Yaks should refuel and return for another try.

To anticipate such a possibility, I sent off an urgent dispatch to Tokyo explaining what had happened and requesting an air cover for the next few hours until dark. I took the precaution of adding that the cover should remain well clear of the gunboat, as they were jittery. There was no way we could tell Hyun the planes would be friendly.

Yong came in and Kim told him what had happened. "Yong, will you see if you can get Lee down here? I think a good shot of scotch is in order all around, don't you?" They both gave an emphatic *"hai"* and were off to drag Lee back with them bodily in spite of his protestations. Lim brought out the bottle and cups and set them down. She had been crying hard, from the look of the swelling around her eyes.

"What is the matter, Lim?" Yong asked.

"Nothing, *Yong-san*," she replied, nor could we find out from her. Later, Moon told us that both Lim and Cynn had been scared badly.

Yong and Kim were busily engaged turning the sharp edge of Lee's dour visage with the traditional Korean victory cry, "*Mansei*," chorused by all and sundry gathered around our CP. He finally succumbed to the spirit of the occasion, aided and abetted by the lusty Highland spirits of Glenlivet. These solemn deliberations were brought to a halt by the sullen undulating roar of approaching planes, only to take on added refinement when they were determined to be British carrier aircraft—the cover we had requested but minutes ago. Our sense of security and well-being took a sharp upsurge as a result of this display of concern over our welfare by General Headquarters. Admiral Andrewes was as true as his word. My position and prestige among my colleagues would not suffer from this incident.

Hyun's search for our mysterious nocturnal visitors was fruitless. No footprints could be found. His party had beat the bushes within a mile radius of where the sampan was found and had not flushed the quarry. He was crestfallen, abject in his apologies. Yong, with typical lack of feeling, did not see his way clear to make Hyun's burden easier; he merely growled that he hoped the section chiefs had something more profitable to offer. I had felt strongly that Hyun would bring in some evidence for us to go on. Now I was not so sure we would be able to run the infiltrators to earth.

Figures on time of tide, darkness, and moonlight kept cutting in and out of my conscious thoughts. Never before had these factors meant so much. They combined to form the key to success if properly used. Conversely, they held the threat of death and disaster if ignored. For the days to come, time would be reckoned not in hourly divisions, but by tidal periods. Three hours to flood, three hours to ebb, with moonrise and moonset delimiting our nightly excursions.

Tonight we should have to be under way for Palmi-do not later than 2000 (8:00 P.M.), thirty minutes prior to darkness. This would give us one hour, the last thirty minutes in darkness, to make the approach. . . .

"Mr. Clark."

"Yes, Lee."

"We were discussing a mine patrol before those Yaks came over," he reminded me.

"Oh, yes." It had completely slipped my mind.

"You were saying it would be necessary for us to watch the channels and the harbor," he refreshed my memory.

"Yes. Well, let's see. You will use the boats at Tokchok-do to establish the patrol. Will there be sufficient boatmen at Tokchok, do you suppose, Lee?" I asked, remembering that many of those junks had been captured. Lee had avoided saying what had happened to their crews.

"I think we'll be able to manage. Do you suppose we will need more than six boats?"

"That should be sufficient. I doubt that they will attempt to lay mines anywhere but in the low tideway [ship channel]. Anywhere else, they can easily be spotted when they are left high and dry at low tide. The thing to do is to have at least one junk spotted at all times where it can observe the actions of other junks along the narrow tideway. That should do the trick."

"We can make reasonably certain that they haven't laid a field by running my ship up the channels and into the harbor each day. She draws fifteen feet and will set off any mine up to that depth," he proposed, without the slightest change of expression. Searching his face carefully, I could see that he wasn't pulling my leg. He had meant it.

Considering his suggestion seriously, weighing the loss of his ship against that of a destroyer or cruiser sunk and blocking the channel, with its awful implications, and reckoning the probable effectiveness of the mine patrol itself in keeping the risk to Lee's ship at a minimum, I decided to let him go ahead with it. After all, he had been doing it. Patently, there were no mines planted as yet.

"Go ahead with that plan, Lee. But for God's sake, see that those boatmen you put in the mine patrol know that you're going to risk your ship daily to prove that they are alert. We know these Red characters are mining. It will be just a question of time before they bring mines in here."

"Yes, sir!" he answered, as cheerfully as though he had been ordered to proceed back to Chinhae for thirty days' leave of absence. "I can run down to Tokchok tonight, get the thing organized, and be back here tomorrow about noon, escorting the first patrol shift to station. Palmi-do should be a good base for the harbor work," he ended reflectively. I concurred, hoping that it would be ours by that time tomorrow.

"Let me have a report of the damage done by those planes, please, Lee, so that Tokyo will have the complete picture."

"Have it for you tomorrow, Mr. Clark."

The shadows were lengthening perceptibly when Cynn announced that dinner was ready. "What is it tonight, Cynn?" I asked, and had my usual chuckle at her reply.

"She-rations, *Taicho-san*," pronouncing her Korean C correctly.

Nautical twilight was fading as our group gathered on the beach at the stern of the junk. A gangplank had been run out from the high stern sheets to the beach, and we boarded without delay. Kim would remain behind and get the woman off to Taebu-do to get cozy with the commissar.

Aboard, the gangplank was hauled in and the fors'l set. The light land breeze quickly filled the sail, and as the bow came around, the boatman lowered away and secured the huge rudder. The mains'l went up with a snap, and we were sailing free with the flood tide for the dark island mass that was barely visible over the high bow.

The run-up to Palmi-do was uneventful, the working of the junk's timbers and an occasional slap of the rigging furnishing the only noise. A few hundred yards out, the sails were gingerly lowered, permitting the tide to carry us in to the sand spit, which could now be made out over the starboard bow. The boatmen had their poles out, probing for the bottom. Shortly, they found it and started wearing the junk around so that she would ground stern-first. The tiller was quickly removed, and two more boatmen were heaving round sharply on a small capstan, bringing up the heavy rudder to avoid its being crushed on the beach. This was not accomplished without some noise, and each squeal and squeak added to my anxiety lest our landing be discovered.

Yong leaned over to whisper hoarsely. "How are we going to get off the beach, Mr. Clark?" he asked. "The wind is setting us right on it."

"Tide will be ebbing again in about half an hour, Yong. Unless a strong breeze comes up, we should have no trouble getting off."

Rhee had clambered into his sampan, which had been hauled up alongside, and was heading around the eastern tip of the sand spit, his single standing lugs'l straining at its halyards. He should make it around Wolmi-do and into the junk "yard," as I came to refer to Inchon Harbor, before moonrise.

A few yards before we beached, the anchor was lowered and the line paid out until we gently grounded. Yong put three of his men over the stern, and he and I followed to make an inspection of our immediate surroundings. The sand spit ended in an almost abrupt cliff on our left. It rose gently dead ahead and presumably fell off into the bay on the far side. To the right, the spit ran into a large cluster of rocks almost thirty feet high, which, in turn, dropped off into the bay. We couldn't see the junk thirty yards away.

Posting our three men at the trail leading up the cliff with instructions to drop back to the junk and report if anyone came down, we went back to the beach. There was nothing to do for the next few minutes while waiting for the moon to rise, so I lay down on the sand and was soon fast asleep.

In what seemed an interval of seconds, Yong was shaking my shoulder. "Mr. Clark, listen." My first thought was that Yong had heard some noise nearby that had alarmed him, and rising on one elbow, I listened intently.

In a few moments, I heard what sounded like distant rifle fire. "You mean that firing?"

"Yes, sir."

It sounded too far away to be on Palmi-do.

"From one of the islands to the west of us. Wonder what the hell they are shooting at," I said, remembering the firing on Taebu-do the other night.

I lay back down again. In a short while, the moon came up. "Okay, Yong. Let's go."

The plan was for the three men, in their bare feet (I'd never seen them with shoes), to precede us at a good distance, tracing out every path as we progressed up the steep slope to the group of houses and, finally, to the lighthouse. If there were troops here, we would make a decision on the spot whether to tackle them or to withdraw and bring in reinforcements tomorrow night.

It was a time-consuming operation. We had no sooner gained the top of the slope than a path forked off to the left. Two men were sent up what appeared to be the main path and one along the other with instructions to keep going until they had investigated whatever was at the end, then to come back and report. They disappeared up the paths in silence, the thick foliage swallowing them completely. We moved off the path into the dwarfed trees, and sat down to await their return.

The moon was going into the last quarter, its brilliance shutting out the myriad stars in its path as it swung through the sky. Shortly, the man who had taken the left-hand path returned. Yong gave two low clucks with his tongue, and we joined him. "This is a path to a little cove at the bottom of this face of the cliff," he announced succinctly. "There is nothing there."

The three of us continued our wait, and in about ten minutes we had a report from the main trail. It forked off to the right a considerable distance farther up. One man had continued on to the right while this one had proceeded on and ran into the houses. A silent inspection had revealed no one in the area. The houses were badly damaged.

Sending one man ahead, we proceeded on to the next fork, where we would receive the next report. I cursed quietly at the unavoidable noise my combat boots made against the stone rubble on the trail. Arriving at the next intersection, Yong gave his clucking signal and our man stepped out from the side of the trail. He told us the trail continued on up the slope to where the Japanese had erected a monument. From there it swung off to the left and on up to the lighthouse. The entire area around the lighthouse had been cleared off.

"Did you inspect the lighthouse?" Yong asked this man.

"I could not approach it without exposing myself. I did not know whether you would want me to do that," he answered hesitantly.

"Perhaps it's just as well. We'll check it later," Yong said.

Proceeding on down the trail to the left, we soon were at the edge of the housing area. The dim moonlight did nothing to enhance the beauty of the scene of destruction that met our eyes. There were three fairly large Japanese-style houses. Two of them were caved in on one side, while the other had taken a couple of shells through the roof. Rubble littered the concrete surface of the communal yard.

Standing quietly, we listened intently for any sound that might disclose another's presence. Only the slight whispering of the trees and the occasional slap-slapping of a dangling board as the breeze caught it came to our ears. Sniffing the air, I could detect none of the odors associated with an occupied habitation—and there were many such odors. Going on, we searched each of the houses as quietly as possible.

"Mr. Clark," Yong called softly. He pointed to another path that seemed to lead circuitously up toward the lighthouse area. That seemed reasonable. The keeper wouldn't want to walk back along the trail only to have to almost retrace his steps by another route. Calling the party together, we took the usual precaution of sending one of the barefooted men on ahead of us, and then followed.

Arriving at the summit after a short, steep climb that had us breathing quickly, we looked out on the white lighthouse a scant three hundred yards from where we were standing. Using my glasses, I carefully scanned the entire open area of the summit, discovering nothing to warrant any concern.

Yong sent one of the men scurrying along the wall to the lighthouse. He was back in a few seconds to report that the lighthouse door was latched shut on the outside. This answered our final question. Unless some Reds were hiding out in the grove of dwarfed trees that enclosed the summit from the cliffs upward, which was highly unlikely under the circumstances, the island was ours. It was hard for me to realize that they had failed to occupy such a strategic point; however, I wasn't inclined to look a gift horse in the mouth. We had our alternate operating base, and that only a bare six miles from Inchon.

Walking up to the lighthouse, I turned my glasses on the city. By George! I thought to myself. If they opened up with their guns, I could spot their location immediately. A query to Tokyo would give me the information on when our planes were going to start softening up Wolmi-do and the city. If I could be here observing . . . The possibilities quickened my pulse.

Yong called my attention to the time, suggesting that we get back. It was 0100 and the tide was fast ebbing. We turned back to the trail. At the sand spit, Yong hurriedly off-loaded the machine gun, a box of ammunition, and other supplies to keep our three-man occupying force going for the next few days. The gun was set up on a small shelf commanding the length of the spit where enfilading fire could be delivered at will. After a recognition signal had been agreed upon against the possibility of our return during some subsequent night, we swarmed up into the junk and were soon anchored off the western promontory of Yonghung-do.

As soon as we were ashore, Hyun reported that Kim did not expect to be back from the ferry for another hour. Evidently he was awaiting low tide before he dispatched the commissar's female package to Taebu-do. Yong and I spent a few minutes congratulating ourselves on our good fortune, waking the girls in the process, and then wearily subsided into our cots without bothering to remove anything but our shoes.

I woke up with Lim playfully waving a cup of coffee under my nose. Yong and Kim were sitting cross-legged on their cots, groggily and noisily sipping their coffee. All the women were in high spirits, laughing, pointing, and making sly jokes among themselves, apparently with Yong and Kim as the targets. They weren't being given the slightest bit of attention by those two stoics. But this indifference was only a ruse. When Cynn and Lim coyly came within their reach, they were grabbed, thrown facedown on the cots, their skirts thrown up and their bottoms roundly spanked and soundly pinched, to the accompaniment of shrieks and squealing from the girls and laughter from Moon, who was enjoying it all immensely.

That item on the agenda taken care of, we grabbed towels and headed for the beach, where the high tide now offered excellent bathing facilities. I was delighted when I found that the soap which had been included in the C-rations lathered in salt water, as were Yong and Kim. The large pebbles of the beach were hard on my feet, and I had to step around lightly. Yong suggested that I borrow a pair of Korean rubber shoes next time, showing me his. We lathered up, dove in, and splashed around until we were exhausted, and dragged ourselves out. Thoroughly awake now, we enjoyed the fresh eggs that one of the girls had again obtained.

My beard was beginning to bother me. After breakfast, I was an object of curiosity as I painstakingly removed it. "How did you make out with your girlfriend last night, Kim?" I asked. He winced as Yong chuckled at this reference to the commissar's package.

"I had to wait till the tide had ebbed and the moon had passed over to get her started. I wanted to plaster her with mud before we left the beach, but she wouldn't have it," he said vexatiously. "By the time she had waded through the mud out to the sampan, she had changed her mind, and realized that the mud on her clothes would put her under immediate suspicion. With that, she un-dressed completely and, finally following my suggestion, rubbed mud all over herself. The boatman said he couldn't see her against the mudflat a minute after she'd climbed out of the boat."

"I suppose she'll wash the mud off in one of the tidal pools over there?"

"She said she knew just the spot to do it."

"Did she appear frightened?"

"No. Just upset at having to plaster herself with the mud. I imagine any woman would feel the same way," he added contemp-tuously.

"Did you have time to get a courier over, too?"

"By the time the sampan returned, it was almost four-thirty. Morning twilight would be just a short time later. We'll have to try to get one over tonight."

We were fairly certain that we had spies on our island. Could be any of the many people who were always stopping by for a casual look at their first American. If they made it back with information, they would be well ahead of us—a full twenty-four hours, to be ex-act. And our courier wasn't going over until tonight. . . .

Chang came down and reported that he expected to float the re-maining junk at nine-thirty, and would *Yong-san* take care of get-ting the sandbags? If so, he would load them on this junk and transfer them at the anchorage to the others.

"The women will be down soon, Chang," Yong replied. "Hyun!" he called.

"*Hai!*"

"Hyun, are these machine guns ready for the boats?"

"*Hai, Yong-san.*"

"When that last junk is in the water, take them up there and load them on board. Two boxes of ammunition for each gun, and a complete set of cleaning gear. Better take an extra barrel for that heavy one. Understand?"

"*Hai, wakarimasu.* [Yes, I understand.]"

Yong was off to the village, and I busily engaged myself in drafting a report to Tokyo on last night's activity. Included was a plea not to bomb or shell our newly acquired advance base. I desperately wanted to avoid any unnecessary harm befalling someone dear to my family, I reflected wryly.

Tokyo was noncommittal in answering my question as to when the softening-up was going to commence. "We have your targets staked out. Just keep the information coming," they said. But I knew it would be within the next three days. I would have to warn my people to remain distinctly aloof from the harbor area during daylight hours.

"By tomorrow, Kim, I hope to present you with some nice live bodies for interrogation. I believe we can anticipate getting quite a few prisoners, but from what we learned from these villagers they'll most likely be innocuous people like themselves. However, there is always a chance for a lucky haul."

"I think that is so, *Kuraku-san,*" Kim replied with his usual formality. "We should expect to get a good number of islanders that will be willing to volunteer for trips to Inchon, also. And, incidentally, I have made arrangements with Chang to send in to Inchon three more people tonight—two men and a woman."

"That's fine, Kim. What about identification papers? Do they have them?"

"They will not be necessary, *Kuraku-san.* These people are well past the Inminkyun draft age. They will not have to show papers. They will stay with their children, having just come up from the south to get away from the hated American devils," he stated blandly. This was a good cover story, although the truth was that refugees were clogging the routes to the south, seeking the protection of United Nations forces.

"They will remain in Inchon?"

"*Hai, so desu.* We will send couriers in to pick up the information they collect. One, the woman, will go on to Seoul. There are many young people who volunteer. Others actually have business in Inchon to attend to and which they carried on regularly until we arrived here. Very few, however, are suitable to this work. It is unfortunate."

"I understand you sent all your suspected Reds down to Tokchok. Did they go with Commander Lee last night?"

"*Hai.* We will need the room they occupied for new prisoners, I think."

That was so. But I was vaguely perturbed about what would happen to them. I guessed they would be shipped on to prison camps where life would be no bed of roses.

Yong came by, and we went up the beach to supervise the placing and mounting of the machine guns on the junks. It was found necessary to shore up the sandbags against the possibility of their shifting as the junk pitched. We finally had a steady platform, with the guns well braced. A few trial bursts and our raiders were ready to go. Chang had his boatmen aboard and Yong his complement of "marines." Besides the gun crew, Yong had put aboard each junk four riflemen and an officer in charge. These crews, motley and untrained though they were, proved equal to the task set for them. Chang had picked out the coaster he considered the best-rigged and the fastest. In this one, we mounted our remaining heavy machine gun. It would be on standby duty for our group.

I was elated with our raider squadron. In the absence of a christening ceremony, we returned to the CP to propitiate at least the demon rum in this venture. Lee must have sensed the imminence of this solemn rite as he chose this moment to appear down the channel towing two junks. One he let go as he passed close by. The other he continued with to Palmi-do, where he dropped it off and proceeded to his anchorage.

"You arrived at a suspiciously opportune time, Lee. You have been consorting with your ancestors again," Yong greeted him accusingly, and handed him a cup.

Lee gave me the report on damage to his ship. No one hurt, only superficial damage. "That junk I dropped off back there, Mr. Clark. They came in to Tokchok from Taemuui-do last night with quite a story to tell. Evidently, it's not known on that island that we hold Yonghung-do, or they would have come here."

"The Reds have been giving them a pretty bad time, I guess," Lee continued. "They'll anchor up by the rest of the junks and will be in shortly."

I recalled what the schoolteacher had said about what was to happen on Yonghung-do if the Red replacements had been permitted to return.

"There is a doctor of sorts here. He'll be needed to take care of some of them," Lee finished grimly.

"Can they be moved?"

"I'd say they can—all but two. They may be dead by this time."

Yong gave Chae instructions to get the doctor out to the junk right away.

"Everything all set with the mine patrol, Lee?"

"Yes, sir. They are stationed in both channels with instructions to make a complete run with each change of the tide, day and night. The Palmi-do patrol will observe from as close in to Inchon as will be safe. I cautioned them to check the beaches and mudflats at low tide."

That seemed to take care of the mine situation, our first order of business. If the Reds had any idea of planting those deadly things, I hoped the constant presence of one of our junks would cause them to think twice.

One of the section leaders came in with a belated report that the tracks of two people had been discovered earlier in the morning at the south cove. They led out of the mud and were lost in the high hills. He and his men had been trying to run them down—without success. Were there any instructions?

Yong looked at me. "Have the usual check made," I said dispiritedly. This thing was going to get out of hand. They were using their blasted infiltration tactics, probably building up a small force somewhere on the island, and would attack when they felt themselves strong enough. What the devil could we do. . . .

Perhaps some system whereby we could identify all known residents. The old system of identification papers again. I hated to do it, but it could expose any Reds that might try to mingle. I called Lim. "Lim, bring me a package of paper from that box, please."

Tearing open the ream of paper, I asked all to watch. Drawing a circle, I ripped a single sheet in four uneven parts through the circle and numbered each piece. Then, on another piece, I set down the numbers, and opposite each wrote in the names of Kim, Yong, Lee, and my own and handed each the piece with his number. "Now, write on your slip your own name in Korean. We will consider that the circle I drew is a *han* [government] stamp. Perhaps the headman has an official one. This piece will serve for a spot check. Anyone found without it can be run in for investigation. If we're not sure and want to make a final check of anyone, we call together the four holders and put all the pieces together. If a piece doesn't fit, well . . ."

They studied this for a while, and finding no objections, I asked

Kim to take care of the project right away. "I doubt that there will be any more of this type of paper on the island, Kim—so as added insurance against forgery, watch this supply closely," I said.

"Yong, when you next meet with your section leaders today, will you please institute a check system of these identification papers? Better make the time at odd hours, so that no one will be able to anticipate the checks and duck off to the hills. Also, better have a curfew from now on—say an hour before sunset to an hour after sunrise. Put some teeth into it, but don't allow the guards to shoot unless the curfew violator starts running away."

I liked curfews even less than identification papers, knowing from experience that some perfectly innocent but frightened people were likely to be shot. The people on Yonghung-do would find it hard to obey rules that restricted their freedom of movement on their home turf.

Chae reported our four armed raiders standing out, and we all took the opportunity of watching our shining hope for victory at sea come around on a port tack, finally sailing free on a westerly course. It was Chang's plan to sail west until he had cleared the Taemuui-do mudflat and then north to Changbong Channel, where he would lie in wait near Sin-do to intercept any traffic coming south on the ebb tide. During the night, taking advantage of high tide, he would move across the mudflat between Sammok-do and Yongyu-do and anchor on the windward side of the little island of Sinbul-do, there to await any morning ebb-tide traffic from Inchon to the southern islands. If a capture was made, he would dispatch it to Yonghung-do with an escort until all four raiders were back.

Down the beach, a sampan was shuttling back and forth between beach and junk, landing the people from Taemuui-do. There appeared to be a good many women and children in the group already on the beach, and I wondered what significance this might have. By two o'clock, Kim had the substance of their story.

"Political Officer Yeh of the North Korean People's Republic was assistant to the chief political officer of the Inminkyun garrison forces of Inchon and its off-lying islands. Whether Yeh's selection for assignment to the area had been deliberate on the part of the Red High Command, in view of his intimacy with the area, was not known. But at any rate he had been so assigned, and this spelled a certain doom for more than a hundred of the innocent peaceful inhabitants of Taemuui-do, sacrificed on the blood-drenched altar of Communism to the ambitions of the traitorous and false Korean prophet, Kim Il Sung, the Soviets' puppet president of North Korea, a more despicable and contemptuous thing than the Japanese abortive Manchukuo's Pu Yi. [Henry Pu Yi, last emperor of China, was made ruler of Japan's puppet kingdom of Manchukuo in 1934.]"

Anger mingled with detestation in Kim's voice as he continued: "Yeh's mother had been born on Taemuui-do, the daughter of one of the larger landowners. After the custom, her family accepted the best offer of a matchmaker, and she married and moved to Seoul. She came back to Taemuui-do to have her first child, Yeh, who spent many years with his grandparents on the island and in Inchon. He entered Seoul University, after the Japanese withdrew, where he became associated with the Communist clique and became an active party worker. During his visits to the island, he made attempts to organize Communist cells with the support of his father, a close friend of Kim Il Sung. The efficient South Korean counterintelligence organization apprehended and later executed Yeh's father. Yeh barely managed to escape to North Korea, where, presumably, Kim Il Sung rewarded his services with an appointment to his political corps.

"On the second day after the departure of the United States forces from Inchon, a platoon of Inminkyun had arrived on Taemuui-do as a security force. Except for commandeering three houses, and daily requirements for food, and a girl now and then, they did not bother the islanders. For the most part, they conducted themselves no worse than would reasonably be expected. This situation existed, however, for only a few weeks, when a commissary officer of the Inchon garrison delivered a requisition on the island for twenty-five large *mal* of rice [about fifty bushels] and many pounds of vegetables. Payment was to be made in North Korean won upon delivery at the garrison warehouse. North Korean won had a much more favorable rate on the black markets than South Korean won, so the islanders considered that they would get at least half the value of their products. But they were disappointed, receiving only what amounted to a promise to pay.

"Two weeks later saw another requisition, another, and still another. Their entire winter's food supply was gone, and they were filling the last demand out of the fast-dwindling house provisions. Soon the island would be faced with starvation.

"The headman called a meeting of the elders and it was decided that a delegation of prominent islanders should go to the garrison commander and lodge a protest against further food requisitioning, and to try to extract some payment for the supplies already furnished. With this money, perhaps the village could manage through the winter, although it would be very hard without fish. All fishing boats were either being sunk on sight or captured by the South Korean navy.

"At the city commandant's office, their petition was heard with patience if not commiseration, and they were referred to the city's political commissar. There they were subjected to a long and loud harangue on the virtue of sacrifice for the cause of the proletariat and, menacingly, on the dire punishment meted out to deviation-ists. None of this they understood, and so, unhappily, they contin-ued to press their argument.

"Whereupon the commissar became very upset and had the en-tire group, which included Yeh's grandfather, escorted to the office of the garrison commander's political officer, which was in the big green building on top of the hill. Ushered into a spacious office, they stood before a desk, behind which sat Yeh, busily wielding a *fuda* [writing brush].

"The police escort unconcernedly slouched over to the window and leaned against the wall, while the delegation shifted about un-easily, waiting for Yeh to give them his attention. About twenty-seven years old, Yeh had the usual shock of black hair, its color accentuated by an ample application of an aromatic pomade that faintly permeated the air of the room. His thick-lensed glasses, characteristic of the student, rested against the bridge of a diminu-tive nose. His skin was sallow and he appeared overly thin, but per-haps this was an impression given by his rather long, pinched face.

"After about five minutes, he looked up and searched briefly the faces of the five elderly men in front of him. No flicker of surprise or recognition crossed his face as he rose from his chair and went into the adjoining office. In a few minutes, he returned with his chief and they stood for a short while in the doorway, discussing the visitors in low tones. The chief returned to his office, and Yeh walked slowly over to his desk and sat down.

"By this time, a definite feeling of uneasiness had come over the group, all of whom had known this man in front of them since childhood, except for the past three years. Up to this moment, the matter of the petition had seemed simple. No great hope had been entertained that they would receive payment, but at least they had hoped to ameliorate their situation by stopping future assessments on their island. Now, suddenly, the atmosphere of this office had erased from their minds all thought of their mission. They were desperately trying to fathom the unnatural emotionless expression on Yeh's face. The grandfather's stolid composure broke down at last under the telepathic urging of the others.

"'Yeh, my daughter's son,' he said haltingly, after the fashion of those addressing their superiors. 'Our island is in desperate straits as the result of the many rice levies made against it. The commissary has not kept their promise to pay for . . .'

"'Silence, old man!' Yeh commanded crisply, permitting a slight leer to creep into his masklike countenance. 'Are you so childish, so blind, so stupid as to think that I do not know what is going on in this area?' he asked mildly, yet with the sword's edge exposed.

"'I do not understand, my son,' the grandfather ventured.

"'Do not understand? You stand there and to my face you tell me you do not understand? You, all of you, who have sent my father to his death along with many of my brave comrades?' he snarled, his voice now rising steadily. 'You think that our skillful secret police did not find you out? That your whole dirty plot has not been uncovered? You set your daughter to it, old man. You and these beasts with you. She was your spy, worming her way into our midst, listening to our secret meetings, running back to you so that you could inform those butchers of Syngman Rhee's.'

"His speech was thick with hate and invective as he clutched at his collar and dropped back into his chair. The group stared at him numbly, not daring to move or speak. They understood clearly the import of his words. It had happened to others. No islanders, but the stories had come back from Inchon and from as far away as Seoul. Now the dread thing was with them.

"The horror of the brainwashing, with its demand for confession. The trenches filled to the brim with the innocent victims whose names had been torn in blind terror from their throats by those like Yeh. Expiation for real or imagined crimes against the dictatorship of the proletariat. Then the power and the lust for still more power that followed acceptance of this bloody tribute by the Red aristocracy.

"Yeh could not have believed that his mother or these people in front of him had betrayed him. Yet he must believe, and to assist him in the lie, the secret police would present him with irrefutable evidence of their guilt. Irrefutable to a man whose mind had been conditioned to accept this evidence as proof and to nurture it. And when it had grown to full stature, conditioned to pluck the fruit which were the lives of those who must die, and in their death would his loyalty to the cause be ensured and the Party's demand for human sacrifice surfeited.

"The office was quiet again. The blood that had rushed to Yeh's face during his psychopathic outburst was slowly receding. 'Your daughter was executed by my hand the day after we entered Seoul, old man,' Yeh stated calmly now. 'Only the higher policy of General Kim Il Sung, which requires peace with the civilian population, has saved your miserable lives. But now,' he said menacingly, 'we are faced with resistance from your island.'

"'My daughter is dead?' the grandfather asked dully, his mind trying to accept this casual pronouncement. 'Dead,' tonelessly, disbelieving.

"'We have no thought of resistance, Yeh,' an elder interposed desperately. 'Always we have cooperated willingly with the commissary requisitions. We do not know of resistance. No, we do not know this thing.'

"But Yeh had gone back to his brush and soon handed one of the police a paper to which he had affixed his *han* [official seal]. 'You are free to leave now, except for your leader, who will be sent to jail,' said Yeh grimly. And the police roughly laid hold of the grandfather and hustled him off.

"The next day, six policemen arrived on the island. The police are the most dreaded of the occupying North Korean forces. They are not the secret police. They are not the military. Perhaps it is this factor of 'not belonging' that drives them to extremes of cruelty— a subconscious or conscious urge to surmount this slight to their warrior character. These police announced their intention to remain on the island to 'correct' the deviationists, to expose the spies and traitors, to find the saboteurs. The headman was literally thrown out of his office, and his family—and those families living with him—were turned into the street. The police took over the island, and at first the Inminkyun soldiers supported them in a desultory fashion, as if to say, 'These dogs, they should be killing cattle.'

"Yeh's grandmother was their first victim. She was to confess her part in the plot to resist the rice levy. Imprisoned in a small closet, she was kept standing all night while a small smoke fire was built under the floor so that it caused her to cough and retch. In the morning, she was questioned again, but was almost unconscious. Her eyes were puffed closed and a rasping cough coursed blood from her lips. She died and was thrown into the street for the villagers to bury.

"All the landowners and boat owners had been imprisoned in the school building. They, too, were to confess their part in the plot. One at a time, they were taken to the office and questioned. First, there were expressions of sympathy and friendship. The police did not like this business. They wanted to get back to Inchon, where there was good wine and nice Chinese girls. But they could not return until the plot and its instigators had been exposed. Yeh was a very powerful man. If the police did not produce results soon, he would come himself. Then it would be much worse. What are the names of the others in the plot? You can go free. Your family will not be harmed. . . .

"It was not long. Before noon, four of the younger boat owners had admitted their part in the plot, and, as directed, had named the four elders who had accompanied Yeh's grandfather to Inchon. And others. Signed confessions of the four were obtained in front of other witnesses. That afternoon, the four elders and their families, twenty-six women and children in all, were shot to death and shoved into a common grave they had themselves been made to dig. The same evening, two of the four who had falsely confessed committed suicide by cutting their throats. The other two escaped to the hills in terror of the other villagers.

"But the young men of the village were not idle. Secretly they were meeting to exact revenge. The older people cautioned them. They would bring down death upon the village, but the voices of their elders went unheeded. Some went to Inchon and returned at night with twelve stolen rifles and bayonets and ammunition, and they instructed each other in their use. Four nights ago, they waylaid four policemen and killed them and threw their heads into the police office. The two remaining police immediately left for Inchon while the Inminkyun took the headmen of six families into custody and shot them to death in the center of the village street, while six more were held with the threat that they, too, would be shot if any further crimes were committed.

"The night before last, Yeh came. With him were twenty policemen. He announced that unless the perpetrators of the death of the four policemen were surrendered that day, the six men in custody would be executed forthwith. And if not by the next day, one member of each family would be executed, and so on until the entire population of the island was wiped out.

"That evening, four young men surrendered themselves as the ones who had killed the policemen. They were tied to corner posts and bayoneted to death and left hanging. But Yeh was not satisfied. The police had bungled. All he had to show his superiors to prove the existence of a plot on the island were four confessions. The six men he had in jail would have to implicate others—or their families would die. The prisoners managed to get out word of the danger to their families, with instructions to send them to Tokchok-do, where they might be safe with the South Korean navy. Last night, the families had left, accompanied by four youths and a fisherman. Their junk had reached Tokchok early this morning, and Lee, after hearing the grim tale, had brought them to Yonghung-do, where he thought the information might be of interest to Mr. Clark."

II

THE RUMBLE
TURNS HOT

7

TAEMUUI-DO RAID

THIS RECOUNTING by Kim of the tragedy transpiring on Taemuui-do was delivered with considerable feeling. It was punctuated only by the listeners' quiet cluckings of the tongue or polite hissings from air drawn in quickly through closed teeth. Reports of such atrocities were continually filtering through to General Headquarters from refugees passing through our lines. Such acts were not unknown to me from the last war, but I was dismayed at this tendency on the part of the Koreans to slaughter women and children of their own race. Civil war of such bitterness could only lead to extinction of the race itself.

"We must do something about this, Mr. Clark," Lee said, a note of determination in his voice.

I agreed with his view completely, but any action I might take had to be considered in the light of our mission. A reasonable risk could be taken in pursuit of information, but information and not revenge must be the objective. It could be assumed that the men who had come over and were ready to fight would know intimately the situation of the enemy on Taemuui-do—provided, of course, we were to strike soon. Their knowledge would supply information on the military situation of the island. What else was there of value to be had by a raid? A captured soldier or two might give us further data on the garrison force.

But wait . . . What about Yeh? A political officer would surely sit in on top-level military conferences. Within the Red organization, the political officers were potent figures. They could even overrule the military within certain limits. Of course . . . Yeh would be an absolute gem—if we could take him and if we could get him to talk. Two great big "ifs."

"How many soldiers did they say were in that platoon, Kim?" I asked.

"Their numbers didn't agree, *Kuraku-san*. A platoon should number about forty, but there are no heavy weapons, so it may be short a squad. They say between twenty and thirty. Add the twenty policemen and we should figure a total of fifty."

"What places do they guard? If we were to set up a raid, would we be likely to run into alert units in the night?"

"They had little information on that. Quite a few had been pulled off their regular duties patrolling and are now protecting their quarters against surprise raids from the hills. I'm afraid we know very little about what else they are doing, except that there are soldiers guarding the junks hauled up at the northern and eastern coves.

"Although the islanders don't know that we are on Yonghung-do, undoubtedly the soldiers know and certainly Yeh. We should expect that they would be guarding their best beaches against some attack by us. However, their routine has been definitely upset, and perhaps they might have relaxed their watches."

This was disappointing. In planning a night raid with greatly inferior forces, certainty of the enemy's force disposition was a must. We could not plan intelligently on mere conjecture. "It would mean a delay, Mr. Clark, but suppose I were to take a couple of the men from that island and a few of my sailors and scout the situation out tonight and tomorrow? A party of about six. I could put my gunnery officer in charge. He has had a good deal of experience on other operations," Lee proposed.

"That seems sensible, Lee. The business doesn't sound too good to me right now, but if you can come up with some definite information on where they have their guards disposed at night I'll have to reconsider the matter."

"Kim, do they have a curfew over there?" I asked.

"*Hai, arimasu.* [Yes, they have one.]"

"How about identification papers? Have they started that?"

"*Iie, mada desu.* [No, not yet.]"

That wouldn't be too bad, although Lee's party would have to stay out of sight until night. With natives of the island to guide them, they should be able to scout the trails leading to the village and the village itself.

"It might be well to issue each of your men a hand grenade, Lee—just in case. What do you think?" I said.

"Good idea, Mr. Clark, but I don't have any. Have you?"

"We took a few they left behind here. Yong, will you give Lee what he needs, please?"

"You will need our junk, Lee. Unfortunately, Chang left with the raiders and we'll have to find you another skipper. I'll send the gun crew along, too. You may need a little cover fire getting back on board if you're discovered. Anything else you can think of?"

"That should do it, Mr. Clark. I'll start getting the men lined up and briefed. Probably shove off a couple of hours before high tide."

Kim and I left for the village to see the refugees, taking some

C-ration candy and gum with us. A couple of rooms in the school building had been converted into a dispensary. When we arrived, we found practically all the refugees clustered about outside the two rooms, anxious to help those less fortunate inside.

It is the custom here for a member of the family to act as full-time nurse to the patient, including such matters as cooking the food that the family furnished, washing dirty linen, and tending to the bodily wants. In most instances, this relative slept in the sick-room. The relative was practically always a woman. This practice was undoubtedly born of necessity, due to lack of funds other than those required to pay for the doctor's services. But it also has a strong tie-in with the close-knit family system of responsibilities, wherein each member is literally and figuratively his brother's keeper. The practice is common even among the well-to-do.

The doctor was busy, so I looked around. There were about thirty women and children, and a few men. There should have been more young men, I thought, and questioned Kim. They had been left behind. All but five of the men had protected the departure.

A thought suddenly struck me. What if these men should chance upon our scouting party? I would have to caution Lee of this possibility. The chance was probably remote, though. They shouldn't venture down to the beaches or on the main trails to the village.

Something else seemed odd. "How the devil were these people shot up?" I asked Kim.

"Their absence was discovered by the police and a search made. Before their boat could pull out of range, the Inminkyun took pot-shots at everyone on the open deck of the craft. If it hadn't been for the dark, they probably would have killed them all."

"I believe the details of their escape might be instructive, Kim. May have to do it ourselves sometime, you know," I said.

"*Hai, so desu.* [Yes, that is so.] The woman who took the prisoners' message is around here. Also Min. He is a sturdy one and should be able to tell us of the escape."

While Kim was locating these two, I tempted one of the more precocious little boys over to me with a bar of aged-white chocolate. His eyes lit up and his mouth crinkled into a shy grin as he accepted the candy, then made a quick retreat to his mother. Other boys were edging their way forward, when a cute little girl with a square bob (they all had square bobs) stepped boldly out, thereby starting a stampede. There was more than enough for the little ones, so I expanded to the bigger girl bracket and was rewarded with not a few charming, if uncertain, smiles and shy giggles. These girls were almost uniformly pretty, and even beautiful, until they reached their early twenties, when the hard work of rearing a large family, usually in pursuit of the essential boy, and the demands of the house and land quickly aged them.

However, their posture remained perfect from the constant carrying and balancing heavy burdens on their heads. They did not have the short legs characteristic of the Japanese women, nor did they style their clothes the same. Their customary outfit consisted of a pair of long pantaloons as underwear, over which was worn a long skirt that was secured at the top by a wide band immediately under the breasts and fell to within a few inches of the ground. The chest was covered briefly by a long-sleeved shoulder jacket secured by a tie at the neck and blousing loose in front, terminated just below the breasts.

Although babies were strapped to the back in the usual fashion, the Korean women had adopted the practice of sliding the baby around under their arm for nursing, where the breast was conveniently exposed and available. Thus, they could continue their labor in the field uninterrupted. I personally thought this was carrying things a little too far, even for the Oriental mother. She should at least be permitted to enjoy her baby without the distraction of having to wield a heavy hoe.

Kim brought in the ones he was seeking and several others. Between them, he managed to develop the details of the escape and related them as follows: "Yi was the wife of one of the six prisoners being held by Yeh and had been given the job of cleaning the dayroom quarters of the guards at the schoolhouse. She had gained permission to give her husband a little food, and while doing so had been informed of Yeh's intentions, and told to gather the six families and escape by boat to the south that very night. When she was through with her work, she had gone as instructed to Min of the fisherman's association and laid out the problem with him. Thereupon, Min had told her to remain silent and do nothing further, that he would take care of everything.

"That afternoon, Min secretly contacted all the young men of the families and explained the matter to them. There would be the soldiers guarding the junks to deal with. The curfew must be considered. It would be a two-mile walk to the east cove, where the junk to be used had been hauled up. They could not use the main north cove, which was in full sight of the village. They would have to catch the ebb tide, and that would mean sailing not later than nine-thirty. This would give them the advantage of darkness, too.

"There were then three things to be done: avoid the curfew, get the families to the cove by nine-thirty, and kill the guards. Avoiding the curfew would be a relatively simple matter. During the course of the day, the women worked the fields and paddies terraced on the hills south of the village. Those that were not already there would be directed by the young men to go at once with their children to assist in one of the usual communal harvestings.

"The children of the other women would be rounded up and taken to their mothers. None would be told the true purpose of gathering until later. About an hour before quitting time, the young men would lead the families to a rendezvous area back in the hills, where they would wait until dark to start their trip to the beach. In the meantime, some of the young men would visit the houses in which the families had lived and notify the remaining families that they were not to make inquiries as to the missing persons' whereabouts. Two others were to recover several of the bayonets and guns not surrendered.

"Min had no particular fear that the group in the hills would be discovered, as the Inminkyun were alert to the danger that had previously struck from that area and were religiously avoiding it at night. The great danger was in someone talking, or that Yeh or one of the others might want to question one of the group and find they had all fled. No solution could be found to this problem, except to give warning of such a discovery by posting two men in the village with instructions to be alert for any such event. Should it happen, they were to leave the village and warn the group immediately.

"Shortly after sunset, the workers started leaving the fields for the village, straggling down the various paths leading to their homes. The group was unobtrusively shunted off to a path that, leading to the village, also wound back around the south side of the hill through the stunted coniferous trees covering that slope. This path ultimately converged with a trail running along the top of the ridge. The group, which totaled forty including the men, slowly made their way along the ridge trail, which twisted and turned, but took them about a mile closer to the boat cove.

"By now, the women had been informed of the purpose of this exodus. Some were extremely reluctant, crying quietly and having to be prodded on by the men. The children started to wail in sympathy with the women's grief. Many, with unreasoning concern, begged to be allowed to turn back so that they could gather a few cherished articles and clothing that had been left behind. Because of this noise, the men called a halt after descending the slope and still about a mile away from the cove.

"Min took one of the men and proceeded quietly on up the trail to scout the situation at the cove. Coming out of the undergrowth at the southern end, they stopped for a short time and carefully studied the beach area. The junks were drawn up at the northern end. The guards should be somewhere near them, so they cautiously moved along the edge of the backshore and around to where they could clearly observe the junk area.

"Min finally spotted the guards. There appeared to be five. Three were lying under the port counter of the last junk, which had been holed and was high and dry. The other two were pacing slowly along by the sterns of the junks, which now had their bows awash. From their gesticulations, Min could tell that the guards were talking, although he could not hear them above the slap-slap of the waves. They watched for about ten minutes, and seeing nothing else, retraced their steps to the far end of the beach and returned to the main group.

"Leaving two men with the group, Min took the other seven and headed back for the beach. Time was growing short. He had noticed that high tide was almost at the stand. The junk would have to be floated in the next thirty minutes, or they would have to wait six hours for the next tide. Such a prolonged delay might well mean disaster. Back at the beach again, Min directed two of the best swimmers to remain, and took the other five who had rifles quietly around to the north and placed them between the path to the village and the guards. These men were instructed not to shoot unless the guards started firing or running away.

"Min then returned to the other two. They stripped, and slipped their fish knives into their breechclouts at the back. Entering the water, they swam out beyond the surf and headed up the shore to the junks, where they let the surf carry them in under the bow over-hang of the last junk. Here they waited in the water and let the pacing guards go by twice, then, as they made their turn back, slid out of the water and quickly up the beach along the starboard side to the counter, where they waited, knives in hand.

"The guards came back, turned, and then Min and the next man leaped on them and plunged their knives hard down to the hilt in the back of their necks with a twist that was meant to sever the spinal nerves. The guards slumped forward on the sand without a sound. Now all three of them quickly ran up the beach to the first junk and edged their way along the starboard side to the counter, then around the overhang of the stern seats to where they could see the three guards lying. There was no way to tell whether they were asleep or not, but their rifles rested against the side of the junk out of reach. A concerted rush by the three landed them astride their victims, and their knives rose and fell like pistons as they cut short the screams. It was over by the time the five others came up on the run to be in at the kill.

"While two of the men went back for the group, Min turned to with the others, soon floating the junk. Everything was with them now. It was dark. They could barely distinguish the shadow outline of the little island several hundred yards to the east. With the junk afloat and a gangplank run out, still the group hadn't put in its ap-pearance. Min impatiently set about checking the lugs'ls and rig-ging, while two of the men cleared the capstan and inserted the bar. A slight southerly sea breeze, dampened by the small headland to the south, rustled the halyards, as Min anxiously scanned the surf and high-water line in the dim light. The stand was past and the tide was beginning to ebb. Shortly the bow would be set down, as the tidal current in its swift descent to the Yellow Sea challenged the holding qualities of the quaint old stock-and-bill-type anchor. Min was thankful for the southerly breeze, which he hoped would carry him beyond the dangerous shoals of the headland before the current could strand him.

"The group at last was emerging from the darkness of the back-shore. They had no sooner commenced filing up the gangplank than two men broke out onto the beach path on a dead run, and were almost shot before they identified themselves as the stay-behinds from the village. Shouldering their way to the junk, they shouted to Min that the families' absence had been discovered, and that Yeh knew what they were up to. A squad of soldiers was probably starting out for the cove at this minute.

"Min did some rapid calculating. They would never get away in time unless the soldiers were delayed. Twenty minutes, even ten minutes, could mean the difference between life and death for all these people. Calling the men together, he assigned those without sailing experience to the certain death of the delaying action. Giving them the rifles of the fallen guards, he directed them to head up the path to the village and lay an ambush. Without a murmur of dissent, they trotted away and were swallowed up by the darkness. It wouldn't be hard to die. What they were to lay down their lives for was right there behind them—their mothers, brothers, and sisters were lost if these mad dogs caught them.

"Frantically now, the rest of the group went up the gangplank, while the capstan was started and others stood by the halyards. Before the anchor was clear, Min gave the order that shot the sails to the mastheads. Putting three men to the huge sweep, he rowed over the anchor, as a flurry of rifle fire broke out almost at the edge of the beach. The ambush . . .

"The sails were not drawing, and Min rushed forward to ease

off the mains'l until it started filling. Ignoring those trying to help, jostling those in his way, he secured the halyards to the starboard cleats and then dashed to do the same with the foresail, belaying the lines. A slight pitch indicated the anchor aweigh. There was no time to glance at the shore. The men were pushing the women and children to the deck, but they were like frightened sheep, huddling together for common protection around the foot of the masts.

"Unshipping the sweep, Min eased down the huge rudder, secured it, and was inserting the tiller when the first burst of fire swept across the deck. He saw a group around the foremast go down in the withering blast. If he could present his high stern to the beach, he could afford them some protection. He put the helm down to luff, when a second volley cracked by his ears, followed by more screams. The men were busy restraining the women from jumping overboard into the false safety of the water. His stern was now protecting those on deck, and Min crouched to avoid the fire that was pouring into the thick timbers behind and under him, wincing as flying splinters dug into his back and arm. Progress was desperately slow, and he was being set down on the headland too fast to clear.

"Realizing that he would again have to expose his passengers to the fire, but having no alternative, he put the tiller up and started bearing away. The increased distance and darkness had now reduced the accuracy of the fire. Everyone had dropped flat on deck. The cries of the wounded made it impossible to tell the effect of the fire, which was becoming scattered and seemed to be cutting through the rigging more than the hull. At last, Min felt it safe to luff again. Within a few minutes, he was clear of the headland and sailing free on a close reach well out of danger. Hours later, he was hailing Lee's gunboat at Tokchok-do."

I couldn't help reflecting, as I studied the squat fisherman named Min, on the qualities in these people that always seemed to pull them through in an emergency. Min, with his unusually narrow squint eyes set in a head too large for his body, would probably have taken last place in any multiple choice for either intelligence or quickness of perception. His broad, moonlike face and rather vacuous expression certainly was deceptive in the extreme, belying the remarkable feat he had just concluded. With all my training and experience, I doubted my own ability to repeat such a performance, and to save some little self-esteem, deliberately avoided such a process of introspection. He was still wearing only his breechclout, which showed the stains of his own and others' blood from last night's work.

"Can't we get some clothes for these men, Kim? And get that doctor to take care of those splinters right away," I directed. Min's back and arms were a bloody mess. We couldn't afford to have this man hospitalized.

The doctor reported one of the women and three of the children dead. Five others had shattered bones, and another nine had flesh wounds from bullets and splinters. Almost half of the refugees . . . Better this than buried in a common grave with their men. How I would delight in taking our men to that island and wiping out every last one of those creatures. But I could not. Such a move would serve only to goad the Inchon garrison commander into sending an expedition after us, ruining all chance of completing our mission. I cursed this type of operation that bound my freedom of action.

"It seems a bad thing, Kim, but you had better question these people after dinner. Our report to Tokyo must go in on schedule."

"*Hai, Kuraku-san. Sono koto wa hanahada judai desu.* [Yes, Mr. Clark. That is a very serious matter.]"

Gene Clark (left) in his role as interpreter to the accused (right) at Guam Class B Japanese war crimes trials, 1948. *(Clark Family)*

Clark (far right) with some of his men on Yonghung-do. Youn is standing at center, with the pistol in his belt. *(Clark Family)*

Clark on
Yonghung-do.
(Clark Family)

The USS *Hanson* provided supplies and a timely bombardment, with only a week
to go before the invasion. *(U.S. Naval Historical Center)*

The pre-invasion bombardment of Inchon, as seen from the
USS *Lyman K. Swenson*. *(U.S. Naval Historical Center)*

The invasion begins: Men of the First Marine Division ride amphibious tractors as
they head for Wolmi-do, September 15, 1950. *(AP/Wide World Photos)*

Marines head for the landing beach in LCVPs.
(Kirchen, U.S. Naval Historical Center)

First and second
waves of landing
craft move toward
Inchon. The USS
De Haven is in the
foreground. *(Colonel
Robert D. Heinl,
U.S. Naval
Historical Center)*

Celebrating on the bridge of the USS *Mount McKinley,* September 15. Left to right: Rear Admiral James H. Doyle, amphibious attack commander; Major General Edwin K. Wright, in charge of joint staff planning and operations for the invasion; General of the Army Douglas MacArthur, commander-in-chief; Major General Edward Almond, MacArthur's chief of staff. *(U.S. Naval Historical Center)*

Four LSTs unload men and equipment on the beach. *(AP/Wide World Photos)*

LSTs on the Inchon waterfront, September 16. *(U.S. Naval Historical Center)*

MacArthur (center) goes ashore, September 17. Vice Admiral Arthur Struble is at left, Marine Major General Oliver P. Smith (gesturing) at right. *(AP/Wide World Photo)*

Marines advance through Inchon, September 18. *(AP/Wide World Photos)*

An LST and an LCM are stranded by low tide on Inchon's waterfront—a stark reminder of why Clark was sent on his mission. Sowolmi-do is in the far right background. *(U.S. Navy Historical Center)*

Gene Clark, now a Commander, later in his Navy career. Among the medals he is wearing: the Silver Star he won for his Inchon mission. *(Clark Family)*

As we passed through the village on the way to the CP, I noticed a long string of people at the headman's office. Kim explained that they were receiving their identification papers.

Lee had completed his preparations by the time we returned. Let's see, tonight's activity would include their reconnaissance of Taemuui-do, the courier to Taebu-do, and the two men and the woman into Inchon.

"How do you plan on making your approach on Taemuui-do, Lee?" I asked.

"Yong and I have been discussing that problem, Mr. Clark. It would not appear to be a good idea to take the junk into a cove, even if we could. Too much of a risk if the men were discovered at low tide when they couldn't float it. The alternative would be to have the men swim in from as close as they can get to the beach without grounding the junk, and then have the junk lie off during the night. In the morning, it could sail around to the northern tip of the island and anchor a few hundred feet off Taemuui-do in the channel. Ostensibly fishing, the junk could remain there until the men swam out to it the next day."

I studied the chart and tide tables carefully. They would land at a point between the north and eastern coves, along a fairly rugged stretch of beach. This was close to the channel, and the junk could anchor even at low tide. Moving north along the coast with the flood tide in the morning, they would probably be assumed to be fishermen as long as they kept well clear of the shore as they passed the village. Come to think of it, Chang would be around there. . . .

"When is Chang coming down to Sinbul-do? We don't want any trouble with his outfit."

"He said he would come through the channel on the high tide tonight," Yong said.

That would be about 2200. He should be anchored off Sinbul-do, then, within a few hours after midnight. Without doubt, he would spot the junk.

"Do you suppose Chang will recognize this junk?"

"He probably will, Mr. Clark. But if it sails on past him, he might become suspicious and try to intercept or fire on it. If I may make a suggestion, I would recommend that we order our men to report to Chang, explain their mission, and then go on. That way, if anything goes wrong, Chang might possibly be able to assist."

That made a lot of sense. "Go ahead with it, then, Lee. By the way, what's the name of the officer you're sending in charge of this party?"

"Lieutenant [junior grade] Ham, my gunnery officer, Mr. Clark. I believe I mentioned that he has done a few jobs like this for me before. Tokchok-do was one when we were planning its capture."

"Splendid, Lee. When your men see Chang, better tell him to return here on tomorrow's morning ebb. We'll need him. Incidentally, your scouting party had better catch the same tide back—otherwise, we won't have time to carry out the raid tomorrow night if the report they turn in is satisfactory."

"Yes, sir. I'll take care of it. I certainly wish Min was able to take this party out. Chang and Min are old friends. They would work well together in an emergency."

"Are you all set for tonight, Kim?" I was inquiring about the information gatherers scheduled for departure to Inchon.

"*Hai, dekimasu.* [Yes, we can do it.] The two men will go in one sampan, and the woman in another. As you have suggested, the men and woman do not know each other, so I am sending them in separately. They will go in on the flood tide about 0400."

"They will need money, Kim. Better give them each about a hundred thousand won, and as much rice as you think it will be safe for them to carry. And warn them to be sure and stay well clear in the daytime of any targets they report. Our planes will soon start bombing every target we relay to Tokyo. Have you had much time to educate them in what information we want and how to report it?"

"This thing is not good, *Kuraku-san*. I managed to talk with them for about three hours. They are of average intelligence, except that the woman seemed very quick to understand. Ten hours would have been much better, but the matter is becoming urgent. I have six others now that I will talk to for ten hours. This will be good, I think. With them I will be satisfied."

"How have you arranged to have their information picked up, Kim?"

"Well, it seemed to me that the need for secrecy is not the same thing as that with the woman on Taebu-do. So I have arranged that the men and the woman direct the first courier to a certain place where the information will be hidden. After that, the couriers will not meet with these people, but will merely go to the hiding place."

Kim was right. The situation was different. His solution was a departure from the railroad station locker and similar Western pickup systems, but it would suffice. Anything too elaborate was bound to go astray in the long run. Yes, it was good.

"Be sure and tell them that if they need more money, to ask for it. We'll get it to them by the next courier. Now, how about the courier to Taebu-do? Is he ready?"

"It is the girl, *Kuraku-san*. The girl I spoke of whose mother is over there and whose father works with Chang in the fishermen's association here. I planned on sending her last, but her father asked me to send her first, as she is very anxious to make sure her mother is well and to see her again. They are very worried."

The girl, Li. Yes, Kim had mentioned her. Younger than Lim, thirteen it was. God, she must look like a baby.

"You are sure she'll come back? Mother and daughter—I don't know. It sounds pretty risky to me, Kim."

"She will come back, of that I am certain, *Kuraku-san*. Her father has told her to do so, and she will not disobey. Such a thing is not done. She will come back. This is true."

There was no other question. Kim knew his own people, and I would not insult his judgment by expressing further doubt, but I would go along tonight to judge the bearing of this child myself. Little children, and girls at that—this was a pretty low business, and I was hard put to reconcile myself to such methods even in the face of necessity. Kim interrupted these bitter thoughts, perhaps realizing their trend.

"She would have gone anyway, *Kuraku-san*. Her father was going to send her over last night, but was stopped. Her disappointment was eased only when I promised to let her go tonight."

I was ready to accept anything to ease this self-recrimination, and thanked Kim for this additional information, then hurriedly changed the subject.

"Moon," I called. "When do we eat?"

Cynn came running out, wiping her hands on her apron, and explained in a placating voice, as if a hungry beast had roared, that we were having something special tonight. There was a little difficulty in preparing it, as it wasn't too well understood, and did we want *gohan* (rice) with it, please?

"That is a little hard to answer, Cynn," I said, putting on a harsh voice. Her eyes opened wide and consternation spread across her small face when I adopted this attitude. "What is this food that Moon does not understand?"

She twisted her apron in a knot, straining to get an answer, and, failing, gave a short whimper and dashed back behind the tent. I hated myself for teasing her like that, but I enjoyed it, too, and it was a relief from the serious business at hand.

"No luck with the search for infiltrators today, Mr. Clark," Yong advised. "Traced those mud tracks as far as they could, but they faded out in the hills. Tomorrow we may get some results from the identification system. Perhaps even tonight, if the word on the curfew hasn't reached them."

"Thanks, Yong. I'd give a lot to know just how many there are. I guess we will be safe in assuming that they'll send more over tonight. This island is just too big, that's all. I'd move to Palmi-do tomorrow if it weren't for the conveniences here, and the fact that they'd probably kill off the population as soon as we left."

"I believe it would be a good idea to double our guards, Mr. Clark," Yong said. "At least until they have made their move. They will have to attack soon. Their food, if they brought any with them, won't last much longer. And with the controls we have placed on the villagers, it will become increasingly difficult for them to maintain any contacts they may have."

"You have the men to do this without depleting our strength at the ferry?"

"Yes, sir."

"Go ahead with it, then, Yong," I said.

Moon came around the corner of the tent, flanked by Cynn and Lim, carrying a cooking pot with her apron. She had a very worried expression as she presented the pot for my inspection of its contents, then stood well back out of reach. I guessed I had overdone my little act with Cynn, but looking in the pot I could see why Moon didn't understand.

Seeing the mystified look on my face, Yong and Kim glanced in, too. I looked at them, and they shook their heads in unison. "By the smell, that is not Korean food, *Kuraku-san,*" Kim offered. So I went back, this time to test more carefully. By its look, it was small brown gravel, intermingled with gobs of a yellowish hue and frying in bacon grease. Testing it carefully with my not insubstantial nose, through the strong bacon fumes I thought I could detect something vaguely familiar.

"Moon, will you please bring the container from which you took this?" I asked.

All three lifted their skirts and ran back behind the tent, deadly serious. If this was what I thought it to be . . .

They came rushing back with two large cans, which I recognized at once. The one can contained dehydrated potatoes, the other dehydrated eggs. Shades of World War II! How in the devil had those cans come to be in our food supply? And while this was running around in my head, the humor of the thing hit me and doubled me up with laughter until my stomach muscles cramped and tears rolled down my cheeks. This first spasm over, I tried to explain to the now thoroughly frightened women what they had done, but couldn't finish as I gasped out another belly laugh and folded up on the table. This unseemly paroxysm having subsided, I rather shamefacedly explained the mysterious cause of my outburst.

"You see, Moon, these are potatoes and eggs which have had all the water removed from them so that they won't take up so much weight and space in shipment and storage," I said. "When they are to be cooked, they are first soaked in water so that they may regain what they lost. After that is done, they are then cooked in the usual manner." I paused to observe the effect of this explanation, but her face was still drawn into a tight grimace of concern, and the girls' eyes were bright with gathering tears.

I appealed to Yong for help; perhaps his Korean could accomplish what my mediocre Japanese couldn't. But he and Kim had now caught the humor of the thing and were having a hard time containing themselves. Apologizing meekly to the women, I offered back the pot, which Moon accepted somberly, and they turned back to their kitchen.

"Don't worry about it, Mr. Clark," Yong said cheerfully. "You don't know these women yet."

He was right. Within a few minutes, we could hear them giggling and laughing in the clear lilting cadences that make women so nice to have around. It was not often, I considered, that a man could fight a war with women to wait on him, and I made a promise to myself to be more careful of their feelings in the future.

"Say, Kim," I said, "let's send a sack of rice up to those refugees. I imagine that they will have a rough time of it, what with food being as scarce as it is here. And see if Moon can't get some more chocolate and gum for those children in the hospital."

Later, Kim got some good information from the refugees, and a lot of it confirmed data we had been given previously by the Yonghung-do people. We sent our message off to Tokyo, after which I made a final check on Lee's scouting party and saw them off shortly after sunset.

It was ten o'clock when we reached the ferry landing, a few minutes before high tide, and dark. There would be plenty of time to get the sampan across before moonrise, which was good. I wanted nothing to happen to this courier. With her father, Li was in the ferry building, which was nothing more than a thatched hut, waiting impatiently to leave. Looking at her small figure and pigtails, I had another twinge of conscience. They were in earnest conversation with Kim for about twenty minutes—a final check and instructions, I presumed. At last they were finished. Kim said that they had both thanked me profusely for helping Li get over to see her mother and had reassured him that she wouldn't fail to come right back as soon as she received any information from "the woman."

Taking the opportunity while I was here, I looked over the defense setup. They had remodeled their machine-gun emplacements, digging shallow trenches around them and covering them over with thatch that had been crudely blended in with the surrounding area. A straight trench had been dug fronting the beach area just beyond the low scarp. Not bad. Not bad at all, everything considered.

Kim had been talking to the section leader, and as we made ready to go back he issued an urgent warning to be very careful. The two-mile walk back to camp wound through the lowland and skirted the big marsh area where they thought the Inminkyun infiltrators to be in hiding. Maybe he had better send a couple of his men with us? No, thank you. We have our guns. Those pesky infiltrators again . . .

The men were becoming worried, and that was definitely not good. Recalling the story of Min on the beach of Taemuui-do, and the ease with which they had picked off five men, I no longer wondered at that trench. It was good insurance for the back as well as the front. Couldn't afford to let our guard get jumpy. I determined that when the Taemuui-do business was over, we'd take some positive action to flush those characters from their cover. That is, if they didn't decide to do something first.

We walked back silently enough, and we went past the marsh gingerly, if not without trepidation. It was a beautiful stretch for an ambush, and I hoped that our unwelcome guests were not also aware of the fact. Fighting for this island was like fighting for a pair of pants with the seat out. If you do win, you're still exposed in an embarrassing spot—the rear.

We turned in at the earliest hour for many a night, two A.M. Kim would have to get up again at four to see his people off to Inchon. I even decided to enjoy the luxury of taking my clothes off, but it proved a poor decision. It seemed as though I had no sooner fallen to sleep than Chae was shaking my shoulder urgently.

"*Taicho-san, Taicho-san!* They have caught a man in the village. Caught a man . . . Do you understand, *Taicho-san?*"

"Yes, Chae. I'll be right with you. Just a minute," I said. Slipping into my boots and trousers, I slung my holster on and followed him out. It would be so nice to get a good night's sleep again.

They had him in the headman's office, and he was a very sorry-looking individual.

"No identification papers?" I asked the section leader who was obviously in charge.

"No. No papers, *Taicho-san.*"

"How was he caught?"

"The village patrol caught him at the rice storehouse. He was trying to break in through the window. There were several others, but they ran away up the hill."

The man was cowering on the floor, bleeding from a bad cut in the scalp, and from several lacerations on the face and arms, probably from a bayonet knife.

"Tie him up good and bring him down to the CP. If we leave him here, they may try to break him out. Kim will question him in the morning."

They all looked at me in surprise at this. "What's the matter?" I asked.

"You don't want us to kill him?" asked the section leader in a bewildered tone.

"No! Don't kill him. You should understand that this man may tell us where the others are, perhaps their plans, many things we want to know. If he is dead, we cannot get that information," I explained patiently to these proponents of immediate action.

"Chae, you remain here and assist the section leader," I directed, feeling sure that he would do his best to see my orders carried out, then trudged wearily back to the tent, too tired to try to analyze the possible value of this windfall.

Lord, but I was sleepy. Beginning to catch up on me, I guess. Felt sorry for Kim. Wonder how they stand it. I never heard them bring in our prize and bed him down for the night. Three hours later, Cynn was shaking me out of the torpor into which I had fallen. The strong black coffee made its way up the nasal passages and pried my protesting eyelids open. Kim was still in his rack, dead to the world with Lim trying to coax him to life, but he would have none of it and I asked her to knock it off.

"Is the tide in yet, Cynn?" I asked hopefully. God, how I needed a cold bath.

It was an unthinking question. It would not be in for another three hours at least. In lieu, I asked Moon to fix a hot basin of water. After shaving, I began to feel somewhat alive again, but my shoulder was tender where I had slept on my forty-five.

Let's see, now, we have a prisoner. "Chae!" I called.

Paikyun came on the double, and I was unreasonably vexed at this display of alacrity.

"Chae is off duty, *Taicho-san,*" he explained. Of course. He was around at the kitchen, subjecting his hunger pangs to the tender ministrations of Lim.

"Paikyun, where is our prisoner this morning?"

"Yonder, *Taicho-san,*" and he pointed to where Choi and Yang were sitting.

The poor devil had been patched up, but was still a bloody mess. "Wake him up and give him a bowl of rice and some tea," I directed. He had to be alert enough to answer questions, if he was so inclined. . . .

It wasn't until ten-thirty that the section leader reported the bad news to Yong. The Reds were at least being diverse in their methods of putting people on our shores. This time it was a battered old junk, obviously on its last cruise, derelict in furnishing fuel for Davy Jones' locker. It was hard to say just how it had arrived at the northwestern tip of the island, but from where it sat they must have put in before midnight last night and had abandoned it on the rocks.

The spot was no farther away than one mile from the western promontory on which we had guards posted—and there was no way of telling how many men there had been on board. It could have been two or it could have been twenty. Why the devil didn't they accommodate my plans and try to land where the guards were stationed? Those grenades the guards were carrying would rot at this rate. Well, a pattern was established, at least.

"Yong, will you please have the section leaders post their beach guards at the more unapproachable spots? Try to pick out places where you would try to get ashore if you wanted to remain undetected. Leave the guards at the south cove, though; that's too tempting a spot for a landing en masse, and they'll probably keep it in mind."

"Yes, sir. Do you want the usual search made? If it is a large group, they'll probably leave some indication of their passage out from the beach."

"Make the search, but have them take a large party with a couple of grease guns."

I didn't want to catch a lion by the tail. Had to give those fellows credit. Here all we'd done was land a woman and a girl against we didn't know how many of their troops. I figured from the way they'd avoided our guarded areas in landing that they were getting up-to-date information on what we were doing.

"See if you can keep this shifting of our guards secret—maybe we can surprise them tonight," I said. A ridiculous request on the face of it. These guileless islanders enjoyed their freedom of speech too much. There was little enough to talk about in their restricted lives. I shrugged my shoulders—nothing ventured, nothing gained.

Yong was pondering what I had said. "You are probably right at that, Mr. Clark. The three times they have come over that we know of, they have landed just where our guards couldn't see them." He emphasized his feelings with a few choice Manchurian adjectives, snapped something at the section leader that made him jump, and was off for the village.

Kim had failed utterly with our prisoner. Not even the kindly gesture of a hearty slug of Canadian Club had dented the man's enthusiasm for a united People's Republic under the heroic Kim Il Sung. I could admire his adherence to principle, but it didn't solve any of our problems—or his. . . .

I had taken a swim and was lying on a poncho, letting the slight surf wash over me, when Hyun came down and reported four junks standing in. With my glasses, I could make out that two of the junks were raiders. The others, then, were prizes. Chang had hit pay dirt. Nothing to do but wait . . . In the meantime, Moon and the girls could whip up a big batch of *gohan*. These men had been on iron rations for quite a spell. A spot of Canadian Club might also help to dispel any feeling that their victory was unappreciated.

Coming up on the radio for our noon schedule, Tokyo assured us that we were doing fine, but could we step it up a bit? The Fifth Air Force was straining at the chocks and would be released on our targets within the next few days. We told them our prospects for increasing the information take were good, provided some characters we were being forced to live with didn't pester us to death.

With only ten days to D-day for Operation CHROMITE, the invasion buildup was going according to schedule. The thirty-six-hour delay in loading out caused by Typhoon Jane had been been made up by working round the clock. In the mind's eye, it was easy to picture the Japanese harbors daily becoming more crowded with fighting and merchant ships.

I had been so busy recently, I had forgotten that this gathering armada was the reason for our intense activity here. If the steps we had taken to date proved ineffective, there was no time remaining to reorganize along other lines. What we had developed would have to work, or we would go down, and perhaps the success of invasion with us.

There was so much still to be done—so much absolutely vital information we hadn't even gotten a lead on, that our effort and accomplishment to date appeared pitiful and ludicrous. If we just had more time to think things out. There were probably many easier and faster methods of getting what we wanted. I wondered with a flash of apprehension if, after all, we shouldn't have moved into the hills south of Inchon on the mainland. But then how could we solve the mining problem, and the beach problem . . .

Well, the die had been cast. It was too late to turn back on decisions.

I was relieved to see Lee making for his anchorage after his morning run, daring any mines to blow him up. "Everything's working smoothly, Mr. Clark," he reported. "Found the mine patrols all on station. The Palmi-do patrol saw Chang's outfit and our other junk this morning when the patrol passed on the way up to Wolmi-do. They said Chang was trying to close a junk running from Inchon to Yongjong-do. Good thing we worked out recognition signals or Chang would have brought him in."

"Do you suppose you could make another run this afternoon at low tide, Lee? If you could pass safely during that period, we would have an item of real value to report." I was desperately anxious to get something concrete back to the fleet on this mine business. It wasn't hard to visualize their concern on this score. Before the bombardment force came in, I had to have some news report on this item in Tokyo's hands.

"Be glad to, Mr. Clark," he replied without hesitation. "You want to know the range of those guns on Wolmi-do. How about me running in a couple of miles to see if I can draw them out? Frankly, my crew is as anxious as I am to throw a few shells into that island."

By George, this Lee didn't mind in the least courting disaster. "What do you suppose Admiral Sohn would say to such a proposition, Lee? Wouldn't he nail your hide to the mast if he found out about it?"

"Nothing of the kind. Our orders are to seek out and destroy the enemy wherever we can find him. I would go in on them at maximum range, just in case they have a couple of 155s."

"If you could stay within a few hundred yards of Palmi-do, and time it so that you could get on the ebb, it might be okay," I thought aloud. "Perhaps you could draw them out. I doubt that the garrison commander would stand the loss of face involved should he not return your fire, even though he might suspect your purpose. I think it's worth a try, Lee. But, for goodness' sakes, if they straddle you, get behind Palmi-do in a hurry. And be sure to use the ebb. If you're hit and disabled, at least you'll be carried down here."

What a way to get range characteristics on an enemy's guns, I thought ruefully. These 155mm guns were Russian-made howitzers reported to be of 1938 vintage—a good deal similar to our own 105s except for size. I recalled from reports on captured equipment seen in Tokyo that their sighting device was very crude in comparison with ours and pinned a little hope for Lee's safety on this deficiency. If they didn't have 155s on Wolmi-do, they wouldn't have them anywhere in Korea, that was for sure.

Much to my confusion, Lee thanked me profusely for this opportunity further to risk his ship. Would I have so generously interpreted my orders in this situation? I felt that I would have been obliged to ask for instructions and strongly suspected Lee of mental dishonesty. His gunboat was here to afford us protection, and not to bombard that forbidding Wolmi-do fortress. These gunboats had been purchased by the sweat and blood of the Korean Republic and were Admiral Sohn's only claim to a navy. If even one of the four were lost . . .

I wavered on the brink of changing my mind, but in the face of our mission, I knew I would compound Lee's indiscretion. I said no more.

"Chang's boats have anchored, *Taicho-san*," Chae reported.

"Suppose you go up and see what they've brought in, Kim," I suggested. "There is a remote possibility that there might be something that will affect our raid tonight."

Although the primary purpose of this raid on Taemuui-do was to capture Yeh alive and bring him back with us, we also hoped to throw such a scare into them that they would hesitate to continue their atrocities for fear of further retaliation. In order to make this threat stick, Kim was having the headman draw up a number of leaflets graphically illustrating this point, which we would leave behind. After all, in ten days we would call them to account.

By 1400, Lieutenant Ham's scouting party had returned in company with Chang and his raiders. Chang had managed to capture another junk, and I was feeling considerable optimism for the ability of this venture to add to our fund of information.

There wasn't much time now. We would have to get under way earlier than expected, for Ham had reported the two main coves to be heavily guarded. Yong, Chang, and I sat down with Lieutenant Ham and laid our plans for tonight's raid. It would be necessary for us to sail west and then north, cutting in to the point where Ham's party had swum out to their junk in making their getaway. This would avoid the guarded areas and afford us an approach to the village, which had proved to be unpatrolled.

In the raiding party, we would take with us the men who had scouted the situation last night, together with the junk's gun crew, Yong, Hyun, Min—who would not be left behind—and myself. This would give us ten men on the raid, plus a fully manned junk with Chang in charge.

Kim would remain behind to see his agents off to Inchon and to evacuate our gear in case the Reds should make good an attempt on our CP while we were gone. Lee would stand by with his gunboat to cover Kim and take him off if necessary.

At seven, Chang had his sails set and we were headed toward Taemuui-do. Taking advantage of the remaining daylight, we made a final check on our guns, and as we came about and started running before the wind, those of us going ashore stripped and rubbed ourselves all over with charcoal. I ran one strip of my Japanese-style breechclout through my knife sheath, hooked my flashlight, slung my holster, onto which I had attached three hand grenades, and I was ready to go.

Plans for the actual attack would await our arrival on the scene, when we could gain a realistic picture of the situation with which we would be confronted. Now everyone relaxed with a bowl of cold fish and rice, while Chang skillfully maneuvered the junk in the growing darkness toward our destination.

It was so quiet out here as to seem almost ominous. Even the slight clicking of the hashi against the rice bowls could be heard above the intermittent sound of the bamboo striking the masts. This atmosphere had its customary effect on me and I started glancing around for a comfortable place to stretch out, being faintly surprised to find that others had also thought of this idea. None of us had had much sleep lately. It would be a good thing to flake out for the remaining hour of the run north.

The activity of the hands at the sails woke me. Chang was winding the junk to bring her in stern-to on the reef now almost underfoot. The tide, still flooding, was giving some difficulty, so we grabbed some of the long bamboos and started poling with a will. She came to at last. Some last-minute instructions to Chang on recognition signals, and we let ourselves down onto the reef. Through the rubber soles of my Korean shoes, I could feel a hundred sharp points and thanked Yong for procuring me a pair. Tonight I shouldn't make so much noise. Last night's scouts struck off for the shore and we followed in single file, splashing a little at first and then getting beyond the water.

It was completely dark. The moon wouldn't be up for two and a half hours. Our guides must be going by instinct, for I could barely see the man in front of me, and distinguished the sides of the narrow trail only by the branches that occasionally brushed by and the deep grass when I stepped too far to one side or the other. Pausing frequently to listen, we pushed on steadily toward our objective. After about a mile of level travel, we started up the steep side of a hill that ultimately led us down to a point overlooking the village and the cove that fronted it.

Here we sat down to study the village from the outline given it by the cooking fires that had not been banked. This effort was futile, but by having Min fill in the details, we gained a fairly comprehensive picture of our target. The police and soldiers had taken over most of the houses along the waterfront, leaving the other houses, three or four in depth, between themselves and the hill area. The schoolhouse, which we had planned on breaking open to free any prisoners inside, was on the left—almost to itself. Yeh's house was located practically in the center of the row of beach houses. With all the men squatting in a semicircle, I gave the orders.

Min and Hyun would take two men and tackle the schoolhouse. The rest of us would go in on the right-hand side of the village and to the last house on the beach. There we would split up, with Yong, one of the village men, and myself approaching Yeh's house by way of the beach. The signal for general action would be given by Min at the schoolhouse, as that was the farthest and he would need the element of surprise in overcoming the guards. Immediately after that, the men on the right would heave a couple of grenades into the nearest barrack house. By this time, we hoped to be in Yeh's house and getting along with the business at hand.

A final check of equipment and we started down the hill. In a few minutes, Min's group veered away to the left on another unseen trail to sink immediately into the inklike darkness. We continued straight on down to the rear of the village, coming out near the well. Thank goodness there was a curfew, I thought. Turning right, we traversed the rear of the houses, now and then passing one showing the faint glow of a kerosene lamp through the paper coverings on the doors.

The sudden grunting of a penned-up sow as her litter disturbed her rest startled me. As we came to the end of the houses, our guide took a broad sweep around, which led us into the rice paddy area, bringing us in on the side of the cove opposite the schoolhouse. If our timing was right, we should have about ten minutes to get into position.

Here the target wasn't difficult to locate. Most of the houses lining the beach showed the light of their lamps, and from several came the sounds of revelry. There might be women in those houses, so I instructed the men to leave them until the last. If there were, the women would probably run out as soon as the thing started. It was useless to give this as the reason, so I just said that those soldiers would probably be drunk and harmless.

The three of us walked out to the water's edge and sloshed up to the middle of the cove, where we headed directly in. When about fifty yards from the house that our guide indicated to be Yeh's, we had to drop flat onto the sand. Two guards had come around the second house and were slowly walking down toward where our men were waiting. They passed, and we eased forward and then made a dash for the darkness between the houses.

Now we were in position. We could hear low voices coming from one of the rooms. Yong noiselessly opened one of the sliding doors that surrounded the porch area, and we stepped in. One of the thin floorboards protested Yong's weight, and we froze. The conversation continued unchecked. Yong was looking into the room through a rent in the paper on the door. I motioned to the guide. He nodded violently. Yes, it was Yeh, and I eased up to take a look and recognized him from his description. There were three policemen with him, two of them officers.

Min should have had time to reach the school. Probably having some difficulty locating the guard. But we certainly couldn't wait here long. We drew back against the wall, becoming three shadows with more than one dimension.

Someone inside was up and moving around. Our knives were out.

Yong, nearest the doors, tensed. His breathing almost stopped. A door slid open and someone stood there for several minutes. A cigarette butt flickered out across the porch into the yard. Whoever it was returned to his place, neglecting to close the door. Well, it would make our job that much easier.

What the devil was holding up Min? I half expected the boys down at the other end to go into action prematurely. Perhaps we could get on with our end of the job without waiting for the others, and I set my mind to this question. We could take them. No trouble there. But there was bound to be noise. Perhaps one of them could get off a shot. That would certainly bring others from the houses on both sides immediately. No, we couldn't get away with Yeh if we did that. We needed the distraction from the other groups to draw the attention from ourselves.

Nothing to do but wait. Someone was moving inside again. A faint hollering could be heard up the beach. I freed my forty-five for quick action, and Yong followed suit. We crouched now, facing the doors. There it was—the slamming of forty-fives and the hacking of Hyun's submachine gun. There were loud exclamations from inside, and before they could reach the doors, the rending crash of grenades a few houses down lit up the outside. They filed through the door now, and as they were fumbling to slide the outer doors aside, Yong jumped the nearest one. I was behind him and in a bound was on top of the man at the door, driving my knife hard up into his ribs. As he went limp, a knee drove hard into my side. But our guide was on the third man before I could recover my balance.

I looked around desperately for Yeh. Yong was pushing a limp body away from him and struggling to get through the door into the house, where Yeh was trying to kick his way out the flimsy door on the other side, screaming like mad. That had to be stopped or he'd have the pack on us. We were both on him. I had to stop Yong from throttling him. He screamed again, and I clubbed him over the head with my pistol. Yong picked him up like a bundle of rags, and we went to the front of the house.

Our guide was in a bad way, bleeding from the side of his head. No way of telling what the trouble was, so I tossed him on my back and we headed out the door. As luck would have it, a couple of soldiers were passing the house and, seeing us, threw up their rifles. We hit the ground as they fired; the bullets kicked dirt in our faces.

Yong was trying to free a grenade as I rolled over and emptied my forty-five into them at point-blank range, just as they got off a final round. There were no others, and we made the beach, dragging our burdens out into deep water. As rapidly as we could, we headed for the rendezvous point, feeling conspicuous in the light of the flames that were reaching up from the houses. Only one of the men was there to meet us. The other two had not come in from blowing up the last house. He thought they had been too close to the blast.

I studied the situation at the houses. The troops were frightened and confused, their officers shouting and brandishing pistols. They were firing at just about everything that moved, including their own people. We had to get around back of the village before they organized. Our remaining guide led off at a fast pace, cutting corners that took us short of the paddies. Soon we were at the point overlooking the village. My legs were so heavy with fatigue that I couldn't control the nervous twitching of the muscles after I had lowered my man to the ground, and I fell down beside him exhausted, lungs on fire.

"You all right, Yong?" I gasped anxiously. It was a while before he answered. Then, laboriously . . . *"Hai."*

Nothing else was attempted for a few short minutes. There was further work to be done, and Min's party had not returned. We were in too poor shape to tackle it alone. I couldn't tell about our guide's condition. The flashlight was too much of a risk. Poor chap would just have to sweat it out. He was still breathing.

Yong was working over Yeh, who was still out. "Don't know about him, Mr. Clark. Will you take a check, please?"

Crawling over to them, I found Yeh's wrist and felt for a pulse. Nothing there, nothing at all. I was dully aghast at the possibility that he was dead. Surely I hadn't clubbed him so hard. Ripping his shirt open, I listened for a heartbeat. Again nothing, but with my left hand I felt smooth oily blood and, exploring quickly, located the hole from which it had issued.

"He's dead, Yong. You've been carrying a useless thing. Sorry," I said, benumbed by a sense of defeat. Where'd he get it? Down in the village, but where? Oh yes, of course. In front of the house. One of those soldiers must have hit him.

A soft clucking of the tongue from a few feet away brought us to the alert. Yong replied, and Min with two of his men came up, carrying another.

"Who?" Yong queried.

"Hyun. Dead," Min stated flatly. What a damnable shame. I hastily reevaluated our capability. Six of us left. One to stay with the wounded man. Five to jump one of the patrols now searching for us along the paths below. It would be enough. A few minutes to allow Min and his men to catch their breath, then we were off down the hill again.

Min took the lead. He knew exactly where he was going, where he knew they thought they would be relatively safe from being jumped. We followed blindly, trusting completely in his intimate knowledge of this area in which he had lived his life. I forged clumsily into the man in front of me, who had stopped. Listening, we

could hear patrols shouting to each other, and occasionally rifle
fire off in the distance. They must have thought we were making
for the cove, or were just plain nervous. Closer at hand, I caught
the sound of voices, which seemed to be coming toward us. The
man ahead started again, almost at a trot, and we made a sharp
turn to the left onto a path paralleling the contour of the hill behind the village.

About thirty yards up this path, Min halted again. This was the
place. I stationed one guide on the uphill side. He was to jump the
last man of the patrol after he had just passed, permitting the others to proceed a short distance up the path to where four of us
would be waiting. The sixth man was stationed well ahead of us to
cut off anyone that tried to escape in that direction.

We squatted silently in the foliage and waited. They were slow
in coming, cautious, and loud in bolstering their courage. The lead
man came around the turn. He was carrying a dim kerosene lantern,
and swinging it vigorously from side to side, more as if to fend off
an attack than to illuminate an attacker. There were four of them.
This shouldn't be bad. The lead man passed our first jumper. We
shrank back into the undergrowth as the light came opposite us
and started to pass by, when a sudden shriek was cut short. A split
second's wait to let this surprise have its unnerving effect, and we
exploded into the path.

A sweep of my pistol butt caught the lantern and sent it crashing and out. The struggle on my left sent my man sprawling into
me, almost knocking me down. Catching hold of his blouse, I
hauled him to me with a jerk and, estimating a point, let go my pistol for his head. Too low, it hit his arm and he was whirling madly
to break away. Grabbing his clothes again, I turned him around
and kneed him. He tried to clutch at my clothes, and succeeded in
digging hot furrows with his fingernails in my bare skin. A short,

painful grunt came from my left, as I finally managed to get a handful of hair and crash a blow against his skull. He went limp. The struggling had ceased.

"Yong, Min—all right?"

"*Hai, hai.*" Cupping my flashlight, I took in the picture briefly. The guide had knifed his man. He was dead. The other three lay like bags of old clothes on the path. "Dump that one into the underbrush, quickly. Clean up the path."

This accomplished, we divided our take—two men to each rag bag. I hoped that this time we weren't lugging an unprofitable load. Back at the rendezvous point, we took another short breather.

"Min."

"*Hai.*"

"Will you remain here for about fifteen minutes? If they find our tracks in that time, throw a scare into them with a couple of grenades and then join us as fast as you can. Otherwise, come along. We won't leave without you, old warrior."

"*Hai,*" Min replied stoically. Five of us now, and four burdens. It would be too slow.

"Yong, let's gag them and try to bring them to. Use their shirts." After about ten minutes, with a little encouragement two of them came around, and we shoved off. With the two soldiers carrying their companion and the rest of us taking turns carrying our wounded man, we made the beach and were shortly joined by Min.

Without feeling, we put our charges aboard the junk, where the gun crew took over. Seems as though all I do is sleep, I thought dazedly as I collapsed on the deck.

8

RED PESTS

CHANG EASED US into our anchorage about 0430. There had been no sounds of gunfire as we came in. Either everything was okay, or the Reds had our base under close control. Only one way to tell.

"Yong, will you please have one of the gun crew go ashore and investigate the situation? We will remain on board until he returns."

If they had just held off while we were gone, we'd do something about them today, I promised myself dreamily. Hard to focus my thoughts anymore. Just about at the end of my rope unless I could get a little rest. How nice it would be to visit the Wakamatsu Geisha House in Hokkaido now. Steaming hot bath. Ice cold rinse. Rubdown; soft, powerful hands coaxing tense muscles into relaxation. Moon was good, too. Surroundings probably wrong.

Those prisoners. Not a sound, not a whimper out of them. Gags probably still in. Stout fellows—too bad they were playing on the wrong side. That tune Chang was humming. Definitely not Korean. Chinese? Mournful with an undercurrent of what? Hard to put a name to it. Nostalgia? No, more of defiance . . .

Yong was shaking me. "Mr. Clark, the youngster brings a message from Kim that everything is okay. We can go ashore."

"Min, please have one of your lads get the village doctor down here to take care of that wounded youngster and yourself, and look over our prisoners."

"Chang," I called.

"Hai, Taicho-san."

"Will you please take charge of the prisoners until morning? Have the gun crew give you a hand. You can remove their gags, but keep them tied up. We are going ashore now—to get a little rest."

"Hai, wakarimashita. [Yes, I understand.]"

Stopping a few minutes after we went over the side to remove our breechclouts and halfheartedly wash off the charcoal and blood, we dragged ourselves shamelessly down the beach to the tent. The salt water should do those scratches some good; it stung sharply enough. Couldn't take chances on infection up here, though. In the tent, Kim had the lamp going, so I rummaged around in the first-aid kit for the Mercurochrome. Moon was up immediately, wide eyes full of concern. She grabbed the bottle and pushed me back on the cot and started dabbing.

But what of Yong? Surely he hadn't come out of the fracas clean. I swung to my feet and went to look him over. He had a couple of deep scratches across his chest and side, and another just below the elbow that looked like a bullet had grazed it.

"Moon, take care of Yong, please. Get some soap and water and wash those things off good before you put on the medicine. Understand?"

"Wakarimasu, Taicho-san."

She promptly roused out her two assistants. That was that.

Yong didn't bother to wake up to honor the girls' tender treatment. Two or three hours' sleep would do more good than all the medicine in the world right now.

The warm sun shining in my face pulled me out of the darkness. It was seven A.M. and Kim was standing by with a voluminous report for Tokyo, a satisfied expression at last on his normally severe face. Wouldn't do Tokyo any good to keep the information here, so after breakfast we went to work on it. Kim elaborated, referring to our town plan map.

"You see, *Kuraku-san,* they have dug holes in the cement surface of the causeway between Wolmi-do and Inchon for machine guns. Sandbags protect them. Estimate is about twenty, perhaps ten at least on both sides. Those nests can cover the sea approach to Inchon from both north and south. They will have to be destroyed if possible. Then along the seawall here, which extends around the tidal basin, many more machine-gun nests. These two items have been confirmed by two sources. There are many Inminkyun billeted in these two churches, and many more in these warehouses. This building here, which was an old American communications center, is now headquarters for Red police. This park, on top of a hill, is where there are four or five antiaircraft guns.

"Several Russian T-34 tanks had been seen on the causeway rumbling out to Wolmi-do. The island is restricted, off-limits. Much activity over there. Also much activity between Wolmi-do and Sowolmi-do. They are doing something there, too. Many loads of barbed wire have been taken by oxcart to Wolmi-do. There have been no unusual troop movements into or out of Inchon, and it seems that there are about one thousand troops in the garrison. About one hundred police. Many people are collaborating, but it is the opinion that they do so to live. The Inminkyun are sending food stores and all rice to Seoul, mainly by junk barges up the Han

River. The people are very unhappy and will welcome Americans' return. Things are very troublesome in Inchon."

This was indeed good news. We were covering some of our specific targets—targets that if destroyed before the landing would save many, many lives. This information would also help our commanders assess the attitude of the populace in possible resistance activity.

After the failure with Yeh last night, I felt this excellent haul recouped that loss in part. But in no sense could it compensate for the death of Hyun and the other two. What our three prisoners could offer . . . well, they were only soldiers and would not be in on the broader military and political picture that had lain in Yeh's sphere of interest.

The information off to Tokyo, I turned my attention to our major effort for the day—rooting out the pestiferous Red infiltrators. Yong had been busy with the safe incarceration of our unwilling guests, and was now reviewing last night's episode with Min, who, for some inexplicable reason, always seemed none the worse for the wear. How I envied these little people their physical hardiness and stamina.

"Yong."

"Yes, Mr. Clark?"

"Our target for today will be those blasted Reds that are somewhere on this island. We've tried everything else, so now let's make an all-out effort. Will you get hold of the headman and all the section leaders? We want to organize every man, woman, and child on the island into one large search party. Leave only a skeleton guard at the ferry and pull off all the lookouts from the west and northern sectors. Take all our own guards here at the CP. It will be an all-day affair and will last until curfew, so better tell everyone to carry a little rice. This may flush them, so you had better issue the necessary instructions to those unarmed to do nothing but surround the spot at a respectful distance. Hold off any action until we are notified and get to the scene."

"What if the guards discover them? Should they try to make the capture?"

"No. Better not, Yong. Unless, of course, there are only four or five. We may be able to talk them into surrendering. Don't want to hurt anyone needlessly. Whatever plan they have to raid us is set to go into action tonight or soon. We want to know what that plan is, for it may involve more than just the group already here. Let's not fight the same battle twice if we can avoid it."

"Right, sir. I'll get started on it immediately."

"Oh, Yong. Another little precaution. When the search sectors are laid out, better look with suspicion on anyone attempting to be assigned to a particular sector or search party. He may be a tip-off."

"Yes, sir," and he was off for the village.

"Min, old warrior, how did you fare with the people at the schoolhouse last night?" I was acutely aware that we had lost Hyun in an effort not designed to bring home information, no matter the humanitarian motive involved. A strict accounting to my superiors might lead to a reprimand for this gratuitous action.

"We were successful in freeing them, *Taicho-san*. There were many men, women, and little children. Just how many I do not know. Perhaps fifty. Maybe more."

"The police guard, or were they soldiers? How did that go? There seemed to be a delay. Better start from the time you left us."

"*So desu ne.* [That is so.] We arrived at the schoolhouse in good time. I was not familiar with the situation of the guards, and the lad that had watched it the previous night and morning explained the matter. There were supposed to be eight guards. We could account for only four around the building and inside. We searched around the grounds and could not find the others. It was thought that they must be inside the building, and that was a bad thing, for there were many rooms. However, only two rooms had lights showing. It would have been wise to look into these rooms, but the outside guards remained close to the windows in the shadows. The door was on the one side with these two rooms on either side, the headmaster's offices. For a while, we watched, and thought about our plan. Perhaps we waited too long for you. I am sorry for that thing. At last it seemed that we could do it only one way: to kill the outside guards and take our chances on whatever guards were inside. Getting as close as we could until we were discovered, we ran in to them, firing our guns.

"This was no trouble. Perhaps they fired a few shots. I could not tell. While the other two finished them, Hyun and I went through the door. Two guards met us in the corridor and fired, hitting Hyun, who fell. I jumped one of them and we fell and struggled, but I managed to get my knife into him, when the other dropped on top of us. He was dead, shot by one of the youngsters coming in the door. I sent one of the boys to release the prisoners while we searched for the other two guards, but they weren't there. So I put out the lamps in case they were nearby.

"The people we had released wanted to know what to do. They wanted to leave the island. I told them they must take to the hills for a few days, as you had told me, when rescue would come. We gave them the leaflets to spread around the village area for the others to read. Then we urged them away. It was hard to get them to leave or not to follow us, for they were desperate people. Such a sorrowful thing to happen. We went back in to look after Hyun. He had been hit in the chest and was dead. As he was not of Taemuui-do, we brought him back for burial."

"About the other two guards, Min?" I asked.

"They were not there, *Taicho-san*. A fortunate matter, for they could have killed many of the escaping prisoners if they had appeared. We would not have had time to run them down in the dark."

That was the way it had happened, simply told with no embellishments, as if he were recounting the day's fishing trip to his wife.

"Thank you, old warrior. Will you please let me know when Hyun's funeral is to take place, for I wish to attend. His death was not in vain if the people he died to give freedom are not soon recaptured."

Chae had reported Lee's ship standing in from his morning mine run. "The ship is doing something up by Palmi-do, *Taicho-san*. Will you come and look?" he now asked, urging my glasses on me.

What in the name of blazes! I looked carefully. Yes, Lee had his gun manned and was running back and forth slowly this side of Palmi-do. There was no particular reason for this odd maneuvering that I could see. Putting the glasses down, I continued to watch. It was only nine-thirty, and the tide would not start ebbing until eleven. Surely he would not be foolhardy enough to put himself under their guns on the flood. Had I warned him of this? I thought I had, but couldn't remember definitely. If his engines or rudder were put out of commission, he could be carried right into Inchon Harbor on the two- or three-knot tidal current. There was not a thing I could do to call him off—and now . . . yes, he was building up speed. This would be it. Those Inchon gunners must be drooling at the prospect of that gunboat coming within range.

The ship was cleaving the calm waters of the bay at about twenty knots when Lee put her helm over for the left turn that would clear the eastern extremity of Palmi-do and take him up the channel. The thing was in the lap of the gods. I sent urgent appeals to all of them to watch over that reckless and foolish, but withal gallant, Korean, Lee.

She came up from her sharp heel and nosed into a course straight down the channel. Wolmi-do was blotted from sight by her bulk. Again she heeled to starboard as Lee came around and opened up. The flash of the second round recorded itself as the first cracked in our ears. A third, and Lee was hidden by Palmi-do as he circled back for another run. I couldn't observe the effect of his fire. He may have fired on Wolmi-do as he had threatened to do.

No answering splashes were visible, as he came into view again and opened up. Still no splashes, and on his next turn he straightened out and moved in still closer. Blast it! Were they deliberately drawing him in? It would be the logical thing for them to try to do.

I waited in an agony of suspense for his next turn. Come around, Lee! Why in blazes don't you come around? They'll blow you sky-high. Ah, at last he was turning. It seemed ages before he opened up. Now there were splashes, well clear to be sure, but they were after him. Apparently, they were walking the fire. That wouldn't give them much time unless they had hot gun crews. Lee finished the run, came hard about, and started cutting back. He couldn't have been more than three miles from Wolmi-do.

The splashes were cascading water to both sides as he presented them with a slender stern-and-bow silhouette for a target. He was certainly drawing them out now. There must have been at least five guns on him, judging from the number and fall of the shot. The slightest turn would broaden the target he made for the Red gunners. Yet he must, or they would range in on him. He would have to judge it carefully.

The ship heeled sharply to a right turn, which he held until they corrected their train and started to straddle. Another turn, and the maneuver repeated. He was coming out, but appeared to be slow-ing down. Now the splashes were behind him, the limit of their range, I hoped desperately. I glanced at my watch—he had been under fire for ten and a half minutes. I just couldn't believe that he had come out unscathed. Why had he slowed before he was out of range? A slight course change to the right and Lee was headed for his usual anchorage.

Off to the left were Chang's four raiders on their way to the northern islands to take up stations. We could expect a few more prisoners. . . .

"Chae," I said, "get a sampan out to the anchorage at once." Yong had appointed Chae to Hyun's job in charge of our CP guard.

Kim interrupted his cataloging of information. "There is an item here, *Kuraku-san*," he said, "which may possibly mean some-thing to us. According to this person that Chang brought in, there is a small group of people in this area here around the Manhak San [Mountain] who escaped from Inchon when the Inminkyun came in. He does not know exactly how many, but several of his kin also went there to avoid arrest for anti-Communist activity."

Looking at the map, I studied the area closely. Not actually a mountain, Manhak San was the highest of a group of hills about four miles southeast of Inchon and about two miles from the main highway to Seoul. At one point, this group of hills extended to within a mile of a tidal inlet reaching north from the bay. Large salt pans covered most of the area of the inlet, but it was obvious that a sampan could get all the way in at high tide. The situation pre-sented some interesting possibilities.

"Is that all the information he could give on that group, Kim?"

"I didn't go into detail with him on the matter, *Kuraku-san*. The item had no military significance, but I made a note to mention it to you."

"It could be important, Kim. If it's something more than just a group of refugees hiding out . . . Perhaps they might be doing a little stealing to keep themselves in food or clothing. In that case, they may have developed some kind of organized activity against the Inminkyun supply centers, or at least a watch along the main highway and surrounding area to protect themselves against surprise."

I considered this for a while. We had good coverage on the bay, but we lacked a reconnaissance element ashore. If we could gain their confidence and support, we would have eyes capable of watching the movement of all traffic on the Inchon–Seoul highway. More than that, probably, if they were seriously engaged in any other effort.

"Let's get the man down here, Kim, and see what else he knows about it."

Lee was taking a little time coming ashore, so I walked over to the paddy field to watch the infiltrator hunt in progress. About fifty people were strung out, moving at a steady pace from east to west. Evidently, Yong had decided to make the broader sweep across the island. The interval between the searchers was wider, but it was probably the only way to finish the search before curfew.

"Captain Lee is coming in now, *Taicho-san*," Chae reported, and I went down to the beach to meet him. The tide was well in, so he landed almost in front of the CP.

Greeting him, it was easy to see that he was immensely pleased with himself. Apparently, everything had gone to his satisfaction. "Lim," I called, "bring the bottle of sake, please." I meant our bottle of Glenlivet, of course, and Lim quickly produced it. If Lee couldn't use a drink, I surely could, but he accepted and downed it with relish, calling for a refill. He certainly was in a fine fettle.

"Did you get a chance to watch it, Mr. Clark?" he asked.

"Watch it! Watch it, you ask? Blast your hide, Lee, I fought that little skirmish of yours. Why the devil did you go in so far?"

Far from being nonplussed at this, he had a self-satisfied grin all over his face. "Had to draw them out. They wouldn't bite until I moved in, so I moved on in."

"But they could have hit you with a rifle, Lee. No blasted reason for you to go in so close."

I could see the twinkle in his eye wasn't going to fade away through this line of questioning. "And the tide," I continued. "Damn it all, if you'd been hit bad, you'd be high and dry on the Inchon mud right this minute."

He cocked his head in amusement at this last. "But I was hit, Mr. Clark. Took one through the engine room coming out. By the size of the hole, must have been a seventy-five-mm. Cut one of my main cooling system lines on its way out the other side. Skin of that ship isn't thick enough to stop a rifle bullet," he ended on a note of disgust.

That took some of the wind out of my sails. "Any other damage, Lee?" I asked with real concern.

"No, sir. That was all. Two holes and a broken line. Holes well above the waterline. Engineer is making a jury rig for the pipe. Going to clamp on a section of fire hose, he said. With all the other leaks there are down there, it won't even be noticed. I must apologize for going in as I did, Mr. Clark. I knew it was dangerous on the flood, but I had just this morning received these orders from Admiral Sohn and I knew that if I had shown them to you, you wouldn't have let me go in. I just couldn't disappoint my crew. . . ."

I took the radio message. He had translated it into English for my benefit. Lee was to proceed immediately to the Taedong Man area and search for a group of barges that had been sighted by the

Air Force moving down the coast from Chinnampo. This order su-
perseded all previous orders. . . .

It took a little while for the full import of this order to register.
Immediately forgotten was Lee's escapade. Kim was giving me a
long look, consternation written clearly on his face.

"We cannot do that, *Kuraku-san*," he said. "It is my feeling that
this ship is the only reason why the Inminkyun have not yet attacked
us. If she leaves, well . . ." He left the potent thought unsaid.

"I must obey my orders, Mr. Clark. Also, I am forced to assume
that the chief of naval operations is fully aware of the predicament
in which your party is left. There is nothing for me to do but to leave
as soon as I give you the information we have learned this morning."

"Yes, of course, Lee. Your orders must be carried out, and I am
deeply in your debt for your having accomplished this morning's
remarkable feat. Your skill and bravery and that of your crew will
be made known in my official report to General MacArthur. Now
let's get to what you learned so that you are not delayed too long."

"Lieutenant Commander Hyun, my executive officer, deserves
considerable credit. As was the case when the Yaks attacked, he handled the ship after I had laid down the general plan of the operation. While the gunnery officer, Lieutenant Ham, fired at discretion
on Wolmi-do and Sowolmi-do, I jotted down what information
there was to be gained, with my navigator doing the plotting. This
chart will tell the story."

He spread out his chart on the table. Meticulously plotted
were his course lines, which closed to within less than four miles
of Wolmi-do. The farthest fall of shot was just over six miles from
Wolmi-do.

"Did you note where the guns were that fired, Lee?" I asked
hopefully.

"Had my glasses on them the first few minutes, Mr. Clark," he replied. "As near as I could judge, they were right in here." He indicated Sowolmi-do and the southern face of Wolmi-do.

I broke out a larger-scale chart. "Can you locate them more accurately on here, Lee?"

He studied it for a few moments, then marked in six points, three on Sowolmi-do. "There was quite a lot of machine-gun fire from Sowolmi, too. Fell short of me. Heavy stuff, though, judging by the splashes. No telling how many, but I would guess not less than five."

Kim was busy jotting down notes as we went along. "Where did you take the shell in your engine room, Lee?"

"Right here, sir," he said, indicating a small X on his chart. I measured it off. Four miles.

"Notice any reduction in the number of splashes as you moved away?"

Lee thought about this for a moment. "Ham did call my attention to the sudden increase in the number of 'overs.' That was when we made this next-to-last turn. From about nine thousand yards to twelve thousand, the accuracy decreased, although the splashes were larger. They had us straddled two or three times, but couldn't make it stick. Larger guns, most likely. Probably 155s."

"Get a look-see at where those guns were that were firing at extreme range?"

"Yes, sir. One was here on Wolmi and the other two on Sowolmi."

I considered all this for a few moments. Anything we had not covered? Oh, yes. "You made the run looking for mines at low tide?"

"Yes, sir. Made it at first light this morning. Nothing showed up. I took the opportunity of notifying the skippers of the three mine-patrol junks that I wouldn't be checking them for the next few days, and that they were to be on the lookout for one of your people to take their reports."

"That's it, then, Lee. You have all of that, Kim?"

"*Hai, arimashita.* [Yes, we have it.]"

With grave misgivings, I thanked Lee and said goodbye, wishing him luck in finding the barges. He was a fire-eater if there ever was one. I hoped that he would get in no trouble with Admiral Sohn over this incident. If he did, perhaps I could get General Headquarters to intercede.

This information was so hot and so reliable that we whipped it into shape and shot it off to Tokyo within the hour. Admiral John M. Higgins, who would command our own bombardment force, should be pleased with this.

But I was very much concerned about our situation with Lee's gunboat gone. Kim may not have been entirely correct in his opinion that the gunboat was the only thing keeping the Reds from attacking, but its presence certainly could be considered a strong deterrent. I added the substance of this thought in our message to Tokyo, hoping they would send the gunboat back.

Kim added another disturbing thought. "We should see that the villagers do not know what has happened to the gunboat, *Kuraku-san,*" he said quietly. "With the Inminkyun on Taebu-do, the Inminkyun on this island, and only ourselves to stand between the villagers and these forces . . . The young men have been reported by their section leaders to be very nervous. They stay close together, and we suspect that they do not patrol as they should when on watch. This is a bad and dangerous condition."

Kim was absolutely right. "Tell Chae and Lim not to mention this thing, Kim."

It was useless to try to reason out just why they had ordered away Lee's ship. It could be anything from a fear that the barges were transporting a dangerous number of reinforcements to Inchon to just plain lack of appreciation for our situation here. If it were the latter case, then it was our own selves that were to blame, for we had given them no indication of any danger except to advise them of the Reds on Taebu-do. I could well understand why, lacking any further details on our predicament, they would think the gunboat could be pulled out at will. But I didn't think it right for us to go "crying wolf" over matters that, up to this time at least, were just beliefs based on nothing more than circumstantial evidence at best. We would look mighty ridiculous if no attack ever came.

"Poor judgment" was the phrase used at Boards of Investigation. It was only one step from that to the final degradation, "cowardice." I shuddered involuntarily at the thought and, snatching my radio message, carefully reread it. No, it wouldn't give the wrong impression, I felt, but words, like coquettish women, are such coy things. Try to hold one too closely and it might up and slap your face when you least expect it.

"I'll go on up to the village and see if the man, Chi, is there. Yong may have sent him out with the others on the search," Kim said.

"Chi. Who is Chi, Kim?" I didn't recall the name.

"He is the man with the information on the Manhak San people, *Kuraku-san*," he replied. "Also, I will see if the three soldiers that were captured are ready to tell something after our kind treatment of them."

I did a double take at this last announcement. Kind treatment. Hah! Kim, you old Manchurian tiger, you don't know the meaning of the word, I thought to myself. Then I wondered whether any of these three had taken part in massacring those women and children on Taemuui-do.

"Chae," I called. "Find *Min-san*, please, and ask him to see me right away."

I looked around and was surprised to find myself alone, and with nothing in particular to occupy my time. It was a strange feeling, like having been forced to hold my breath for a long time and then all at once being able to release it. What could I do with this freedom? One look at my arms and hands told me what I had to do—they were still streaked with charcoal.

I reveled in cold seawater and the somewhat less than luxurious lather of the saltwater soap. This was the life, cavorting around, making like a seal but undoubtedly appearing like a wounded hippopotamus to the women who were now watching and laughing on the scarp. I wondered if they gave a thought to the constant danger they were in. They would surely be killed if the Reds ever took them. I had to see that it never happened.

Min came down as I was stretching myself out on the beach to see if the sun wouldn't encourage my slight tan. "Sit a moment, Min, old warrior." Reaching in my jacket, I offered him a cigar. As in the case of Chang, I was certain that he would take and smoke it with great enjoyment. In this, I was not disappointed.

There was no hurry. I would carry this off in the leisurely manner of the Orient. Closing my eyes, I could hear him drag heavily and exhale with zestful appreciation. The noise represented his thanks for this gesture of comradeship. He would say nothing until I made the point of our discussion.

It was unfortunate that the information of Lee's departure would have to be told to still more people. However, it could be disguised. No reason for Min to know the entire truth.

"There has come up a very important matter, old warrior, in which we must again seek your strength and wisdom," I said with appropriate emphasis, and closed my eyes again. The Gods of the East were with me on this junket, I mused. Men like Chang and Min didn't just happen. They were placed in my path by omnipotent forces, whether for good or evil only history would judge. The barbaric hordes of Jenghiz Khan had once swept to the east and west, yet today only the student will philosophize about the effect on contemporary civilization. Truly, mortals are puny creatures reaching ever and ever—for what? . . . If we could just burst our shackles, have an awareness of our goal. The East was deep in this pursuit. How far ahead—how far behind?

"Captain Lee with his ship will be gone for several days, *Min-san*. It will be necessary that you check and receive the daily reports of the mine patrol that he has established. Do you know of this mine patrol, old warrior?"

I could hear him puff slowly on his cigar as he turned what I had said over in his mind. "No, *Taicho-san*, I know nothing of this matter," he replied with deliberation.

I explained the problem to him at length. The possibility of the fleet coming in. The disaster of a ship sunk in the narrow channel. The types of mines. Mud, and the tides. Lee's final report, which indicated conclusively that as late as this morning there were no mines laid in these channels. The patrol itself and their runs. The daily reports.

During this dissertation, Min listened with rapt attention, letting his cigar go out. I was congratulating myself on my fine delivery, when he effectively punctured this conceit.

"That is a strange manner of thing, *Taicho-san*," he commented in a bewildered tone.

"Strange, old warrior . . . What is strange?"

"These mines. Such things really exist? The Inminkyun have these?" he elaborated.

Gad, I thought, was it possible that the fact of their existence was unknown to some people in this world? Obviously, from Min's unbelieving expression, it was not only possible but true. Such being the case, it was necessary to go into much greater detail with my illustrations. It was like explaining a bullet to someone who had never seen a rifle, but he grasped its potential threat readily enough.

"You may use the raider with the heavy gun to make your rounds, *Min-san*. Captain Lee has informed the patrol captains that you would be around tomorrow morning on your first check."

If I only had a powered boat of some kind . . . Rhee—what had happened to him? Sent him in to Inchon days ago. But that was a long shot. Hope he hadn't been caught.

A runner came down with a report from the ferry. There was a sound of heavy firing coming from Taebu-do. The section leader couldn't tell what it was, nor the cause for it. Said it didn't sound like mortar fire, but very loud. Well, they couldn't carry a howitzer across the channel, even at low tide. I was to regret my quick dismissal of this information.

Well done on both sides and in the middle, I slipped on my trousers and jacket and returned to the tent for my glasses. Another little lighthouse was provoking my interest to no end. On the chart, it was named Pukchangja So Light, height forty-five feet. Like Palmi-do Light, it would shine down the two channels approaching the harbor. Lee had been complaining about there being no lights. First opportunity, we would go over and check it. The fleet could certainly use a light coming in here. Radar was good, but in my experience, for close-in work there was nothing to beat a heading on a light.

The fleet. By George, here it was the sixth and I still had nothing except general information on that mud or the seawalls. One of the islanders had told us that it was common practice for people to drive their oxcarts out onto the mudflat near Inchon and load junks in the channel near low tide. Good dope, as far as it went. But how wide were the wheels and how heavy the load? Presumably a soldier could walk on it in certain areas in safety. But what areas? Would a tank spin its tracks or sink? I was certainly going to have to get those answers, and soon. Last-minute changes in invasion plans aren't accomplished with any great ease, and as far as planning was concerned, we were long past the last-minute stage.

Paikyun came in with a message. Yong-san wanted me to come right away. Had they found something? Hai! On the way he explained that the searchers had flushed someone in hiding in the hills at the southern end of the island. It was thirty minutes' fast walking before we arrived. I could see the line of searchers still moving forward, extending as far as I could see. I hadn't visualized there being so many. Altogether, close to a thousand in the search, though. Paikyun led the way to a small group in a clearing halfway up the hill. Yong was busily engaged in berating a young man whom I took for one of the enemy, until I caught the idea through his gesticulations that he was our man. I wondered if this had been going on since Paikyun had left to fetch me, and dryly considered what a wonderful master-at-arms Yong would make.

His brief diatribe completed to his liking and the subject's petrifaction, Yong explained: "This stupid creature of the impossible," he said, transfixing the unfortunate individual with a venomous look, "took it upon himself to disobey my orders and killed this." He kicked the body of a man patently dead from a bullet in the head.

"How did it happen?"

"The villagers flushed him out of that outcropping of rocks down the hill. There's a small area in the crevice where he'd been hiding. He started running up the hill, and this man shot him instead of following to see where he might go. He may have led us directly to the others and saved further searching." Yong spat violently, indicating the extent of his disgust and disappointment.

It was too bad that the man had been killed, but . . .

"He may have been instructed to run in an opposite direction to the hiding place of the rest of the group, Yong. Certainly, we would have so instructed one of our people," I reasoned.

"Don't see how that could be possible, Mr. Clark. We've covered thoroughly all the ground in the opposite direction. There's the sea to the left, and more hills straight ahead. I figure that they must be up there someplace," he said, indicating the area ahead.

"You consider that he was a lookout, then?"

"Yes, sir. No sign of food down where he was, or anything else to indicate he has stayed there any length of time. If he was here alone, he surely would have moved in closer to the village in order to steal food."

"Have you searched him yet?"

"Nothing on him at all, Mr. Clark."

He was clothed in a pair of dark cotton slacks and the usual cotton shirt, which looked as though it had been washed in mud. Probably had been, come to think of it. Wouldn't do to run around here with a white shirt.

"Don't know what tricks these people have up their sleeves, Yong. Take off his clothes and search the linings. Check his shoes. No particular reason why he should be carrying anything, but there may be something."

There was nothing.

"All right, Yong. He's your property. Let's follow along the line he was taking and see what shows up. If that outfit is around here someplace, they're onto our little game after that shot." We started off at a fast pace to catch up to the line of searchers.

"I think if I were running an operation like theirs, I'd put out more than one lookout. Several in depth perhaps. May scare up another one or two before we reach the main unit," I commented.

"Know what I've been thinking, Mr. Clark?" Yong said. "I think that those section leaders never made a real effort to find these Reds. I should have gone with them myself."

Yong was probably right. It was no great reflection on our defense force, though, I considered. No training, no background. Likely no stomach for a firefight with a hidden enemy. Couldn't blame them a bit. Didn't like it myself. It's a rotten feeling to think that someone itching to get your scalp is in an excellent position to put one between your eyes before you even see him.

We caught up to the search line and started zigzagging over the landscape as we advanced, in an attempt to cover any likely hide-out spot. It wouldn't be sensible, I reasoned, for them to have an outpost so far advanced as to be completely out of contact. There must be somebody around here close. Yong motioned to a clump of trees on the summit of a small knoll we were approaching. We headed for it, the only likely spot this side of the rise. Nothing happened, and we entered.

Our man on the right called out, pointing excitedly down the hill. Running over, we were just in time to see a pair of legs disappear into a rocky formation about four hundred yards away at the start of the rise of the next hill. We lit out after him at a lung-bursting pace.

This was definitely the wrong thing to do, as we immediately came under fire and had to hit the ground but fast. We rolled and crabbed over behind a low rock outcropping, and took stock. They were firing from a good distance, evidently intending to keep us away rather than kill us. They could have let us come right up on them and then blasted us. Two or three rifles, at most. More than likely a reinforced lookout post.

"Send a man over to the guards in that next group, Yong, and tell them to come in on the right flank of these jokers." The man attracted some attention, as indicated by the dirt kicked up all around, as he shot off like a scared rabbit.

"Holler back to those people up there, Yong, and tell them to get word to all the defense force men in the search party to get down here on the double. We'll probably have good use for their guns if these boys want to fight it out."

One of those Garand semiautomatic rifles I couldn't get back in Sasebo would come in mighty handy right now. You could hit a man at seven hundred yards with one of those things. We popped up and down now and then just to ensure that the Reds were still with us. Evidently, at this range, their guns weren't too accurate, for their shots fell wide consistently.

"Were there any reports of boats beached around here anywhere, Yong?" I asked. I was disturbed by the thought that the purpose of this little action might be to delay us so that the main group could get away. Oddly enough, the thought didn't enter my mind that they might be planning to attack us and were merely buying time to organize.

"None were reported, Mr. Clark."

"Have you been over this area at all?"

"No, sir."

We couldn't see a thing beyond those rocks but trees and underbrush. They could move a small army around in there and we'd never know it. I thought of a radical move to flush them, but abandoned it. Setting a fire would endanger us as much as it would them, what with everything dry as tinder. Yong was indulging a few Manchurian epithets, presumably impatient with the slowness of our men arriving on the scene.

In spite of the efforts of the section leaders, the villagers were crowding in about us in a respectful semicircle. Nothing to do with them. Like sheep. Push them back in one spot and they surge out in another. Some men started forward on the right, closing the flank.

"Yong, I don't think whoever's in there is going to try to break through all these people behind us. Supposing you take charge of that group on the flank and bring them in close enough to harass our little friends, while I take a couple of your grenades and ease around the other side, up through the rocks, and see if we can't put them out of commission. When you hear the grenades go off, close in on them fast. Got it?"

"Yes, sir," and handed me his grenades. Wicked little Korean jobs. Looked like beer cans.

"I'll be about five minutes," I said, and quickly crabbed back up to the tree line. It was a clear run down the left slope, along a small ravine into the rocks, and then a skin-scraping, shin-banging job of going up, trying not to make so much noise that I'd be heard over the din of the rifle fire now drawing sharply closer. It was slower work than I had thought, and I had to try five or six different cracks through the huge mass before I finally spotted them. I was in a poor spot to heave a grenade. It would have to go up about four feet and then through the break without anything but the slightest angle, or it would carom off and our quarry would scatter.

I clambered up and was finally standing astride two of the inverted-V craglike rocks, making like the Colossus of Rhodes and just as exposed. Crazy thing to do. From here, the view down was now partially obscured by foliage. With our own bullets ricocheting from the rocks under me, I jerked the string off the grenade's safety and tossed it down, another to the left to discourage any retreat, and promptly fell down the exposed side of the crag, as rock and debris from the explosions pelted my hide. Fortunately, the incline was gentle because the rocks at the bottom were sharp. I stayed there until the action ceased. No use getting caught in a crossfire.

"Clark. Mr. Clark." It was Yong calling. I felt bruised and skinned all over. What a way to make a living, I thought disgustedly. I walked over to the trees and joined Yong, who expressed concern over my torn clothing.

"Get any of them alive, Yong?" I asked eagerly. It was beginning to look like we'd never get a break with this outfit. They were either dead or wouldn't talk.

There were only three of them. One badly mangled and dead, and the other two with so much dirt and blood on them it was hard to tell what had happened. But they were conscious, and Yong managed to get the dope we needed. Telling the villagers to take the prisoners back to the schoolhouse and turn them over to Kim, we considered our next move.

There were twenty of them at the top of the hill, in among the huge rocks that formed the summit of an escarpment falling off into the sea. This rocky formation provided numerous crevices and indentations ideal for concealment and defense. The only feature of the terrain in our favor as we scouted the position was the thick underbrush and foliage of trees that covered the side and top of the hill right up to the rocks. They had definitely drawn in their horns. Not a sound out of them.

"How are we going to handle this one, Mr. Clark?" Yong asked.

"I'll be blasted if I know, Yong. They're covered on both flanks and rear by that cliff, and trying to get at them from the front would be like hunting a tiger in a maze. They'd have the drop on us at every turn."

We had our defense force with us now. Plenty of firepower, but no way to use it.

"Suppose we toss grenades in on them," Yong suggested. "Maybe that will make them scatter or surrender."

Grenades were a possibility. But they probably wouldn't hit more than one man at a time, if we were lucky enough to drop them in an occupied crevice. Grenades like to spread around a little to make their presence appreciated. Still, it was worth a few of them to try.

"Okay, Yong. Scatter about ten of them around. Let them go at about one-minute intervals, for the nervous effect if nothing else. First, though, better send three or four men down to the beach to cover, just in case any of them try to break out that way."

It didn't work. A little hollering and jabbering in there, but nothing else. What the devil did you do in a case like this? A flamethrower would do the trick, or even a barrel of gasoline. We'd used both on Okinawa getting the Japanese out of their holes. Nothing like that in my supplies.

"Let's go in after them, Mr. Clark," Yong was urging.

"I'd rather make them come to terms from lack of water than risk any men in there, Yong. It's a lengthy process, but we have time on our side right now."

The idea of a fire came back. The crevices were narrow. Perhaps they might draw a little. A slight breeze up here, a sea breeze. Just what was needed. Still . . . I grabbed a handful of dry grass, set it in one of the openings, and put my lighter to it. It didn't do anything. Not enough fuel.

"Have the men gather a lot of wood and grass and stack it in that crack, Yong. We'll see what happens."

"It'll set fire to all this other grass around here and spread down the hill, Mr. Clark."

"It may, so stand by to fight fire after we light it."

In a few minutes, we had a raging inferno going in the crack. It didn't draw in either direction appreciably, but it was red hot.

"Break off some long green branches and start shoving the fire back along the floor of the crack." It worked, so we started stoking and pushing fire back along all the cracks. Gad, but it was hot. In a matter of minutes, the men were to the first breaks in the crevices.

"Toss on some of the green stuff, make it smoke. Then split the fire and take it on in."

I hoped the smoke would afford some cover for our men. The shooting started, and we ran in our submachine guns, spraying lead as the advance was accomplished. It was a long, hot, and murderous job. Three men came out seriously wounded, many more badly burned in their eagerness to close with the smoke-hidden enemy. Grenades were useless in the close quarters. Two cavelike flaws in the escarpment had shielded seven of the Reds, all of whom were now dead or wounded.

"Mr. Clark, they're firing from down on the beach," Yong reported, and we dashed over to take a look. The remaining Reds were making a break for it, not realizing that we had them covered from below. Running back, we led the men through the rest of the maze and out onto the top of the cliff. Below us was a fairly steep sloping face of the escarpment, undulating roughly like an uneven washboard. Our quarry were fully exposed to our fire either from above or below. Yong called on them to surrender. Seven of them managed to do so before our eager beavers below cut them down.

Dead tired, aching, scorched all over, but probably less worse off than the others, I asked Yong to have the section leaders dispose of the bodies, and bring in the others for Kim's attention.

"Better have them make a check of the rest of this area, Yong. See what these jokers had in the way of arms and supplies. They certainly must have an interesting story to tell—if Kim can persuade them to give out with it."

On the long hike back, we didn't exchange a word. Yong was a sight for the books. Hair singed and curling whitely at the ends, hands and face blackened, eyes points of black in rings of blood. He'd been right in the forefront all the time, but concerned with the safety of his men. No rash head, his. How he managed consistently to be in the thick of it and still available when I wanted him was a profound mystery to me.

It was after three when we gave ourselves over to the worried care of the women, and before they had finished, Kim was in with a report. "The first two men you sent back, *Taicho-san*. One of them says that this group of theirs is but an advance party. It is all I could get from them before they died. In his delirium, I think this man did not know who he was talking to."

"Too bad, Kim, but it's more information than we had. You are searching their clothing carefully?"

"*Hai.* I have the man, Chi, *Kuraku-san*. Shall we talk to him now?"

Chi? Who the devil was Chi? Oh yes, the man with relatives in the Inchon hills. I couldn't think anymore. It'd be nice to get into that cold bay again, but the tide was out. Suppose the water wouldn't be good for the burns, anyway.

Kim was waiting. "Let's relax for a while, Kim. Sit down and join me in a drink, please. Lim, will you get the sake [scotch] bottle and fill three cups?" I had to have something to get going on again. Yong looked dead.

After a couple of stomach-warmers had kidded me into feeling better, I tackled the matter of Chi. "He's here, you say, Kim?" I asked.

"*Hai, so desu.* He is outside waiting."

"You know what we want, Kim. Get any further information he may have on those people in the Manhak San area. Particularly anything he knows about their activities. Would they be receptive to a proposal from us to exchange rice for information? Perhaps even some of these rifles we've captured today. How far does he think they'd go if we gave them rifles and ammunition? You know, Kim. If it looks good, we should do something about it tonight, if possible. Time is growing terribly short."

9

BATTLE OF
THE JUNKS

W E W E R E A L L greatly relieved at having removed the
threat at our back. If they just hadn't taken Lee and his
ship away, things would really have been looking up. Without our
realizing it, the threat of nightly attack had taken its toll on all of
us. The guards around the CP were jubilant, mimicking their recent opponents while they dressed their fire and battle scars. Chae,
who had followed us against orders, had managed to get into the
fray and was deigning to let Lim clean up some particularly ugly-
looking burns. These lads didn't know the meaning of patience or
discretion, but I was thankful for those very characteristics. They
had played an important part in winding up what could have been
a long, drawn-out affair.

Ahn reported two of Chang's raiders standing in with tows. By
George, if we could just get a steady flow of material like that from
the mainland, we'd have it made. This Chi business looked better
to me all the time, and I impatiently awaited Kim's report. Little
Cynn, figuring that our banged-up condition placed us in a conva-

lescent category, was giving several beautiful renditions of Korean songs, and Yong perked up sufficiently at this to join in on a few choruses. Wonderful voices. A race of tenors, the Korean men— with apologies to Caruso.

"We might be able to work something out on this thing, *Kuraku-san,*" Kim said at last, conservative as always. "Chi says he knows approximately where they are located, and is willing to make the negotiations. But he says someone must come with him and bring rice and guns so that they will be convinced we can give them support. He requests that you go with him."

"Me go with him? Why should I have to go with him, Kim?" I asked dubiously. Right at this moment, I couldn't see myself getting off my cot.

"He says that if an American officer meets with them, he'll guarantee that they will do anything asked. He says that when he saw you here so close to Inchon, everything for him was changed, and for the other people, too. Everyone has been told that the Americans are being driven out and will never return. They do not know that an American is right here fighting for them."

He stopped, then added, "I think that he is right, *Kuraku-san.* From what I have learned talking to all these refugees . . . But I am afraid for you, if it is a trap . . ."

Yong had listened intently to what Kim was saying. "What do you think of it, Yong?" I asked.

"Kim knows these things, Mr. Clark. No doubt he is right about your going, but there is the risk. Still, this man Chi didn't know he was going to be brought here by Chang, so he couldn't have planned anything like a trap. It wasn't until we asked that he suggested it could be done. No, I don't think it is a trap."

"Yong and I could go with you, *Kuraku-san*—" Kim said.

I interrupted to ask, "How long do you estimate it would take to make this contact and get back, Kim?"

Kim went back to talk to Chi again.

"I don't see any reason for Kim to come along, do you, Yong? He has plenty of work here interrogating all these people."

"Yes, sir. I don't see any reason why you and I can't handle it," he replied, inviting himself in as though there never would be any question about that point.

The tables showed low tide at 1711 this evening, with high at 0019 in the morning. We'd have no moon until midnight. Those factors were eminently satisfactory. A light sampan could do the trick and get us over the shoals if necessary. Kim came back in with the rest of the story.

"It is not more than two miles from the reach of the inlet to where he thinks his people are. He estimates the time he will take walking up, contacting them, and coming back shouldn't take more than ninety minutes. Maybe two hours if he has trouble locating them."

"Okay, then, Kim, let's do it. You'll have to stay here and continue your work with the prisoners. Ahn reports another two junks captured by Chang coming in, so that will mean more work tonight. Yong is pretty well beaten, so will you please have Min get a sampan ready, with a sculler who is familiar with that stretch of the bay. Load four sacks of rice, and all the rifles and ammunition we took today. We'll leave when it gets dark, about eight."

"*Hai, dekimashita.* [Yes, I will do that.]"

"Yong and I will get a little sleep, Kim. We'll have to get our report out to Tokyo before I leave tonight, so wake me up in a couple of hours, please." I lowered the tent flap to shut the sun out of my eyes.

The information Kim wrangled out of the Reds from Taemuui-do wasn't too bad, but it couldn't be confirmed. The Inchon garrison commander was dispatching a heavy-weapons squad to that island, including two 120mm mortars. They intended to use these to cover the channel to the west of Palmi-do. These things carried a tremendous wallop and would cause all kinds of damage to a ship, although I didn't consider them too good a weapon against a moving target. They hadn't come close when the Taebu-do outfit used them against Lee when he was bombarding them.

There was additional information on their barracks in Inchon, but an outsize estimate of the number of garrison troops. They claimed over two thousand. By working backward on their tables of organization, Kim was able to point out that so many men in a squad, so many squads to a platoon, platoons to companies, et cetera, including a generous allowance for service troops, just didn't add up to two thousand. They backtracked and shut up.

It was still a couple of hours before dark, so we ran a sampan over to Pukchangja So Light. The tide had just turned, and most of the huge rocks that the light was set to warn against were uncovered, making it a nasty business to get to the narrow, perpendicular steel ladder that ran up the side to a small platform. The door at the top was open, with room for two small people inside. A thorough inspection of the light and its fuel and power system revealed that through the simple mechanics of cleaning a few badly corroded terminals, refilling the small fuel container from a can on the deck, and lighting the wick, we had a perfectly good light again. We were back at the CP in time for *gohan* (rice) and (ugh!) beef stew.

Having become rather dexterous in the act, I slept practically all the long haul over to the mainland. The sculler finally awakened us—Yong was asleep, too—when he became stuck fast on a mud bank. We accommodatingly hauled ourselves over the side, thereby lightening the load, and slubbed through knee-deep mud to meet him on the other side. The salt pans extended out to within a few yards of us. Apparently, the sculler was using the sharply banked edge as a guide up the inlet. As we proceeded on up, the scull oar was abandoned and he began to pole, maintaining a good rate of progress with the help of the incoming tide. We finally beached at our destination at about ten-thirty.

There were a dozen or so lights around from houses. Our boatmen said they were nothing to be concerned about. Mostly huts of the people who tended the salt pans. The most they wanted was to be left alone to carry on the work of their fathers and forefathers. In fact, while we were waiting for Chi to return, he would gladly take us to a nearby hut of one of his friends. Yong frowned on this suggestion. Whether for the same reason that I had, I didn't know, but I wanted to get a little more sleep. I was dead for sleep, and for that matter, if I didn't watch myself I would be dead because of it. So the three of us discharged the rice, guns, and ammo, and dragged the sampan high up on the beach, and Yong and I took turns watching and napping. It's odd that when you're so tired, you can forget such little things as bruises, scratches, burns, and wet, clinging mud. In fact, nothing seems to matter a great deal. I guess the nervous system just hasn't enough pep left to snap back anymore.

Yong was awake when Chi returned with his friends. He woke me quietly. They were wandering around the area trying to find the sampan, making enough noise to wake the dead. At least they were sure of themselves and their surroundings, I thought, to make so free and easy with their presence. We let them hunt for a few minutes, while Yong and I scouted the area behind them to assure ourselves that we weren't buying a pig in a poke. They might have friends in the Red Army. . . . There were three of them besides Chi, and were probably a little surprised when we clucked at them from the area through which they had just passed.

It was no strain at all arranging a deal with them. Their spokesman seemed highly intelligent and a very bitter and determined man. Their stories, which they briefly gave to assure us of their sincerity, were of the usual arrest, imprisonment, and summary execution of friends and relatives, themselves escaping to avoid similar treatment. Most of them had sent their women and children on down the Suwon road to the south with instructions to get behind the American lines. The men were remaining, for the most part, to keep what watch they could on their properties in and around Inchon and Yongdungpo, hoping to steal some of their more valuable belongings and spirit them away to the hills.

They would do more, but they lacked guns and ammunition and, therefore, had to spend most of their time foraging for food. With the rifles we brought they could take more rifles, and more food. But—slyly—rice was hard to come by even in stealing, so they would appreciate it if we could now and then give them several *mal* of rice, please.

Not a bad argument, I thought to myself. Particularly as it appeared these people were going to be worth their weight in gold as a source of information. We agreed to have a boat in here every night at high tide to pick up their reports. Every third night, the boat would bring three *mal* of rice. They would furnish a twenty-four-hour guard to cover the area of the boat landing, and warn off the boat with a rifle shot if the arrangement was discovered by an Inminkyun beach patrol. An alternate landing point was agreed upon. These details out of the way, I gave them a general briefing for half an hour on what information we wanted, and we shoved off. From here on in, Chi would be our contact man.

The moon was well on its way up as we poled our way back

along the salt pans, and, unfortunately, my nervous system was working, albeit sluggishly, again. Why the devil didn't somebody open up on us from the nearby beach, or at least challenge us? I was not in the least unhappy that the tide was again with us, adding a few knots to our speed as we came out of that tight corner.

From the complete lack of attention paid us by the Reds as we leisurely sailed down the narrow inlet and into the bay under the embarrassing moon, it was logical to conclude that the Inchon garrison was small in number or decidedly listless in their guard duties. In either event, it was to my liking, and I filed the impression away for further consideration. We arrived at our base without incident.

Our morning contact with Tokyo disclosed a sharpening concern over the danger of strategic Wolmi-do. It was reiterated that they considered this island the whole key to success or failure of the Inchon invasion. The task force commander, Admiral Doyle, wanted it knocked out at any cost. From Lee's experience, it was easy to see why. The tactical situation in which the fleet would find itself, as it steamed up the narrow channel past Palmi-do toward Wolmi-do, would be somewhat similar to the one that had faced the German High Seas Fleet under Admiral Scheer at the Battle of Jutland. There, the British Grand Fleet under Admiral Jellicoe had been deployed in such a manner that all of their guns could be brought to bear on the lead ship in Admiral Scheer's column. Only the lead ship of the German column could return the combined fire of the British, and then only by coming about—the principle of crossing the T. Here, Wolmi-do occupied the advantageous position of being able to bring all its guns to bear on any lead ship steaming up the channel, while only the first ship in the column could return the fire. This threat had to be eliminated, regardless of cost, before D-day.

The information on Wolmi-do that we had obtained so far, that we considered good, was limited to Lee's heroic sortie. It looked as though a little personal reconnaissance job was in order. Besides, there was more than guns that we had to know about that place. . . .

Kim had managed to get two of our Red infiltrators to open up, and we had full coverage of information on Taebu-do. But the rascals had failed to cut us in on one vital piece of information that made just about useless all the rest of what they had disclosed in such detail. However, we weren't kept in the dark long on this critical point.

About noon, Chang came breezing in with two more prizes in tow, and promptly marched down to the CP a group of seven pretty *kisaeng* girls for our inspection and appreciation. Their *mama-san* was beside herself with grief and worry. She had paid the junk skipper a small fortune in money and jewelry to smuggle them out of Inchon and down the coast to Pusan. They had been treated very badly and were being persecuted by the Reds in Seoul, where she had an elaborate and famous teahouse. As luck would have it, Yong and Kim both knew the house and the *mama-san,* having often frequented it in prewar days. Yong reassured her of our intentions, and the cloudy atmosphere cleared at once—particularly when I was pointed out as living proof of our intimate connection with the American forces.

Our old barbarian, Chang, was definitely disappointed at this revolting development. This was war to him. What was taken was the spoils of war. This rule, naturally, applied to this particular chattel article, as well. His vociferous declaration of this principle in front of the girls brought on another display of female handkerchiefs before we could quiet him down. A subtle reminder to him that in dealing with the fairer sex, sugar was always preferable to vinegar, apparently gave him a satisfactory degree of reassurance that his prizes weren't altogether beyond reach. Yong then took the woebegone group up to the village, while Chang and Min immediately went into a huddle.

Pirates. I'd bet my bottom dollar Chang and Min were both pirates, the way they covertly watched those girls as they headed up the path. Certainly, we'd not heard the last of this little matter, and at that moment I heartily wished Chang had missed that one junk. I considered sending the whole batch on their way, but relented when I thought of the heartbreaking two-week trip they would be in for, and the fact that in half that time we could put them ashore again in a friendly Inchon.

The doctor came down and surprised me by reporting to Chang on some of his men. Two were dead, and two more seriously wounded. He had dressed some minor damage from splinters on three others, and was concerned about Chang. Was he all right?

"Of course I'm all right, you old butcher," Chang replied angrily. "What did you do to those boys that they should die?"

I was completely ignorant of what had happened, but this short-tempered outburst of Chang's was going to do nothing for harmony in our closely knit little group.

"What's this all about, Kim?" I asked, always liking to get the story from him. My Japanese fell far short when it came to details. Kim launched a salvo of Chinese at Chang, effectively diverting his attention from the obviously discomfited doctor. Chang quieted down almost at once, as Kim's eyes and authoritative questions drew him back to the incident in which I had announced my interest.

It must have been quite a fracas to cause so much damage, I mused. Just like Chang to consider it so minor as not to warrant mention.

"I can't get too much detail out of him, *Kuraku-san*," Kim reported, "but it seems as though the Inminkyun are onto Chang's raiders. With the exception of the junk that was trying to smuggle the *kisaeng* girls out, the other three junks he brought in yesterday and today had policemen hidden in the holds. This accounts for the six police that I noticed at the schoolhouse. They are in bad shape. Haven't questioned them. After Chang's first unopposed captures, his captains relaxed their caution and were surprised when the police in the second group tossed off the hatch tops and cut into them with their rifles."

It was bound to happen, but I hadn't figured that it would be so soon. Their liaison was very good to be able to pick up the ball on the second day and put guards on board.

"What upset him about the doctor, Kim?"

"Chang just didn't consider the men's wounds bad enough for them to die, but the doctor says they were both hit in the chest and abdomen and never had a chance to live."

"What medical training has he had?"

"These are not real doctors, such as you have, *Kuraku-san*. According to your standards, they are not much more than trained nurses, yet they do have the title of 'doctor' in Korea. Higher training will give them a higher degree, but even so, it is nothing too good because of lack of laboratory and competent staff. But this man has performed an appendectomy on one of Lee's sailors, and he lives. He is very good, as our doctors go, and had a good practice in Seoul before he was forced to flee."

Chang had stomped off in a huff at the end of Kim's questioning, chewing the end of his mustache. He was having a hard day all around.

"Did Min have anything to report on the mine patrol, Kim?"

"*Iie*. Nothing was seen. They reported that more rice was

needed, and some charcoal if we could spare it. I will see that he has it for them on the next round."

After lunch, Yong and I began work on our plans for tonight's activity. When Tokyo chose to emphasize a particular requirement, it meant that we put it to the head of our priority list. Tonight we would tackle Wolmi-do. It would be another early-morning job, so we promptly turned in for a little more of that necessary, sleep, only to be disappointed. Chae had a messenger from the ferry. Yong took the report, and it wasn't good news.

"The section leader at the ferry says there's a lot of junks moving around in the cove over at Taebu-do. It's his opinion that they're heading over here."

An item flashed through my head, and I was on my feet instantly. Kim had said that our infiltrators were but an advance group. This, then, would be the main force, if they were coming here. Our information-gathering setup on Taebu-do, based on the woman friend of the commissar, had obviously been a flop. A hasty conference was in order. If Lee were just here. But if he were, those people wouldn't dare venture out in the daytime. We were agreed that, if at all possible, we would have to get them before they landed. Once they got ashore, we would be in a bad way against a large force of regular troops. It was hard to believe that they didn't know we had already destroyed their fifth column. Still, the firing had been a good six miles away from Taebu-do, and unless they correctly interpreted the smoke from the fire, it was possible they were going to be in for a surprise.

There was no time to lose. We explained the situation to Chang on the way up to the anchorage. The tide was at the ebb, and in our favor. The huge lugsails were run up almost in unison, and our five raiders began moving out into the stream before the anchors had been heaved to the cat. Chang ordered men to the sculling oars, as the vagrant sea slipped away into a dead calm and the tidal current threatened to set us back on the rocks. By skillful application of oar and rudder, the promontory was cleared.

Fully expecting Chang to take the shortest route to intercept the Red junks, which was the very narrow and shallow channel between Yonghung-do and Taebu-do, I was taken completely aback when he came about on a port tack and set a course for the East Channel. This would require at least another two miles sailing. I hurried to the helm, where Chang patiently explained.

"The tide is our only friend now, *Taicho-san*. On this course, we remain in the lee of the island until we come about for the approach on the Inminkyun. Should we take the other passage, we will have a much weaker tidal current, and shall receive the full effect of the sea breeze. I should say that we will save at least thirty minutes by taking the East Channel, keeping the men at the oar."

This lesson in local sea lore learned, I returned to my seat on the sandbags that buttressed the heavy machine gun. There was no rhyme or reason now to the positions or maneuvers of the other junks. They were just making their way down the channel as fast as they could. I could make out Yong on the junk, hugging our starboard quarter. He was going over his machine gun. A precaution I should have thought of, as I belatedly turned to checking ours.

Completing the check and adding a short burst for a test, I tried to estimate if they would have time to land at the south cove before we could intercept them. The tide would carry them south as they made their way north-northwest on a port tack. The afternoon sea breeze was very weak, between three and four knots. For every foot westward, they would be carried a good fraction of that distance to the south, and away from Yonghung-do. It stood to reason that they, too, were using oars if they hoped to make a landing before nightfall.

All factors considered, I felt that we would be able to close them well before they could land. It should be plain murder when we went into action. I patted the gun affectionately, then started to consider whether they might have thought of the same thing. Well, why shouldn't they have thought of it? My confidence started to ebb with the tide. Their machine guns weren't bad, but their heavies couldn't measure up to ours—I sought to seek refuge from my doubts. This dangerous possibility weighed on me until I had to do something about it. I hailed Yong.

"Yong," I shouted, "Tell the other skippers to remain about a hundred yards behind me as we start approaching the Reds. If they have a heavy machine gun, it will outrange your thirties. We'll close them first and see what they have, then you can move in. Got that?"

"I understand, Mr. Clark. Will do," he replied, and called out the instructions to the others.

We were coming up on the little midchannel island of Soobol, when we heard a hail from that direction. I had to look twice before I made out the small junk lying close in and almost hidden by the rocks and overhanging foliage. It turned out to be our East Channel mine patrol passing a friendly greeting. A very lonely vigil he was keeping.

As we came clear of the island's lee, the sails filled and Chang jibbed to come about on the starboard tack that would take us down to confront our enemy. We were sailing free on a broad reach as we passed Pang Am Light close aboard to starboard. I made a mental note of the fact that perhaps this light, too, could be placed in commission. In another ten minutes, we were clear of the long narrow headland that extended southwest from Yonghung-do.

Chang shouted and pointed. Yes, there they were. I had expected to see them clearing another headland almost due east, but had not allowed for drift. Evidently, the tidal current from Yonghung Channel was stronger than they had counted on—or perhaps they were so confident that they just weren't concerned with an hour or so delay. I turned my glasses on them.

There were six of them, one a huge Kwantung junk and the others coasters like ours. The Kwantung was under foresail, mainsail, and spanker, grasping hungrily at the breeze. I estimated the distance at five miles.

The tide was well on its way out now—a great expanse of mudflat showing itself to our left. I hadn't considered this, although I certainly should have done so. The Reds couldn't have been intending to land at the south cove, for the simple reason that they couldn't, except at high tide. There was almost two miles of mudflat to cross at this time. Then they must have planned on coming in on the East Channel side, the side we had just passed, where there were no mudflats. That would mean they intended to make contact with their fifth column group. But that didn't make sense, either. If the fifth column were to make a diversionary attack, they would be up by the village—a good three miles away. There would be no joining of forces in that event. Probably they just wanted to avoid a frontal attack and were choosing the most likely place to land.

Chang came forward. "If we continue on this course, we will get in the tidal eddy ahead and be swept ashore, *Taicho-san*," he informed me.

His knowledge of local conditions was invaluable. The danger of the lee shore had been driven home to me in typhoons and was a factor to be respected even in powered craft; it had to be feared under sail.

"Thank you, Chang. Come around a few points until you're clear of the eddy, then set a course to bring us between the In-minkyun and the island."

Evaluating our situation as it slowly developed, I saw that little advantage could be gained by any maneuver so long as the wind held from the south—and that would not change until late tonight. The tide gave us our only advantage as we were carried down on them. Shortly before we were in position to open fire, we would have to cram on full sail in a hurry.

I walked back to Chang, who was studying the enemy sails closely. "Chang, will you please tell the other skippers to take up their positions astern in a line abreast? Keep them several hundred yards clear of us on either side."

"*Hai, Taicho-san,*" he answered spiritedly. The old pirate was in his own element here and caught the significance of the move at once. We wanted to be able to lay all our guns on any single target that we chose when the time came.

The Reds had been straggling also, but were now closing their intervals to bring them abreast of the Kwantung. There was a sudden sharp clap and a brief flare from the bow of the Kwantung. A shell smacked the air overhead as it passed on its way far beyond our junks. Chang and I exchanged surprised looks, and Yong was shouting for attention, to be sure that we hadn't missed the disturbing news.

"Have them open and stagger their intervals, Chang." Another clap, and a crack overhead. Still way over, and to the left. They hadn't corrected at all.

"Keep your present heading, Chang. They're going to have to change course, if they want to keep that gun on us. We'll be able to sweep their entire line if they do." I studied the Kwantung closely through the glasses. They had a breechloader of some kind. Had to be fairly small caliber, to be accommodated by the junk. A mountain howitzer? I couldn't recall one of less than 76mm. Too big. It must be some such gun, though, and not being on a swinging swivel, it could only be fired within a few degrees of dead ahead. The maneuverability of the junk would determine the effectiveness of the gun.

The third round seemed to go through our rigging, so sharp was the passing crack of air. That trajectory was very flat for a howitzer of any caliber. They were firing point blank at us, I realized, with a very high-powered projectile. Then I had it—an antitank gun, and it was in clumsy hands or they would be firing a great deal faster. My immediate consternation at this wholly unanticipated development faded appreciably. An antitank shell is armor-piercing—made to explode after passing through several inches of treated steel. I should have had the clue as to the type of gun we were facing from the fact that the shells did not explode when they hit the water. Unless there was a faulty shell, they would not detonate when they hit our wooden craft, but would merely pass on through and spend themselves in the sea. Even the problem of splinters was minimized.

I had been tempted to open up with our heavy machine gun at this distance of about nine thousand yards, in an attempt to disconcert their gunners. Now I could bide my time, taking what damage they could inflict while we closed in to let go with our own little surprise. If we could get to within several thousand yards, we could cut them to ribbons in a few minutes.

I looked around to see how the other junks were doing. Not too well. Either they didn't understand the interval business, or just didn't choose to do anything about it. But they were on the same course, at least. I should probably be thankful for that. *Tactics* was undoubtedly not a word in their dictionary. Yong's junk and another to our left were hit several times in succession, the latter with a shell that raked a gash almost the full length of her starboard side. We had closed to within five thousand yards, and were assured of crossing well above them. A little deception was in order.

"Yong," I shouted, "open up with your machine guns. Don't make it too accurate. I want them to think that's all we have, so they won't fear closing with us."

For answer, he opened up at once and walked his fire to within a thousand yards of them. The men on our other junks started shouting, wanting to open up also, and I could hear the faint shouts of our enemy. I could make out the decks of their junks now, and they were crowded with troops. We should certainly have to stay clear of any possible boarding or they'd slaughter us with all that manpower. There had to be a good eighty or ninety of them altogether.

The Kwantung's gun was firing a good deal faster now, and with increasing accuracy. Coming up to cross them, we were deliberately, if slowly, opening our sides. Two shots hit us in succession, but we felt only slight jars as they passed through the starboard bow and out the port quarter. A shout from the junk astern to our left told us they'd been holed below the waterline and were taking water fast.

"Tell them to pull out and make for the Yonghung Channel, Chang. Beach it on the mudflat up there if they can't make it." They had been taking a lot of punishment, getting most of the fire intended for us, but which had gone over. It wouldn't have happened if they'd kept an interval. She was the only one that had been in the way of enfilading fire.

Yong's junk had been receiving some divided attention because of his belligerency with the gun, and more shouts announced that a lucky hit had raked the deck, causing several splinter casualties. I estimated the distance to the Kwantung at about three thousand. She was leading now, and with better discipline had herded the others fairly well in line astern. Barring any accident, we had them. Another fifteen minutes and we'd be in position. A shot suddenly bounced me off my perch on the sandbags, and sprawled me on deck. Picking myself up, I hastily inspected the damage. The thing had passed through the pile of shoring sandbags, and the gun sat askew in its position, but evidently undamaged.

We quickly manhandled the tripod back into position and shored it up. The ammunition belt had taken a bad twist, and to avoid a jammed gun it was necessary to remove it and advance it beyond the ruptured links. This accomplished, I checked our position again, just as the top of our mainmast sagged, and slowly toppled down, covering the people aft in a blanket of sail and broken bamboo. It was an unfortunate blow, but Chang kept a steady helm, seemingly not in the least perturbed. Seeing that the loss of the mainsail was no disaster, I took a final calculating look at the Kwantung and her shouting, gesticulating troops. The time was ripe for the kill.

"Chae, pour everything into her bow," I said, and I backed away to avoid the flying brass. He poured it in, and accurately. The other junks opened up on anything they could hit with their thirties. I concentrated my attention on the Kwantung. With perfect control, and utilizing standard short bursts as Yong had instructed him, Chae was just plain melting away the entire bow. The long narrow barrel of the antitank gun rose slowly and toppled over backward. The entire length of the deck was exposed, and soldiers knocked each other down trying to fling themselves into the sea, as a holocaust of death and destruction cleaned the entire topside.

Chang now came around on the wind, heading for other targets but keeping the Kwantung between the remaining enemy craft and ourselves. Light caliber machine guns on these other vessels were taking their toll on ours, in addition to the concentration of rifle fire that the troops laid down. Another of our junks was out of action, and I could see no stir on board as she drifted helplessly between wind and tide.

Passing the hulk of the derelict Kwantung, we came down on the next in line. The high poop of the huge junk had hidden the devastation we had wrought from her consort's eyes. As we nosed out from behind the towering stern, our next objective lay within a bare three hundred yards of us. Chae had used the breathing time to run in a new belt and check his gun.

"Open on the nearest one, Chae."

Without the modest protection afforded the Kwantung by her heavy bow timbers, this coaster literally flew to pieces—and her troops with her.

"Don't sink her, Chae," I cautioned, as he started to lower his fire. "Move on to the next one."

But now the handwriting was on the wall, and the Reds were all jumping overboard to avoid the ravaging hail of steel-and-splinter death. Our remaining two junks were calmly and carefully picking off every head that floated. The blood left a faint discoloration in the murky waters, which quickly diffused. There would be no survivors from this engagement, for we could not afford to permit a single one to swim or otherwise land on Yonghung-do.

Boarding the junks, decks ghastly from a mixture of blood, gore, and broken bodies, we removed everything of use. Chang recommended keeping two of the coasters that had remained fairly well clear of the firing. Putting crews aboard them, we sank the others. Yong came about to recover our own derelict, which had drifted a short distance south, and soon we were straggling back up East Channel, licking our wounds as we went. I wished that I had thought of bringing the doctor, but he had been busy with those men of Chang's. Too, if he had been lost it would have been a terrible blow, considering all the people he had under care in the combination prison and hospital.

Chang had been nicked by a bullet in the right arm, and had a miserable-looking patch of splinters in his thigh, which he was industriously removing, now and then sending up a torrent of abuse at his fallen mainmast. Chang had occupied the most exposed part of the junk, giving orders and alternately grabbing the helm on the raised stern sheets. His two crewmen had suffered bruised heads, shoulders, and indignities from the crashing bamboo yards. Chae, Ahn, and Paikyun—the gun crew—and I had come off with nothing worse than a few splinters.

Chae and his two cohorts were avidly reliving the brief engagement already, spirits soaring, enthusiasm and energy undampened. Chang hurled a couple of futile imprecations at them, which caused only temporary lulls. Finally, they burst into song. What peculiar people these were, and I was even more astounded when it was taken up on the other junks. Yong and Chang were dominating the stage when we finally anchored, but what outlandish tunes! They probably stirred old Jenghiz Khan in his grave. If the occasion or spirit that was moving them was the temporary freedom from fear of our vicious little neighbors—and I felt that it was—I was sorry that I was unable to join them. The loss of so many men would, I hoped, discourage any new attack—perhaps until D-day, but that was wishful thinking. . . .

The crew of the junk that had been holed had managed to bring her back and beach her below the anchorage. Now they were cheering "Mansei" as the sampans took us in to the beach. It was a major victory for the island forces, and the villagers were out to make sure that appropriate honor was done their men. Seeing the way the wind blew, I thought it wise to lift the curfew—an order that couldn't be enforced was a very poor thing indeed.

The big bowls of rice and two fried eggs that the women had ready minutes after our arrival put much-needed energy back into our systems. The doctor came down as we were enjoying a second cup of strong black coffee. He wanted medical supplies; several of the men were in much pain. Could we spare anything? Yong looked at me questioningly.

"Give him everything we have, Yong. Throw in all but one box of those morphine syrettes, and keep out a little cotton and Mercurochrome." I explained the syrettes to the doctor. A single shot should deaden pain; if not, then two. No use keeping the stuff. If we were to need it, I'd just as soon be in his hands as those of anyone else available.

Then Kim came down to throw a cloud across our clearing sky. More information from the Taebu-do men we had captured on the hill indicated a big attempt on the island for tonight.

"But Kim, we just had a big attempt. Surely they were not planning two such tries for the same day. It just isn't reasonable," I concluded impatiently.

"I agree that it is not reasonable, *Kuraku-san*. It is my own opinion that what they have told me refers to the operation this afternoon. It is likely that they are confused. Perhaps the schedule was set up for the attack to take place tonight."

Ah! That was more than likely. We had intercepted them well out. So they could have planned the landing for tonight, just as Kim said.

"Furthermore, these men insist that if today's operation fails, they have plans to try again at once. The garrison commander has upbraided the battalion commander on Taebu-do for his failure to re-move us. He has given him several special-type guns, and has added new units to his heavy-weapons platoon. They say, too, that they are now in radio communication with the garrison commander."

This report didn't make for any peace of mind. I couldn't help but wonder if our recent raid on Taemuui-do hadn't invited this un-welcome attention. Stick even a Red with a needle and he'll feel it.

"Anything pleasant to report, Kim, you old rascal? We're in a mood to celebrate this evening—not to give ear to a deteriorating situation."

"Well, yes, I have. Their informants have evidently tried to im-press the battalion commander by exaggerating our strength. They are of the opinion that we have three platoons of regulars here, in-cluding a heavy-weapons squad in each platoon. To date, at least, they do not know the gunboat has left for good, but they do know it is gone temporarily. That word traveled fast."

"That is good news, Kim. It means they'll take a little time to prepare for another go-round, and perhaps we can get Lee back by that time. Still, if the pressure is really being put on our lit-tle playfellows, we had better advise Tokyo of the new state of things. Maybe they will review their decision on withdrawing Lee's support. I'll add it to tonight's report, along with your other information."

"Those girls from Seoul had quite a lot of information from the capital," Kim added. "As of the fifth, everything appeared perfectly normal. No unusual troop movements, either north or south, or to Inchon. They located several tank hideouts; one is the old cotton mill on the road to Seoul. Several fuel dumps, and even an ammu-nition dump hidden in the woods. There are highway checkpoints on the road to Inchon about every half mile, but they only check men of military age not in uniform. They don't check packages going to Seoul, but inspect everything coming out of the capital. Their stories agreed independently of each other, so I consider it to be very good information."

We sat down at once and got this off to Tokyo. It was the first good report out of Seoul we'd received. Dusk had settled before we were free to look into our plans for tonight again, after the rude interruption of our abortive afternoon nap. This was certainly not the humdrum existence of Tokyo. I was absolutely out on my feet, and as the nervous excitement of battle wore off, the thought-benumbing demand for sleep grew. For this ailment, I had brought with me a cure—Benzedrine tablets. I had put off using them as long as I could. Now I slapped one in my mouth and washed it down with coffee, making Yong do the same.

"Come on, Yong. Let's get going." Outside, we picked up Chae, our key to tonight's operation, and headed up the beach to where our sampan and sculler were waiting. Climbing in, we shoved off on a flooding tide that we would trust to carry us noiselessly down past Palmi-do to Wolmi-do, our destination. The moon was rising later and later in its last quarter. Tonight it wouldn't put in an appearance until after 0100. There would be a critical interval of thirty minutes between moonrise and the ebb tide that would carry us back out again, but we hoped to finish our work in time to get away by use of our single sail and firm application of our sculler's brawn. I hoped we weren't placing too much faith in the land breeze, but after several nights' observation, it seemed a sure thing.

"You have many casualties in your junk, Yong?" I asked, not having received a complete report on the killed and wounded. It was Yong's junk, I recalled, that had taken a gouging shell across its deck.

"Their machine-gun fire was inaccurate, Mr. Clark, but their rifle fire caused us several casualties, aside from the splinters. One of

Min's boatmen took a slug in the groin shortly after we all opened up. Then a big splinter took Choi between the shoulders as he was feeding the gun. Came out through his chest. Dead before he hit the deck. Same batch of splinters took Yang in the back and neck, but the doctor thinks he might pull him through. I doubt it. Just before the Reds started jumping overboard, another boatman took one in the leg. Cut through an artery. He put on his own tourniquet."

Four casualties out of eight men, whereas Chang had been our only case. We had been busy engaging the Kwantung in a bow-to-bow duel, and had been protected by her huge bulk from the others' fire. Our other junks moving on down to engage the smaller enemy craft had taken the full brunt of the firefight. It had been rough, but not nearly as rough as it would have been if those jokers had landed.

The Benzedrine had taken hold now and we were both wide awake. It was a good feeling to be free of the weight of drowsiness. The tide carried us effortlessly on to Inchon. The boatman's sole concern was to steer for the city's lights. Without moon or stars, we seemed to be suspended in black space, the darkness was so intense. It was quite impossible to make out any line delineating land, sea, or sky. What lights there were appeared suspended in the same plane, and had it not been for the soft noise of the water under our keel, it would have been wholly an eerie feeling.

Little Chae had been trying for days to get us to let him scout out his old haunts on Wolmi-do. The older people assured us that he knew the island like the palm of his hand, having spent just about all of his vacation days at the swimming pool there. Wolmi-do had had two major attractions under the Japanese. First and foremost, it was the principal resort of Inchon—its hills, now embracing guns and ominous caves, had then been the mecca of picnic parties. Secondly, it was the location of the Standard Oil installation. Chae was certain that he knew the beaches and walls well enough to discover just how they were being guarded.

The swimming pool was constructed of rock after the Japanese style, with high walls to keep out the tidal waters. It was situated on the northwestern tip of Wolmi-do, and it was here that we beached. Chae stripped to the skin and hopped over the bow into the mud, which he promptly plastered all over himself. It was quiet. A few lights shone down toward the cove. Otherwise, there appeared no sign of life. Yong whispered the recognition signal, handed Chae his knife, and pushed off. A few yards out, Chae was lost to view.

The boatman steered the sampan out into the stream, then started sculling against the tide. It took a good thirty minutes to travel the few hundred yards to where the long causeway leading south from Wolmi to Sowolmi began. The plan was for Chae to cover the beach area from the swimming pool north to the causeway, while we would cover the comparatively safe area of the causeway and what parts of Sowolmi-do we could without blowing the operation.

We beached at a group of outjutting rocks, and quickly donned our mud uniforms. Instead of a knife, I carried my binoculars. The sampan was to wait. If anything happened so that he had to leave, he was to pick us up at the little lighthouse island of Seito Gan, about fifteen hundred yards up the channel.

Rounding the rocks, we could barely see the beginning of the causeway. Using my glasses, I could see it clearly. I was continually amazed at how effective binoculars were at night, and using them wisely, I was certain that I should see any exposed enemy in the dark before he would see us. This knowledge afforded me a proportionate degree of confidence in nocturnal operations.

As we moved in closer, we could hear low voices, and finally located the guards by the burning ends of their cigarettes. They were squatting on the ground, and were apparently the causeway guard. Waiting about fifteen minutes to learn if there were a patrol in addition to the guard, and none appearing, we made a wide swing back to the water's edge and then in again to a point well clear of our talkative friends. Here, we climbed the side of the slightly inclined seawall and searched the area around us.

I had anticipated seeing barbed wire stretched along the causeway, and perhaps even a system of trenches. With my glasses, I could see a good fifty yards toward Sowolmi-do. Nothing but causeway. We slid back down and walked up another hundred yards. Still nothing, and so on till we were almost on the little island itself. Here, it became ticklish work. Sticking our heads over the top of the wall, we were looking squarely into a machine-gun nest. We ducked back instinctively and held our breath. We hadn't seen anyone, just the gun and some sandbagging around it, but it wasn't wise to observe anything from such a vantage point. We moved back down the wall and came up again about ten yards away.

There were several machine-gun emplacements, but no evidence of guards or gun crews. From a careful inspection, it appeared that the road that ran along the top of the causeway continued onto the island around the eastern side. A crouching run took us across the road and we dropped over the far side, where we promptly slid to the bottom. Yong cursed under his breath. We were up to our shin-bones in mud. The other side had merely a coating of mudlike silt over a hard clay subsurface. Here the subsurface was more mud, hardpacked. We had rubbed quite a lot of our new-look uniform off and took time to replace it, and I regretted not having done so earlier. This particular mud had a smell akin to that of rotten fish and other things I couldn't quite put my finger on.

We slubbed along the bottom of the wall for a few yards, alarming ourselves at each step with the noise we made, and finally halted. This was definitely no good. A whispered consultation and we crawled back up the wall, only to throw ourselves flat against it as a group of soldiers passed by so close we could have grabbed their ankles. When they had gone on toward the causeway, I used my glasses to inspect the area from which they had come. There were a few cement structures down to the left on another level, apparently buildings and not gun emplacements. The road itself wound on around the hill into the darkness.

Another whispered conference, and we decided to cut across the road into the foliage at the bottom of the hill. Being the quieter of the two, Yong would make the first dash and I would follow. Just as he was tensing for the run, I grabbed at his back and pushed him down. There, just a few yards up the hill, I had seen a small red spot glow bright. A cigarette. Pointing out the area to Yong, we waited. There it was again. We were stymied on this approach, so, retracing our steps, we crossed back over the causeway. This was taking a devil of a lot of time. One absolute rule to follow in such close-in work was to halt frequently and watch and listen for several minutes.

It was impossible to estimate how long it would take to work around the profitless west side of the island to where we might run across something of value. Having come this far, I would have done almost anything to spot one or more of those guns that had fired on Lee. However, we made better and safer progress, even though there were many huge rocks to traverse. Once past this area, we ran into a vertical seawall and had to backtrack. Climbing the mass of rough, tumbled boulders to the top was hard on the skin—and required all our concentration. Consequently, we could do nothing but freeze in our stance when someone spoke up almost alongside of us. My mind was in a whirl of undecided moves, one discarded as rapidly as the next. Only a subconscious command to stand and utilize my only protection—camouflage—kept me from pouncing on the speaker immediately in an attempt to neutralize the danger.

What Yong must have thought, I don't know, but he stood as still as a rock. The speaker was answered from a short distance to the right. Yong put out a hand and pushed me down, following suit. As he could understand what was being said, he must have known that we hadn't been seen or heard. The conversation continued in a sporadic manner for about ten minutes that seemed like ages. Then Yong pulled back on my arm and cautiously felt for a step down. We backed down the rocks like a couple of ungainly honey bears.

I was almost beside myself with mortification. All this effort, and nothing to show for it but a couple of machine-gun nests. Stopped at every turn, we could only trudge back to the sampan. I hoped he hadn't been forced to pull out. A fifteen-hundred-yard swim would be the last straw right now.

This Yong is an admirable fellow, I thought. I felt like a babe in the woods when I was with him on these jobs. He never made a wrong move and was silent as a ghost. I often wondered on this and other occasions whether he wished I'd leave the whole business to him and stop endangering his life. For that matter, I was of the firm opinion that I hadn't begun to sound the depths of his capability or ingenuity. I comforted myself with the thought that at least I wasn't hampering the operations of little Chae. What an indomitable people this was, and I reflected with regret that a good half of them were fighting on the other side.

The sampan was still there, the boatman answering Yong's soft clucking at once. Chae hadn't made his way up as yet, but he had a much longer stretch to cover. By making the rendezvous at this end, he wouldn't have to retrace his steps to the swimming pool. We took the time available to slip into the water and wash off the camouflage, which had stood us in good stead. From the number of burns that cropped up as the salt water took effect, I was going to need a little of that Mercurochrome.

Yong was firmly sold on this business of wearing no clothing whatever in these nightly affairs, and the experience I'd had on Taemuui-do had sold me. In that one little scrap, I had managed to quiet my man by grabbing his clothes. He had desperately tried to grab mine and, of course, failed. So it would be in any tussle in the dark, where only the sense of feel could be engaged. However, I was a long time overcoming a certain sense of insecurity as it concerned private well-being.

A good forty minutes had passed, and I was becoming concerned over Chae, when we heard his clucking from the dark of the rocks. He came on in, exhausted but beaming.

MUD, MUD, AND MORE MUD

NATURE'S LAWS BEING more or less immutable, my pre-
diction that the gentle southerly wind of the summer monsoon would be replaced by a northerly breeze off the land was
confirmed, and our small sail filled immediately. We ran lively before the wind, and the crisp gurgling sound as the blunt cut-water
of the sampan opened a path down the bay and the gentle heeling of
the diminutive craft to the wind formed a soporific combination
that soon had Chae sound asleep. We were well out of the way before the waning light of the crescent moon could reveal our presence to hostile eyes.

"This thing about the wind," Yong said, "it puzzles me, Mr.
Clark. Why should you be able to say that the wind will come in
another direction at a certain time? I've asked the boatmen. They
just say that it always does, but do not seem to know why."

This question was typical of Yong. Always eager to learn—to
get to the bottom of things. Never satisfied with just knowing, but
searching for the reasons. "It's a very interesting subject, Yong.

During the warmer seasons of northern areas, the land during the day is commonly warmer than adjacent waters. The air overlying the land is heated, it expands, and it is pushed upward by cooler air that runs toward the shore from the surfaces of adjacent water. This is a sea breeze. At night, the land surfaces lose the heat gained during the day, and as they become cooler than adjacent water surfaces, the wind direction reverses. This is a land breeze and is what occurred tonight. In the absence of relatively strong prevailing winds, such as the winter monsoon in this area, it is fairly safe to depend on it."

"These monsoons. How do they work?"

"In general, the same as land and sea breezes, but on a much larger scale. With the monsoons, it is the cooling and heating of the tremendous landmasses of Asia and Siberia. When this area turns cold in winter, it is the same as when the local land surfaces turn cold, except that the monsoons occur seasonally, whereas the land and sea breezes occur daily. The winter monsoon blows out of the north and into the south seas. The summer monsoon blows out of the south into the summer-warmed landmass of Manchuria, Mongolia, and Siberia."

"This is a very interesting thing. I have been wondering about it for a long time, Mr. Clark. Does anything ever occur to change it?"

"That's a really involved subject, Yong. The answer is, yes, but only temporarily. This is when we have storms and typhoons, and these exceptions can be fairly well predicted by the various instruments, including the barometer with which you are already familiar. However, for such sailing as we do around here, where distances to shore are never great, it is generally enough to be able to read the clouds and the unusual changes in wind direction."

Soon we were approaching Palmi-do. I would have to look into the possibility of putting the Palmi-do Light back into commission, I thought. Might be able to take care of that today. It would be visible down Flying Fish Channel for twenty miles, while the Pukchangja So Light could be seen for only about twelve miles.

It was almost three again by the time we beached and shook Chae awake, and made him go over the side to wash off his mud coating. Then, with him thoroughly awake, we took him down to the tent and bled him of his information. We had to get this dope while it was fresh. How many times had significant details slipped out of the mind with the passage of a few hours? We could not afford this.

With a talent for graphic illustration, little Chae promptly drew a sketch and filled in the detail of what he had observed—not omitting the five patrols and two guard points he had cautiously circumnavigated. Although these latter had effectively stopped his exploration in depth, he had thoroughly scouted the beaches and embankments. The cove south of the swimming pool was entirely free of any form of underwater obstacles and was suitable for bringing in large landing craft, including LSTs. Some work with bulldozers would have to be done to make adequate exits for tanks and larger vehicles. A hard-surfaced road passed within a few yards of this exit, which he knew extended across the narrow neck of the island with the causeway.

This, of course, assured our landing force of a ready means of getting tanks into Inchon—so long as the causeway remained intact. It was a most important piece of information. Further, the entire western side of the island had been ringed with trenches right up against the seawalls. Taking no chances, the Reds had fronted these trenches with high barbed-wire fences—no doubt the wire that had been previously reported coming over on carts. At two points, Chae had seen entrances to caves beside the roadway running around the west side. A ramp that was shown on the chart, and which I had hoped we could use to land personnel and equipment, was nonexistent. Chae said it had been destroyed years ago, but that it was still a good point to rig a temporary ramp, for it extended farthest out into the deep water of the channel.

Piecing all our information together, we gained a fairly comprehensive picture of how our forces could land and, partially, with what defenses they would find themselves confronted. It was important and urgent from a planning viewpoint for Tokyo, so we fixed it up and sent it off before the effects of the Benzedrine wore off. Kim had some excellent items that had been brought in by Chi from his friends on Manhak San, including gun positions, barracks, troop strength—and a request for more guns. I chided myself for not having thought of sending in the arms we had taken from the Reds' junks, which included four machine guns and several submachine guns of Russian make. Well, we'd send them in on the next trip. It should make them happy if that's what they wanted.

As far as we'd been able to extend ourselves in the week we'd been here, we still had an insuperable task facing us. It just wasn't possible, with the moon and tide to consider, to conduct more than one operation a night—and the nights were running out on us rapidly. We figured that any operational information we sent in after the thirteenth—five more nights—would be impractical to place in use. By that time, the plan for the invasion had to be sewn up tight. The troops would long since have been embarked, and part of the invasion fleet on the way to Inchon. Only data of momentous significance could be used. If we'd just arrived a week earlier than we had . . .

Providentially, beginning tomorrow night we could ignore the moon. It was going into the dark phase. Just the tide then . . .

In spite of the Benzedrine and strong coffee with which Moon had worriedly plied us, getting to sleep didn't require a second thought, although we probably would have slept much better had we known the good fortune which was to favor us that afternoon.

Through the combined good offices of Moon and Kim, we slept through until nine—a good, solid four hours. Moon suggested in pointed terms that we were filthy and reminded her of fishing boats, and that we should shed these disgusting relics of last night's activity in the sea—before breakfast, please. This was made inconvenient by the fact that the tide was all the way out, but she had the answer in a tidal pool at the foot of the east promontory. Being a male of the species, I was not at all chagrined to find Lim, Cynn, and others of a mixed company also indulging in their ablutions. Chae, the lucky little rascal, was not going to be disappointed in the physical aspects of connubial bliss if that body of Lim's portended all it seemed. Moon, of course, railed at us when she saw our scratched bodies, but we took our Mercurochrome like men—wincing.

Paikyun came in while we were dressing and in a shocked tone announced that a battleship was standing up the channel.

"You mean Lee's gunboat, Paikyun?" Yong corrected pointedly. I gave a sigh of relief and thanked Tokyo for heeding our request for its return.

"No, *Yong-san*," he insisted stubbornly. "This is a battleship. Come and see, please."

What the devil. He had seen Lee's gunboat enough times to recognize it. Surely the bombardment group wasn't coming in to start softening up so soon. We hurriedly threw on our jackets and walked out to the scarp. Paikyun was definitely right. It was not Lee.

"Get my glasses, please," I asked Paikyun. It looked like a light cruiser or destroyer. What with these new big destroyers, it was difficult to distinguish between them anymore. It was a destroyer, I decided. We speculated on what she might be doing in here. I couldn't see any other ships coming up the channel. Shortly, three planes went over—high. I turned my glasses on them—ours, not Yaks this time. Marine jobs, by their markings. They were probably with the tin can, since no others had shown up around here since our fracas with the Yaks.

It was something new and distracting, and for that reason among others of a more soul-satisfying nature, gave us an excuse to sit down and contemplate what would happen when the bombardment group came in. Man, would they scare the living daylights out of those Reds. We laughed and joked about this eventuality for about fifteen minutes, when Ahn directed our attention to something else. It was a destroyer's motor whaleboat easing its way around the western promontory.

What a curious development this was. Undoubtedly that destroyer's boat. What was it doing nosing around in here? I immediately came to the conscience-ridden conclusion that Tokyo was dissatisfied with our work and was sending in another party. Oh, Lord, I thought, this is it. I mentioned this possibility to Yong. He merely shrugged. He wouldn't try to analyze the ways of Westerners, but if I was right, he would stay on. He was a Korean officer with a mission from the Korean government and would see it through, with or in spite of the unfathomable Americans. His philosophy didn't help me an iota, and I chewed nervously on my cigar. As the boat came closer, we could see that it was crowded with sailors armed to the teeth. Perhaps they thought we'd turned Red or something and were going to arrest us. It was not beyond the realm of possibility, but I couldn't assign any reason to such action.

The boat officer was evidently familiar with the shallow depths over which he was sailing, for he kept about five hundred yards offshore. When the boat was almost opposite the large congregation of villagers who had gathered around us, I and Yong stepped out and hailed.

"Ahoy! In the boat! Looking for something in particular?" This was just in case they were not looking for me.

There was a nervous fingering of guns by the grim, determined-appearing landing party. The reply came immediately. "Is there an American on that island?"

Yep, doggone it, they had me tagged for return. Couldn't understand why, though. I gave an answering hail, and I supposed my two-day beard was sufficient evidence that I wasn't a Korean. The boat officer was taking us all in carefully with his glasses. He was in a very uncomfortable situation, actually. I was soon to learn that neither his captain nor he himself was certain that we were on Yonghung-do. Such being the case, they had scouted along the islands on the way in until they had found our group. We could have been the enemy and, except for a quirk of fate, our group would have been the enemy. Still, they came in close enough to have been riddled by hidden enemy machine guns—"sitting ducks." The boat officer couldn't accomplish his mission of finding us had he remained farther out. He could and did subject his boat and men to possible murderous enemy fire by moving in as close as he did.

"Can we move in closer to the beach, Mr. Clark?" the boat officer called. "The captain would like to see you on board."

I waved him on in, there being several feet of water over the mudflat by this time, and climbed in the boat. There were a few curious stares at my unkempt state, and I suddenly remembered to toss my cigar over the side. Smoking was prohibited in navy boats—if not in junks. There seemed to be nothing of common interest to discuss on the way to the destroyer, so I gloomily surveyed the bay and surrounding islands that had so unexpectedly become a home away from home. It wouldn't be such a bad thing to be recalled, I temporized with myself. It had been rough going. I estimated from the new holes I'd made in my belt as I cinched it up that I'd lost a good fifteen pounds. The only saving grace of the job was that it had been interesting—too much so at times.

Wisely, the captain hadn't anchored in the channel, and was maintaining just enough turns to keep steerageway. The boat coxswain brought us up under the davits where the falls were cleared, and the hooks rove smartly through the hoisting links. In a matter of seconds, the boat was clear of the water and we stepped out on the main deck, where the executive officer took over and hurried me to the bridge. There I was introduced to Commander Cecil Welte, captain of the USS *Hanson*.

"I have orders to evacuate you and your party, Mr. Clark. Do you have any casualties on the beach?" he asked.

Casualties? What did he mean by that? "Yes, Captain. We have casualties. About forty, I guess. But how did you know? Who sent you here to evacuate us?"

"Why, Naval Headquarters, Tokyo. Dispatch said you were under attack and that you should be evacuated. But let's get along with it, please. Don't care for these waters. Do you know whether they are mined or not?"

"No, Captain. No mines. If you don't mind—I don't like to delay you, but I must get this straight. Were your orders to evacuate my party left within my discretion or not? You see, we have eliminated the danger for the time being. The casualties we have are being taken care of by our own doctor, and are all Koreans. We never requested a ship to evacuate us, although we most certainly appreciate the interest shown."

The captain sent for his dispatches. Reading them over, we saw immediately that this whole thing was the result of our two radios to Tokyo expressing concern over the departure of Lee's gunboat, and advising them of the recent attack in force—which had, apparently, been due to the direct interest of the Inchon garrison commander. My fears of an involuntary recall blinked out.

"In that case, is there anything we can do for you, Mr. Clark?" Commander Welte asked.

Exercising what I thought to be remarkable restraint, I promptly stated two requests. "Taebu-do, that island over there," I said, pointing, "has some unfriendlies that have been bothering us considerably, Captain. We would appreciate it greatly if you could give it a short-time bombardment."

"Be glad to. Can you give me an idea where to unload?"

We walked over to the chart which was being used for conning. I pointed out the junk cove and the small island of Sonjae-do, which lay in Yonghung Channel.

"It would be a big help if you could destroy the junks and sampans in this cove. It would prevent them, for a while at least, from coming over and troubling us. Along the top of this little island, the Reds have dug some trenches, which they man against the possibility of an attack from us. A little attention should upset them."

The captain studied the chart carefully, tracing his natural approach course down East Channel and around the southern tip of Yonghung-do. There was plenty of good water for junks, but extremely tight quarters for one of our larger destroyers. Commander Welte would have been well-justified in reconsidering his offer.

"If I do get stuck in the mud down there, this flooding tide should break me loose in a hurry," he commented, without much conviction. "How about mines?"

"There are no mines in this entire gulf area south of Inchon, Captain. And, incidentally, when you pass Paegg Am Light, you will see a small junk. It's our mine patrol."

Didn't want that junk sunk. Couldn't imagine why Tokyo hadn't given out our information on the mine situation. Certainly Commander Welte had reason to be concerned. Red mining activity was going on everywhere, and this was a key area. Being ordered into these close waters without such vital information must have caused him no end of worry.

"That's it, then, Mr. Clark. I'll bring my air cover in to spot. No reason why they shouldn't use their bombs and rockets if they see good targets, is there?"

"No, sir. Please avoid the village, though. The people are good South Koreans—just under the Reds' control for the present. No reason to shoot them up."

"Check. Anything else?"

"I've learned that these jokers are deathly afraid of phosphorus. If you have any, I'd suggest you use it on them. It'll scare the devil out of them, if nothing else."

"Don't you need a few supplies? How about cigarettes? Glad to help in any way we can, you know."

I considered briefly, then asked for the two things that could, I thought, help us most through the next week—sugar, and medical supplies for our overworked doctor. The captain sent for an assortment of drugs and bandages, including some badly needed penicillin, and sulfa—and a hundred-pound sack of sugar put up in ten-pound bags. It was more than I had hoped for. Sugar was worth far more than rice for barter, we had belatedly discovered. Inside of fifteen minutes, I was back on the beach. Ahn and Paikyun happily unloaded our precious cargo. The whaleboat cut back to the *Hanson,* throttle wide open.

In less than an hour, Taebu-do was taking salvo after salvo of deadly phosphorus shells into its beach area. The trenches on the heights of Sonjae-do came in for their share of punishment, while the Marine devil-dogs lashed the beaches into a lather with five-hundred-pounders and rockets. Yong dampened my feeling of accomplishment by putting forward his opinion that the bombardment and bombing were probably a mistake. He reasoned that the battalion commander on Taebu-do could not stand the loss of face occasioned by the attack, and would try to strike back as soon as he could. In this view, I was inclined to agree, but then, I rationalized, he had already suffered such a loss of face in the junk battle that he would do what he could anyway.

It was about two when Ahn asked to borrow my glasses. Something up by Palmi-do. He couldn't quite make it out, but it looked like smoke. After a while, he came running back and reported a pompom (a junk with a one-cylinder diesel engine) coming down the channel from the direction of Taemuui-do.

I studied the pompom and the area astern of her carefully. I wouldn't put it past the garrison commander to send down on us a fleet of junks. If he had a pompom, this would be the place to use it. But I couldn't see another craft in view. There was only one answer—the boatman, Rhee, whom we had sent in days ago to steal a pompom and had given up on. Somehow, he had accomplished his mission. It was such an important development that I didn't dare estimate its potential value until I had had a chance to see what shape it was in—both engine and hull.

"Wonder if we can use it in tonight's operation, Mr. Clark," Yong said, no doubt recalling the long, tedious haul in to Manhak and out with the sampans. Dependence on wind and tide would be gone with a powered craft—and our problems simplified greatly.

"I'd certainly like to, Yong," I replied, "but I think it'll make too much noise for as close in as we want to go. However, maybe we can give her a trial run over to Palmi-do when she gets in. We want to take a good look at that lighthouse and see what needs to be done."

The tide was high, and Rhee brought his boat right up to within a few yards of the scarp and anchored her. She had an old coat of white paint on her and carried an Inchon Harbor registry number on her bow. Built with heavy wooden members, she measured roughly thirty-five feet from stem to stern, with about a ten-foot beam. Tossing some rice and other supplies aboard for the Palmido guard, we followed and shoved off for the lighthouse island.

Yong and I joined Rhee in the small wheelhouse. He accepted our thanks and compliments without change of expression, but I could tell from the grand manner he assumed at the wheel that he was bursting with self-satisfaction. The pompom had been ready on the fourth. There had been no danger at all once he had disposed of an individual that Rhee's friends around the waterfront thought to be a Red lookout. Perhaps he hadn't been. Rhee shrugged. All the boat owners had dismantled and sunk some critical parts of their boats in the mud so that the Inminkyun would not commandeer them and send them up the Han River on the Seoul supply run. Too many had been sunk by the American fliers to risk it. Others had deliberately holed their boats. There had been three pompoms that could have been used, but this was the best. When Rhee had assured the owner that he was taking it away from Inchon to a safe place, the owner promptly volunteered to go with him. We would find him now down in the engine room.

Anxious to learn the ways and means of accomplishing little tasks like spiriting a full-grown boat out of an enemy-held harbor, we pressed Rhee for details.

The Inminkyun had suspected nothing as they were getting the boat ready, for families lived in all the boats with a variety of activity going on all the time around the junkyard. It wasn't until last night that there had been a sufficient interval between the beginning of ebb tide and moonrise to permit them to float the boat out into deep channel water. They had met with hard luck before reaching deep water, grounding on a shoal spot. By the time they had worked themselves free and floated silently out into the channel, the moon was up. Dim as it was, they feared passing the guns of Wolmi-do, so they started the engine and headed north, making a wide swing of the northern islands, finally anchoring in Chang-bong Channel to await today's 1230 high tide. They had then crossed east over the mudflat north of Taemuui-do and south to Yonghung-do.

Looking down a light well into the engine room, we could see a grizzled, toothy old man oiling, wiping, and otherwise nursing his diesel monstrosity along. It was the type of engine found in this region, which worked on a "hot-top" principle. The single cylinder stood about four feet high, and burned anything that smelled as though it had oil in it. To start it, a separate mechanism charged with compressed air and fuel shot a blowtorch flame onto the top of the cylinder until it became red hot. At this point, the engineer gave the cylinder a squirt of fuel and it was off to the races, bucking so violently that the boat itself would nog with every stroke of the huge piston. At the extremes of the boat, this nogging motion would be exaggerated so much that I had difficulty keeping my glasses steady enough to study any object.

Our little tour finished, I asked Rhee a few questions. How much fuel left? There was enough for two days, providing we didn't use the boat all day. Did the stack always throw off so many sparks? It always threw out sparks. Last night they had thought those sparks would cause them trouble. Hmm. No nocturnal activity for this buggy, that was for sure, and unless Lee returned, we'd soon be out of fuel.

Rhee beached the bow on the Palmi-do sand spit, and our island guards assisted in off-loading their supplies. We had thrown in a few cartons of cigarettes, and they overwhelmed us with their thanks. Quite obviously, they weren't faring too badly on this isolated duty.

It was necessary that we get back to Yonghung-do quickly if we wanted to get any sleep before tonight's mission, so we went straight to the lighthouse. A standard-type facility, it was round and about forty feet in height. Opening the bolt, we swung wide the double doors set in the structure at the top of about five steps. Inside to the left was a triple row of heavy-duty batteries, similar to the kind we'd found at the Pukchangja So Light. They appeared in bad shape. Someone had opened them all and they were dry. A couple of five-gallon distilled water bottles sat on the floor, empty. Several of the wire leads to the light above us had been jerked loose. It didn't look good from down here. On the right was a single iron-rung vertical ladder extending through a round hole into the deck level of the light itself.

We climbed up. Here everything appeared in good order. A kerosene can was on the deck, half full. An inspection of the lamp and wick showed it to be operable, so without further ado I lighted it. The flame wasn't high enough. A little cleaning fixed it. If we couldn't get the batteries working, which was the power source for turning the shade, we would at least be able to have a fixed light shining directly down Flying Fish Channel. I noted with some surprise that the whole rig had been made by some outfit in Paris, France. Back below, I went over the batteries carefully. All definitely dry, no water, no battery acid. The wiring could be fixed, but without the batteries it was useless. Well, it was the light down the channel for those critical hours of early-morning darkness that was needed. A fancy flashing light would only serve to give a navigator a flashing instead of a steady light on which to take bearings.

Making a final check on the lamp, I blew it out. I'd have to advise Tokyo and ask when they wanted Palmi-do Light in operation.

It was luxurious riding in the pompom, and we were soon back at the CP, having accomplished what would have normally been a four-hour job in two. Yong was puzzled by what I had written on the lighthouse door before we left. It was the time-honored phrase "Kilroy Was Here" and the date. I became rather entangled in explaining the subtleties of how the thing would baffle the U.S. Marines who would come later. I managed to get across the idea that the charm of the saying was its inexplicable appearance where it was least expected.

Inside the tent, there was all kinds of female chattering and activity. Kim explained that it was occasioned by two events: One, Lim's and Chae's parents had finally agreed on the marriage and they were now engaged; and, second, the village fathers, in celebration of yesterday's victory, were throwing a party. In deference to their status as our servants, the three women were designated as maids at the party. This, of course, was an honor for them and the reason for all the preparations.

Scrubbed to a rosy pink, and in varying stages of dress, they were doing their very best primping with a minimum of makeup material. I dug into my ditty bag and offered them a can of Mennen talcum powder and face lotion, which promptly changed their entire attack on the problem. Soon the tent was in a white haze as the powder was splashed around freely to effect its proper body tinting.

A delegation of notables—namely, the headman, the schoolmaster, and Chang—came down with a formal invitation for our attendance. From the libidinous look in Chang's eyes as he caught sight of Cynn pulling on her dress-up silken pantaloons, I gathered there was something else on his program tonight besides food and drink.

"*Shicho-san* [Mr. Mayor]," Yong said, allowing the headman considerably more honor than was his due, "we have much work to do this night and must leave the island early. However, the Taicho and myself will be happy to accept for an hour or so, after which *Kim-san* will represent us." Then, anticipating me, Yong added, "We would like to contribute a few bottles of American sake to the party, if you can use it?"

The headman accepted this gesture, and we dug out three bottles of Canadian Club from the case. As they headed for the village again, I saw old Chang take charge of the bottles and hoped he would leave a little for the others.

Ignoring the girls, we turned in for a few more precious hours of sleep. Time, tide, and moon were all in our favor tonight, and it would be a full night's work.

Kim roused us out at seven-thirty. We all donned the kimonos sent down to us for the occasion and walked up to the village. The party was at the headman's house, and removing our shoes, we were ushered immediately into the party room, which had been enlarged by the simple expedient of removing the sliding doors between two smaller rooms. The arrangement was the same as in Japan, except that here there were no tatami mats on the floor. Wide pillows were furnished the guests, on which they sat cross-legged.

There were about fifteen guests in all. I could appreciate the brave effort that had been made in scouring the village for enough of the proper dishes and paraphernalia to do justice to the occasion, and, even so, the result was pitifully lacking to a sharp-eyed observer. This was forgotten at once, however, when the *kisaeng* girls came in dressed in their best finery, looking like a spray of

brilliant flowers in a swamp setting. The merriment began immediately following the customary round of speeches. The interpre-
tive dancing of the girls was at least comparable to that of the
Japanese geisha, if perhaps at times more on the suggestive side.
Chang was literally beside himself with impatience, chewing on
his drooping mustache, downing copious quantities of straight
whiskey, and not being too discreet in fondling the girls assigned to
serve him. Now that the girls were assured of their privilege of re-
fusal, their vanity satisfied, they seemed completely fascinated by
the ruthless Chang.

Regretfully, Yong and I pulled ourselves away from the party.
Passing along the street, we could hear smaller parties going on in
the other houses. A victory for freedom is something well worth
celebrating, I thought. If fortune favored our side, soon all of Korea
could be repeating the gay activity of this village.

Neither of us looked forward to this night's work. It was going
to be just plain dirty. The stretch of Inchon's outer harbor from
just south of Doku Gan point around to En-do island was to be
looked over to see if any area could be found suitable for landing
craft. From there, we had to go inside the harbor and check the
consistency of the mud and the height of the seawalls.

We were very lucky, in that Rhee, who had just spent four days
prowling the beaches north of Inchon, had all the information
needed for that area. In fact, he had spent most of that time on the
boat looking down the muzzles of the machine guns being placed
on the Wolmi-do causeway running to Inchon. The old man who
was the owner of the boat had watched many guns being moved
onto Wolmi-do and had been able to pinpoint some of their locations. Tokyo had welcomed this information. Slowly but surely, we
were filling up the vital gaps. This would be one of two final major
undertakings before the invasion.

We'd had some ropes braided for tonight and the lenses of several flashlights covered with heavy red cloth for signaling purposes. Using adhesive tape, we secured our knives to our backs with the hilt just below the nape of the neck. A single grenade we cross-taped as usual slightly above and behind the right hipbone. If worse came to worst, neither of us could be taken alive because of the nature of the information we possessed. Should one of us be unable to kill himself, then the other had a duty to perform the task, unpleasant though it might be. It was melodramatic perhaps, but we never considered it a laughing matter.

Flood tide started at 2050 and we shoved off for Doku Gan point. There was no particular hurry. The tide should be flooding for at least two hours before reaching our destination—a spot about a mile off the point. While the boatman guided the sampan along with the tidal current, using the sail intermittently, we took the opportunity to doze.

The slight halting motion when the sampan grounded on the mud was not perceptible to us, and the boatman woke us. Pointing to some lights in the east, he said they were from villages just south of Doku Gan. If we walked straight toward the lights, we would arrive at the beach we wanted to survey first.

Unlike some things to which I could become accustomed with repeated use, the thought of another application of mud filled me with disgust. Grabbing the pole, I shoved it down in the mud and pulled it out. About three feet. Too deep to make any progress. We knew there to be quite a few winding channels up through the mudflat. These creeklike depressions were eroded by the water running off at low tides. The boatman poled back along the water's edge until he found one, and turned the sampan into it.

A few hundred yards up this impromptu stream, we grounded again. The pole indicated two feet of mud. Tying ourselves together with the line we had brought, we went over the side. It was like stepping into a big can of grease. Giving the boatman his directions, we commenced slubbing toward shore, keeping as much distance between us as the line would permit. If there were a quickmud area, we didn't both want to be caught in the same one.

About five hundred yards and we were exhausted. I had taken about thirty minutes to progress that far, but now the mud was below my knees. Yong, having much shorter legs, was still in for a grind. We slubbed on, gradually reaching firmer footing. About five hundred yards out, it was a fairly firm bottom. I picked up a handful of the stuff and it felt like a mixture of sand and mud, with a little shell. It would be good for a landing area if it was of that consistency the entire length of the beach.

Continuing on in, we searched for obstacles to a landing, man-made or otherwise, and then turned south to skirt the beach itself. Finding nothing further of interest, we crossed into the backshore. There we found extensive rice paddies, but they were dry. The earth banks built up between the paddies would cause vehicles some trouble. There appeared to be only one exit from the beach—a narrow passage between two knolls at the south end. It would need considerable widening. Troops could get in, but vehicles would have a hard go of it. Large landing craft were out. The gradient was too slight; it would cause them to ground a good half-mile from the beach. Smaller landing craft could be used.

Doing an about-face, we headed north around Doku Gan point. After our little experience running up the inlet to Manhak San, we had been inclined to treat any beach guards the Reds might have with contempt. As a result, we weren't expecting the challenge that rang out as we rounded the point, hugging the jagged rock formation. We immediately ducked in among the rocks and waited for developments. The challenge had come from a point well above us and, I estimated, a good fifty yards distant. It was repeated, but in a doubtful tone this time.

Yong whispered that the guard must be alone or he would have called for other guards right away, and proposed that we get him. Bloodthirsty character. Didn't he know he could get me killed that way? I promptly canceled the proposition. There was no sense to it unless the joker had really discovered us. Nothing further happened, and after about fifteen minutes of playing possum, we moved quietly on around the point, sticking close to the rocks. The stars were out in their full-dress glory, extending across the entire firmament. We needed the dim light they afforded, but I was begrudging the scenery they exposed to the enemy.

Yong was mumbling something under his breath and finally stopped. His short legs had put him in dire straits. Mud had worked up between his legs and was chafing him. Impatiently, he started trying to get it off, and I could scarcely restrain a chuckle at his efforts. Like a cub bear . . .

Continuing on around the point, we approached a roadway skirting the shoreline and running into the Inchon suburbs. This was an excellent landing area, except for the fact that it would be extremely shallow water even at high tide. I estimated eight to ten feet of water at most—enough for the smaller landing craft and perhaps Amtracs. The exit highway was immediately available to the invasion troops.

Landing here, they could cut into the city from the rear, closing off the Seoul highway and preventing reinforcements, or advancing up it to attack the smaller inland city of Yongdungpo. I considered whether the invasion commander would be willing to split his forces in the assault. If so, then he could land troops and light equipment here and put his heavy tanks, trucks, and howitzers ashore across Wolmi-do into Inchon. Troops landed here could depend on call fire from the destroyers and cruisers in the harbor in support of their advance, and to knock out enemy strong points until their own heavy equipment arrived from Wolmi-do.

The trouble was the tide again. Even small craft could use this landing area for only two to three hours at most during the interval of flood tide. Could enough troops and equipment be put ashore in that short interval to launch a major drive up the highway? They would have to sustain themselves for over eight hours, until the next tide permitted reinforcements to land. And the beach area itself was extremely short to accommodate such an effort.

I tugged on my line for Yong. "If our troops landed here, how could they get their equipment out?" I asked. "Do you remember from Kim's information whether there are any exits?"

Yong thought for a moment. "Seems that there were some, but we certainly didn't pass any," he replied.

"We better make sure, Yong. They may decide to use this place." We retraced our steps, checking the shore carefully, finally coming to a large fill. This had been a way out, but had evidently been filled to provide a foundation for the road. Farther, there were two others—both filled. That question answered, we turned back, hitting the mud several times as truck headlights opened holes in the darkness above us. Mud-caked rocks, that was us.

If equipment was to be landed here, the retaining wall would have to be breached. Yong and I briefly discussed where it could be done with the greatest facility, just in case headquarters asked us to undertake the job. It would have to be done the night before the landing, or the Reds might suspect and fill it up again, or worse— booby-trap the whole exit area and zero it in with guns and mortars. As it happened, we weren't asked to blow it—the marines apparently deciding to take care of this little matter themselves.

Getting in closer to the outskirts of Inchon now, we had to slow down and listen. It could be they had a patrol along the top of this wall. We wanted to hear it before we were heard. As we moved in closer, we could hear a lot of noise. Yong said there were factories up over the seawall. The refugees had reported that here were many machine-gun nests spread out along the top of the wall. Inasmuch as the wall was almost vertical, I preferred to take their word for it. We might be able to get a look at it from En-do island, provided that place wasn't too well guarded.

We ran into a lot of big rocks along the bottom of the wall that looked as though they had been discarded by the builders. To pass them, we had to move out into the mud fifteen or twenty feet, and were once again slubbing along.

"How are we going to measure the height of that wall, Yong?" I whispered.

"I was thinking of getting the poling stick from the sampan," he answered.

That would take too long. The sampan was waiting for us at a little island off En-do a good half-mile away. There was only one way to do it without wasting time. Yong agreed, and we headed in over the rocks. At the wall, we explored it carefully. The bottom rocks had not been cemented and held a great many niches that could provide adequate, if precarious, footholds. Setting myself firmly against the wall, I aided Yong as he climbed the slight slope of the bottom half of the wall and then braced him as he cautiously straightened out to reach for the top. I prayed fervently that his exploring fingers wouldn't find a Red's face.

Yong was stretched to his full height before he started easing back down. Supporting his muddy hide on the way was a slippery business, but he came down safely and without a sound. Now all we had to do to determine the height was to measure to my shoulders and add to it Yong's outstretched inches.

The survey of the rest of the beach area around to En-do produced nothing feasible in the way of landing areas. En-do itself
was apparently unguarded, but we may just have missed them. I
couldn't conceive of its being unguarded. However, we couldn't see
far enough from it to determine the extent of enemy activity in the
vicinity, so we headed for our rendezvous.

Halfway to the little island, Yong blinked his flashlight to reassure the boatman that we were still his charges. A few seconds
later, he flung up his arms wildly, trying to catch his footing, and
slid off into a hole of quickmud, the stuff itself stifling a muted
outcry. I grabbed desperately for the line before it could tighten on
my waist, but my hands slipped. The line came taut and I was
dragged, sliding, toward the hole where Yong had disappeared. My
feet caught suddenly and I hauled away on the line as fast as I
could, taking single turns around my wrist to avoid the slipping effect of the mud on the line and my hands.

Yong came up, still flailing both arms, and gasping for air. Hauling him over to me, I helped him for the next few yards to where we
were standing in water. Coughing and blowing his nose, he cleared
up some of his trouble, and after a few minutes was able to talk. It
hadn't been a hole he'd slid into, but one of the tidal channels.
Considerable mud, but mostly water. I was relieved at this, but it
was a harrowing experience and I suggested that we might return
to camp. He wouldn't hear of it. As the little snakelike channels
seemed to run on a course diagonal to ours, I went ahead—with
added caution. Without further incident, we found the sampan
and rolled into it.

What a life for a sailor . . . Yong was grumbling to himself as he
splashed the cleaner water out here onto his face and in his ears.

"Shove off on the bell, coxswain," I said in English, and was surprised when the boatman applied his oar in response.

"How about the tidal basin, Mr. Clark?" Yong asked. "Shouldn't we take a look at it while we're here?"

"I think not, Yong. It would be impossible to get out of that area into the city, except along the narrow seawall. I'm afraid the Reds would pick off our men as fast as they mounted the wall. No, it would be a waste of time."

The boatman had rigged sail to buck the tidal current as we headed out due west for the south breakwater. It had taken us more than four hours to cover the few miles back there. We hadn't been pressed for time, of course, and had taken only a minimum of precaution. I had a suspicion that we had relaxed our guard too much. It was a hard thing to counteract—this thing of familiarity breeding contempt. We would have to tighten up. . . .

A large searchlight flashed on from Wolmi-do and swept down the channel. I was concerned until I realized that we were practically in the shadow of the breakwater that was between the light and our boat. No one could see anything moving within range of its beam, and after a few minutes it blinked out.

"Wonder if that could have been started by Rhee's getting away with the pompom?" Yong asked. Not being quite so objective at the moment, the thought hadn't occurred to me.

"Very probable, Yong. I wouldn't be surprised if they had assigned a couple of squads to watch the rest of those boats. It must have been a bitter pill for them to swallow, considering what they could have done to our boats had they been able to put it to use."

We were moving around the extinguished breakwater light, and the boatman dropped the sail to let the tide carry us the rest of the way into the harbor. If that searchlight came on now . . . This ride would, we hoped, land us against the seawall fronting the city itself. There should be many junks and sampans afloat in there at high tide, but if we were careful we shouldn't cause any excessive amount of attention. It was still about twenty minutes to high tide.

We wanted to have the sampan against the seawall so that we could measure the distance to the top from the high-water stand. It would be a simple matter for our assault planners to add to this figure the predicted rises on the fifteenth, and then they would know how far the troops would have to climb to get over the top.

The lights on Wolmi-do were receding on our left. As the lights of the waterfront began to take form, we all searched anxiously for a likely spot to ease in to the seawall. Quite a few junks were bobbing around over by the Wolmi-do causeway, but only now and then did we see one around the waterfront wall. The boatman pointed to a ramplike structure that thrust itself into the harbor water up to the level of the town, apparently a means of loading or discharging cargo when the tide was not all the way in. Dark areas appeared under it, and as I nodded, he steered for it. If we could get under the ramp between the pilings and the seawall, we'd have it made.

Silently, we were guided between two junks and then several more, as the boatman attempted to keep as many craft between ourselves and the shore as possible. Then, as we were making a final swing to bring us under the structure, an eddy caught the sampan and swung it out and past the ramp, setting us inexorably into a nest of junks and sampans. We were going to crash into them for sure and made ready.

Just as the sampan hit, we went silently over the side, and were holding to the stern of the junk by the time the occupants came on deck to investigate. Seeing first that no real damage had been done, and then that the disturber of their rest was nothing but a lowly sampan man, they started to upbraid him loudly and roundly. The poor chap, worried as he must have been without benefit of our guidance, had the presence of mind to whip up a hasty excuse for his presence that luckily held water. He had gone to sleep in his sampan up-channel, and it had broken adrift.

Two soldiers or policemen appeared on the seawall about fifty yards away. When the junk people saw them, they started their altercation all over again. The Reds chimed in at this point, wanting to know the whole story. As Yong interpreted, it seemed that the junkmen were determined to have our man's scalp. Oddly enough, it all ended with the Reds shouting imprecations at the junkmen and ordering our man away to wherever he came from. Promptly, our boatman started sculling down-channel, but making very little headway. The junkmen returned to their living quarters in the hold, and the Reds walked away from the wall.

As soon as we were free of possible surveillance, we kicked off for our sampan and grabbed the low offshore gunnel. This time as the sampan came in, we were able to bring it close enough into the eddy to grab the ramp, and in a few seconds we were ensconced under it against the seawall. Yong had lost his flashlight when he floundered back in the mud, and in searching around the bottom of the sampan for mine, I realized that all of our clothes had lain in plain sight of anyone flashing a light into the boat. My marine outfit would have been pretty hard to explain—but at least not as hard as two weird characters dressed in mud.

Marking the wall, we commenced our vigil, which was to last only a few minutes. The affair with the junk had delayed us almost too long. The tide began receding as we took the bamboo pole and put it up to the top under the ramp. I marked the distance on the pole with my knife and the job was finished.

"Say, Yong," I whispered, "how wide is the seawall on top?" If the troops were going to need scaling ladders, those ladders would have to hook on to something.

"Wide? I don't understand 'wide,' Mr. Clark."

"Width, Yong. Something is long, wide, and high. Like this sampan is wide from here to here." I illustrated.

"No, no. I know what you mean by word 'wide.' I don't understand it with the top of the seawall."

It was necessary to illustrate again using the gunnel as an example. It was a seawall keeping out the water. The top of the gunnel was so wide, thus. Then it dropped down again to the bottom of the boat. Yong grasped the point, and calmly said it just wasn't wide at all. The seawall went up to there, and he pointed over our heads, and then it was level all around. It was a sudden drop-off from ground level. I got it through my head at last that the top of the wall just wasn't "wide," and wondered how the devil the scaling ladders were going to be made so that they'd hook on to a flat stone surface.

With most of our mud washed off by the enforced swim, we were getting cold. The caked mud was good in that one respect: It did keep us warm after our body heat had worked on it for a while. The nights were rapidly getting colder. . . .

We'd have to get out of here so that we could put our clothes on. This time, our boatman had a course of action figured out, and by utilizing slight, fine holds in the rocks of the wall, we were able to drag the boat along its face until we were well free of the eddy. Once clear, it was a simple matter to push off and drift down to the channel with the ebbing tide.

Dawn was spreading itself across the eastern skies when we dropped sail and beached in front of the CP. We took a few minutes to wash off a little more mud, before going up to the tent. The lamp was out—the first time I'd seen it out, come to think of it. Kim had that thing going all night as a rule. He worked long and conscientiously cataloging, checking, and evaluating the information he elicited from his various sources.

Ahn was on duty at the tent and reported that nothing unusual had arisen. Asked about the party and if he'd had a good time, he said that many *kampai* (bottoms-up) had been drunk to Chae—maybe too many.

Listlessly sprawling on my cot and pulling the blankets up, I ran through the usual mental calculation. Nine days down, six to go to D-day. I was feeling pretty good about the offshore and beach information we had. But we were still lacking in the information that would cut anticipated casualties to a minimum. Tomorrow perhaps, we could figure out some new angle. This night's visit had shown me more than words ever could what a spot our troops would be in going over those walls unless every gun possible was spotted and destroyed before the flag dropped.

SPOTTER'S
PARADISE

COMMANDER LEE SUNG HO returned in the afternoon from his assignment up north. His trim patrol boat was a welcome sight. But he came only for a short stay. Taking advantage of his presence, we had him transfer a couple of drums of diesel oil to our pompom and then take our accumulated prisoners on down to Tokchok-do.

The victory celebration was marred by a report which came in at noon that one of the outpost watchmen had been killed, his head almost severed by a vicious knife attack and his body badly cut up. It was an obvious attempt to intimidate our other lone guards. Doubtless, it would have such an effect, not for this reason, but because someone must have leaked the information as to where these watchmen had been posted. After considering all the factors carefully, we concluded that it had been done by trusted men or by nocturnal visitors who had met with a trusted man—a bitter pill to swallow. We countered by posting the men individually and in new spots and shifting the section leaders, hoping that if it occurred again we could pin it on the proper person.

Our contact with headquarters in Tokyo brought three highlights. Another typhoon was making up. On the seventh, Navy patrol planes flew out to look at the depression area. The storm was producing moderate swells along Japan's east coast. By the eighth, the storm had become a baby typhoon and had the name "Kezia" assigned to it. At its present course and speed, it would hit the Korean straits on the twelfth or thirteenth. As of today, the prospect for a collision between Kezia and Task Force 7—the designated name of the Inchon invasion fleet—seemed unavoidable. Now a 125-knot nightmare, it was headed right for the invasion staging area. So far, however, I could detect no sign of its existence. Lee's barometer gave us no clue.

Tomorrow we would get our first glimpse of what was to come. Two heavy and two light cruisers were heading our way to feel out the Inchon defenses. Headquarters wanted the Palmi-do light put in commission at 0030, 15 September, and wanted our opinion of the accuracy of the American tide tables for Inchon waters. This latter question Lee and I had been studying in connection with our own operations, and had come to the conclusion that the Japanese tables were accurate, whereas ours were not. We made up a report on the apparent time differential and sent it in.

Chang reported an unusual amount of junk traffic, all heading from the islands into Inchon. This report alarmed us momentarily, until Kim clarified the matter by assuring us that the garrison commander was calling in a great number of junks to accelerate his rice deliveries to Seoul. At this stage, we were very apprehensive of any unusual activity, for it might well indicate the discovery by the Reds of our true intention of invading Inchon.

We were busily consuming rice and a nice mess of fish that fortune had favored us with, when Chi put in a belated appearance from making his daily contact with the people in the hills. He was bursting with news.

"Our people have made contact with another resistance group in the Sorae San area near Yongdungpo," he said. "Believing this to be important, I waited the arrival of their representatives."

"How are they set up, Chi?" Kim asked.

"About the same as our group, except they have no arms. They have heard there are Americans around and wanted to make a contact. They are very anxious to help in any way they can."

Word certainly gets around, I thought. It did seem to be a good prospect. It would give us a line practically into Seoul itself—and we could certainly use it. If we could arrange a consolidation . . . Kim was ahead of me.

"Are they willing to join forces?"

"Very anxious to. They say they have over a hundred men of varying ages. About half that many women and children. It has been a problem feeding themselves, but like the others they would rather steal or starve to death than abandon their properties in Yongdungpo and Seoul."

"Are they willing to take up arms against the Inminkyun if we provide them, or do they just want us to feed them?" Kim asked, following through.

"No. They would like to kill all the Inminkyun they can, and know of many places where they can ambush patrols and supply units, but they would like the reassurance of seeing an American. It is difficult for them to believe there are Americans here, for the Inminkyun tell all the people that Americans have been chased out of Korea and will not come back."

The Reds had good propaganda in that story. After all, we controlled only a few square miles around the Pusan perimeter and the

Reds were still pressing in hard. It would certainly make good propaganda for an American to show up to discount this story. Besides, this might be the answer to our problem of getting better dope on the Reds' defenses beyond Inchon.

Kim turned to me. "I don't like this business of you going in on the mainland, *Kuraku-san*," he said. "It exposes you to a much greater risk of capture when you are away from the water. However, this is an excellent opportunity to complete our reconnaissance net. We have the sea and islands covered, and with Chi's group we have a channel into Inchon and even into Wolmi-do. With this addition, should it turn into a good thing, we will cover the rest of our area—right into Seoul itself."

I knew Kim would come to this conclusion, just as I had. It was a natural to round out our organization, and I tried to determine why we hadn't thought of the possibility of the existence of other resistance groups before. Just plain carelessness. Must have been. As for the greater risk on the land, perhaps Kim was right—look at what happened to the Taebu-do men we had cut down the other day. True enough—I wasn't a soldier, nor did I have any extensive guerrilla experience, but I would have Yong with me and there was no question that he knew all the tricks of that trade.

"What do you think of it, Yong?" I asked.

He thought the matter over with great deliberation. I could see readily enough that it wasn't completely to his liking, and he explained. "Taking Chi in to the beach the other night was a fairly safe thing, Mr. Clark. We knew that he had had no opportunity to prearrange a trap, and we had the opportunity on our side to avoid being captured when he returned with the others."

I glanced at Chi, who was taking this in, and at Yong, who was studying his face closely as he said it. Yong continued. "We have given them arms and rice, and Kim says they have given us good information, which he has confirmed from other people. But your capture would make Chi or another a big man with the Inminkyun."

Yong stopped and casually smoked his cigarette, still studying Chi, who was obviously doing his best to avoid appearing nervous under this line of reasoning. I wouldn't have stopped Yong for the world. He knew his people, and he was making sense.

"The good information Chi has given us and which Kim has confirmed could have been planted just for its effect. Perhaps Chi is just an innocent tool—a dupe of the others. It would be reasonable to assume that if this was a plan to trap you, the story of this new group would be an excellent means of springing the trap. It's logical and it holds much promise for our own side . . . if it's true," he concluded.

Kim took up the discussion, leaving Chi in a state of agitated suspense. "This thing is not new to us, Yong. Everything you say is true, but precautions can still be taken. It will be a simple matter to arrange a dummy meeting—then if there is a trap the wrong persons will fall into it. Chi has told us that the people would meet him as usual on the beach, and then everyone would go to the hills where the meeting is set to take place. We will simply dress one of our larger men in the clothes of *Kuraku-san* and see that no lights are permitted until the matter is known. *Kuraku-san* and yourself can land at another point and follow Chi and the group, remaining in the dark until the last. If anything is wrong, you can escape from the hills back to your own sampan."

"Yes, we can do that. But of course I will have to go with Chi in order to give the alarm if it should become necessary," Yong said. They both looked at me for approval of this plan. It was satisfactory, with a slight modification.

"You'll have to stay with me, Yong. We can no more afford you being captured than myself. The propaganda value might not be so great, but the information you have on the invasion plans is practically complete. No, you'll have to decide on someone else to send along with the dummy to give the alarm."

This was decided instantly. It would be Chae. The dummy would be one of the section leaders who approached my size, even though a little short in the legs. Chi accepted all this without comment. I understood these people enough by this time to know that if Chi were in league on a plot, he would say nothing and go to the certain death of our grenades when it was exposed. If there was no trap, he would continue working for us, philosophically accepting our suspicions as part of the ticklish game that was being played.

We would shove off for the inlet below Doku Gan about nine-thirty that night. If things worked out right, we'd return the following night. This would give us time to work out a plan with the Sorae San group, and to run down to Inchon to do the little job I had in mind.

Chang had shifted the heavy machine gun from our damaged junk into the pompom, converting it into a vital unit of our raider squadron. With his flair for the theatrical, he arranged for its proper send-off. On this occasion, a large proportion of the island population gathered at the beach around the craft to witness the short but noisy shaman ceremony dedicating the craft in the service of the Korean Republic. As I saluted with all the formality and dignity I could muster under my old steaming cap, the grizzled and haggle-toothed owner quickly bent a small flag of the Republic of Korea to a ten-foot bamboo pole and secured it to an upright stop on the pilothouse. From now until D-day, the old scow would be our "flagship."

Joining in the lusty *"Mansei"* that followed, I experienced the comfortable feeling of community trust and acceptance—something that had been withheld me at the simple but impressive funerals of the past few days. It must be hard for these people to judge the relative merits of their sons being murdered by the Reds under Red occupation, or being killed by the Reds while fighting with a mysterious American, a creature of nocturnal habits who remained aloof and inscrutable at his place on the beach.

It was a peculiar feeling to be watched covertly from all sides and sometimes to catch one of them in a prolonged stare—the young men crowding in close to us so to identify better their intentions and loyalty to the mooted freedom we represented. I carried off the inevitable necessity for a short speech by addressing the gathering in English, which Yong translated freely into the proper ritualistic Korean phrases. I strongly suspect that my oratorical flight only furnished window dressing for Yong's far more impressive native eloquence. Like any normal male, however, I found no trouble deceiving myself into believing that it was my thoughts that held the gathering spellbound.

In the crowd as it was breaking up, I noticed the woman who had entertained the Red political officer at her teahouse and had gone to Taebu-do to provide similar services, without obtaining any of the information we so badly wanted from that threatening island. I asked Kim whether he had ever found any additional work for her. Yes, she had been toiling night and day with the doctor, caring for the sick and wounded at the hospital. She had redeemed herself completely with the villagers. It was a good thing to know, and I was glad that I had asked. I had thought she would remain an outcast. Atonement would be more difficult in the Western world. . . .

When Commander Lee returned, we had an important task for him. In studying our charts, we had been struck with the thought that some fleet units would quite probably transit the narrow channels to the north of Inchon, thus making a two-pronged approach. If such would be the case, then it was equally important that the northern channels be checked for mines. Lee would depart at once to scout the area south of the big island of Kanghwa-do. Establishment of a mine patrol there would be unnecessary, for the channel bottom was fully exposed at each period of low tide. Thus any planted mine would be easily seen for several hours each day.

Lee had a question. "During our course of instruction on mining at the Naval Academy, Mr. Clark, I seem to recall discussion of a type of mine that couldn't be swept?"

I whipped this around for a while and concluded he was referring to the mine the Germans had started using in desperation toward the end of the war. The British had also developed this particularly vicious instrument, but because they didn't have a way of countering it they had not used it.

"You're probably thinking of the 'oyster' mine, Lee. Technically, it's called a pressure mine. I don't know whether it could be used in these waters without considerable improvement, because of the tremendous tides. It operates on a rather simple principle, and you'll probably recall it. As a ship passes over the seabed in fairly shallow water, the hydrostatic pressure is reduced. Just how much it's reduced depends on such factors as the ship's speed, draft, and size. This reduction in pressure is used to trigger the mine, which lies on the bottom. The thing that makes it so hard to counter is that it can only be disposed of by reducing the water pressure at seabed level—and this is done by either running high-speed craft or by towing hulks over the minefields. That would be difficult, if not impossible, to do in these waters. I'm no expert by any means, Lee, but I think they cannot be used here due to the varying hydrostatic pressure induced by the tides."

I hoped I was right, but if I were wrong, I hoped the Russians had none of these things in the Far East.

"Well, if I find one, I'll bring it back for inspection, Mr. Clark," Lee said jokingly. I wouldn't have been surprised to see him hauling in a ton of steel and dynamite—or my being invited to his funeral, either, for that matter.

"A sampan came in from Taemuui-do last night, *Kuraku-san*," Kim advised. "They've set up their 120mm mortars on the southeastern end of the island. I figure they intend to cover the main channel west of Palmi-do with them."

Looking at the chart, I asked Lee if he thought he could take them under fire without coming within range of the Inchon guns. The answer, of course, was affirmative. With his experience in dodging mortar fire from Taebu-do, I thought the Taemuui-do jokers were going to be in for a hard time unless they were well-entrenched.

The final problem that confronted us before leaving for the mainland was strictly humanitarian in nature. One of the women Chang's raiders had brought in was pregnant. According to the doctor, it was a matter of hours. It was her desire to have her baby at home, and home was in Inchon. Instead of shipping her to Tokchok-do, would we send her home?

"I've questioned her at length, *Kuraku-san*," Kim said. "Chang took the junk she was in up by Yongyu-do, where it was headed for Inchon. There were a couple of Inminkyun on board, but nothing to connect her with their activity. Victim of misfortune. Normally, I would recommend sending her on in, but she knows something of our methods and defense setup here now. I don't think it would be wise to let her go."

In spite of the casualness attending the birth rite itself in this region, the importance of women having their babies at home attained a significance bordering on fanaticism. This, Kim knew better than I. The problem was one of balancing the compassionate aspects of the case against the possible danger to our own situation.

"Let's consider, Kim, that she told all she knew about us. Could it make any difference? I believe the Inchon garrison commander has all the information known to this woman, and probably a lot more. Her telling what she knows isn't going to make him any more or any less anxious to get rid of us. In fact, you might tell her that Lee's gunboat has just brought in a number of reinforcements for us. Then, if she does do any talking, the information will be colored in our favor."

Kim considered this for a while and agreed that we should provide her transportation into Inchon. He accepted my argument so readily, I suspected that his initial objection had been made as a matter of principle rather than out of conviction. Kim had a few children of his own. . . .

At nine-thirty, we hiked down to the eastern promontory where the sampans had been hauled up. Although the darkness of the night was relieved by starlight, we encountered difficulty negotiating the confused mass of barnacled rock at the base of the promontory. Where the others seemed to float sylphlike from one rock to another, Yong and I were far from giving a ballet dancer performance even with the aid of our flashlights. Having sat down several times rather suddenly to prevent a more severe fall, we reached our sampans with nothing more serious than bruised dignities.

Chae and Chi, the section leader wearing my clothes, boarded one sampan, and Yong and I the other. For security reasons, Chi was seated in the bow of his craft with Chae in the stern, so that if anything should go wrong, Chae would be in command of the situation. As an additional precaution, Yong had searched Chi and taken away his only weapon, a fisherman's knife. I marveled at the lack of offense shown by Chi at these obvious measures that impugned his loyalty.

The boatmen ran their poles into the mud and we moved slowly into the tidal current. As Yong gave final instructions to Chae to keep his sampan within several yards of our own, I pulled off my shoes and, stretching out athwartships with my feet over the side, pillowed my head on the rubber shoes to catch a few winks.

It was understood without saying by this time that Yong and I would sleep when we could and would divide the available time evenly. This arrangement we scrupulously kept, although we were both put to it at times to repay the other's generosity. The nature of comradeship developed unconsciously under such prolonged dangerous conditions was one I found difficult to analyze, although it has occurred time and again with me, both with Occidentals and Orientals. A psychologist could probably put a name to it and support it with Latin words of many syllables, but in the final analysis it is exactly that relationship immortalized by the World War I song "My Buddy." A simple thing cutting across race, creed, and color and, without reason or second thought, requiring a man to lay down his life for his friend.

Arriving at the shoals at the upper end of the inlet, where last time we had consigned ourselves to the mud so that the boat could get over, we were pleasantly surprised to find that Chi had made a slight innovation to the passage procedure. The boatmen eased the sampans against the embankment of the salt pans, where we climbed out and simply walked alongside as they were poled over the shoals. Again I was impressed with the fact that, in these operations, there was absolutely no substitute for local knowledge.

Boarding again, we now proceeded silently up the final reach of the inlet, keeping well over to the western shore. In the distance, we could see the loom of the lights from the small settlements we had noted last night, and an occasional flash as the Wolmi-do search-light sought to surprise unwary junk traffic escaping from Inchon with human cargo. Moving in closer to the beach, we heard the croaking of lovesick frogs combined with the gentle gurgling of the water beneath the gunnel. The sounds stamped with a disturbing sense of unreality any thought of danger.

As the inlet commenced to draw its shores sharply together, Yong signaled our boatman to turn in and beach the sampan. The other craft was out of sight against the dark backdrop of the hills. Jumping out, we pushed our boatman off, with instructions to stand by in the stream until first light, when he was to beach at high tide and haul his craft into the foliage along the shore to await our return.

These rather elaborate safety measures upon which both Kim and Yong insisted never failed to make me self-conscious, and of-ten left me feeling slightly ridiculous when everything turned out well. As we covered ground toward the rendezvous point, I felt downright silly about the whole thing. This sentiment wasn't en-hanced in the least as we observed from a hidden vantage point the perfectly innocuous meeting between Chae's group and three men who had materialized from the scrub fronting the beach.

They moved off into the hidden trail, and Chae cautiously let the others take the lead. As he disappeared, we trotted out and en-tered the trail behind them, maintaining a sufficient interval to be guided by the slight noise they made. Within a few minutes, we broke out into an area of rice paddies and had to wait until our guides faded out before we took up our pace along the foot-wide path atop the man-made banks separating the paddies. I hastily gave thanks that the paddies were dry, for I almost immediately slipped and had to jump into one. Normally at this season the rice crop would be only a few weeks from harvesting, but the paddy beds would still be sufficiently soft to sink a man up to his knees in mud and "honey" (human excrement, used as fertilizer everywhere in the Orient).

I quickly regained the narrow path and we hurried on. It wouldn't do to permit the others to outdistance us, for we would be lost, aside from the fact that we seemed to be headed for a small village from the number of lights directly ahead. Getting through or around them would require sticking to our unknowing guides like glue.

I almost ran over Yong as he stopped suddenly. Ahead, they had made a sharp left turn to skirt the village, and Chae had fallen back to be certain that we were taking the proper path. Uninstructed in this regard, his action was indicative of his initiative and alertness to our problems.

The village behind, we toiled up a trail to the back of the ridge and into shrub and small isolated tree stands. This certainly didn't afford sufficient concealment in the daytime to any sizable group of dissidents, I thought. But there was another rise ahead. I considered the area we had passed in relation to the limited information afforded by the maps. If the other approaches to this stronghold were as open as the one we were traversing, these people were as good as trapped if the Reds found out about them. A cardinal rule for guerrillas was to have a reasonably safe escape route. But then, I had given up trying to determine what these people considered "safe," much less "reasonable."

It was well along toward midnight when we entered the tree line far up the face of Manhak San. From the amount of noise the group ahead was making, it was evident that they felt they were in safe territory—which fact helped us immensely in tracing their movements in the dense brush and trees. Taking advantage of this, we dropped well back. We didn't want to spring any guard they might have posted along this trail for the purpose of intercepting just such characters as we might represent. I was pleased to note their good security sense. Within a few minutes, the group ahead stopped, permitting us to ease up and eavesdrop.

Yong whispered that it was one of their trail lookouts, so we struck off into the brush to bypass the point. By the time they had finished their exchange of comments and compliments, we were ahead and waiting beside the trail. As they passed, we again fell in behind at a good distance. There was one more encounter before reaching camp, and following this, voices were raised to normal volume. Yong stopped and pulled me off the trail.

"They're entering the camp. Better wait here until we get some signal from Chae," he said.

Nothing untoward occurred, and we were soon in the midst of an excited and curious gathering. Any surprise they may have felt when Chae brought us in was well concealed, and I couldn't help speculating on whether Chi had succeeded by some covert means in informing the others that we were nearby.

The camp area appeared rather extensive, and in spite of its airiness possessed an odor always associated with inadequate sanitary facilities. The ground was well-trampled and free of underbrush. Overhead, the foliage from scrub needle and broadleaf trees growing thickly around shut out the dim light of the stars. Immediately in front of us as we sat cross-legged on the bare ground, two women were worrying over a large pot of rice cooking on an improvised charcoal grill. A small pit had been hollowed out of the ground to hold the charcoal, and the orange-and-red embers gave off a comforting glow in the chill of the night air.

The representatives of the Sorae San resistance group were three in number and entirely harmless in outward appearance: an old man with classical Korean clothes, long beard, and black stovepipe hat; a youth about Chae's age in appearance; and a middle-aged woman busily preparing tea. After the manner of Koreans, they acknowledged with solemn politeness the introductions, with a slightly more outward show of deference toward the westerner.

Yong engaged them in an extended discussion at once on the details of their situation and requirements. While this was continuing, my eyes grew accustomed to the dim glow of the embers and I studied the faces about us. The sunken cheeks and bony forearms and hands that extended out of long white sleeves showed that the grim specter of malnutrition was present. The normally healthy brown pigmentation of the skin had given way to a sickly chalklike yellow, which effect was aggravated by a loosening of the skin as the stored-up fat tissue burned away. I had seen this before many times, and although it now didn't upset me as at first, still I couldn't control an involuntary shudder at its awful presence. As visual evidence of the utter horror of war, I had yet to decide which was the worse to look upon—death or famine.

Yong concluded the discussion and turned to me. "Apparently, all the people in this Sorae group have a fanatical desire to remain close to their homes and the courage to do anything we ask of them. They have no arms, and they have been able to buy and steal only enough food to keep them alive. This old man is one of the elders but not the actual chief. It was thought better to send down this group, as the most likely to get past any patrols along the way."

The woman passed around tea, which we accepted gratefully. I noticed that the others from Yonghung-do as well as myself turned down the proffered heaping bowls of steaming rice.

"Do you think the others at Sorae San are in as bad shape physically as these three, Yong?"

"I would say so, Mr. Clark, and perhaps worse."

"Then we certainly don't want them to go out and stir up any trouble. They'd be massacred. Seems to me the best thing we can do is to try to give them some food, and just enough guns to make an occasional foray on a supply outfit. There must be a lot of that going on around there and it wouldn't create enough notice to bring Red troops down on their group."

Yong considered this a few moments. "No, sir. I don't think that's right," he said firmly. "Although they are in bad shape from lack of food, still they are capable of long and sustained activity. You must understand that this condition is not uncommon. Although this lack of food has been caused by the war, it happens very often in peace when crops are bad and people go hungry and die. It is why girls are a tax on the family, for they cannot survive the famines as do the men and work the fields living on nothing but grass and roots. There is much life and vigor and courage in these men, young and old, and they will fight cleverly and savagely if given arms. The food they will take with arms, and the old man has said that they only ask for weapons—even knives if nothing else— and their stomachs will be filled. In return for this, they will give us the information we seek," he finished spiritedly.

I had certainly come about on the wrong tack that time, with all the wind spilled out of my sails. As gracefully as I could, I conceded Yong's points and asked him to assure the old man that we would furnish his group with all the arms we could—and as fast as we could. With Chang's daily prizes, we had already accumulated another small arsenal. The problem was to get them here.

"We'd better send Chi and the section leader back to the island tonight with instructions to return with the arms tomorrow night. We'll be able to deliver on our side of the bargain before we leave here as evidence of good faith," I said. Yong agreed that prompt action was in order and so informed our two men, to the patent satisfaction of the three emissaries from Sorae San. The old man in turn said that they would leave at once for their camp and bring back enough help to transport the weapons.

At this proposal, I interjected a suggestion. "There will be something of great interest here tomorrow," I said, "which you will want to see and tell your people. Suppose the young man returns for assistance while the woman and yourself remain to witness this important matter?"

I wanted these two to see the bombardment and to put them under the impression that we had been instrumental in the cruisers' arrival. Knowing their impressionable nature, particularly in regard to matters of armed might, we could depend upon them recounting the story and, in the manner of such things, the story snowballing into a forceful psychological instrument, not just for us but for the United Nations effort. This proposition agreed to, we shifted the conversation around to our plans for tomorrow.

For whatever effect it may have had, we had given our maps to Section Leader Chae to carry for us. Now we spread out on the ground the Inchon town plan and a large-scale map of the area contiguous to the south. The others of the group closed in around the maps, and in the reflected light of the charcoal embers, their crouching figures and drawn, intent faces epitomized everything furtive and clandestine.

Yong knew the plan and proceeded to explore possible courses of action. His approach was indirect, but necessarily so, as we could not chance a leak of the bombardment even at this late hour. "We look for a point from which we may observe this part of Inchon," Yong stated, indicating the area in question on the town plan. "This point must be close enough to the city for *Taicho-san* to study the buildings and the hills through his binoculars. This thing he must do in order to learn where the Inminkyun have placed their guns and housed their soldiers. Is it understood?"

There was silence for several minutes as the maps were studied. The place names on the maps contained only phonetic spellings of Korean ideographs, so it was necessary for them to locate things through physical features alone. The chief of the Manhak group, an unimpressive-appearing individual who somehow reminded me of the fiery little Hyun, spoke up first.

"It would be a simple matter," he said, "to take you into Inchon in the carts. Early each morning, the farmers below us take their vegetables to market. As they are our friends, I am sure we can prevail upon them to hide you in the carts."

Yong glanced at me, and I shook my head. "From inside Inchon, we could see nothing. Either the hills or the buildings would block our view. We must be located somewhere along here," and I indicated the general suburban area and hills south of Inchon.

Suitable sites were reduced to a choice between Doku Gan point and the heights of Ok-tong, the latter merely being an extension of the Manhak San hill range extending almost to the bay. Both heights were guarded by units of the Inchon garrison. Ok-tong was an observation point for traffic checks of the highways below and therefore maintained the heaviest guard unit. The Doku Gan unit, which Yong and I had alerted last night, consisted of only three soldiers. Their main duty was to watch the beaches extending north and south and the bay waters in front of them.

"Do these guards have radio or other means of communicating with the garrison at Inchon?" Yong asked.

"Another man knows about such things. Please wait a moment," the Manhak leader replied, and went off into the dark. Evidently, this little outfit was becoming organized. I hadn't hoped to get such detailed information, but then it was their life and liberty to know about such matters so close at hand.

Another youngster appeared with the leader and the question was explained. "No," he said, addressing his chief, "there is no such communication. There is only the messenger that comes from Inchon at noon each day to take back the reports."

Yong turned back to the leader. "Do you know how many soldiers are stationed on Ok-tong?"

There was a short conference on their side before they replied. When he answered, they all appeared in agreement. "There are twelve soldiers and one noncommissioned officer during the day. Twelve others report at six o'clock, and then, six at a time, they patrol the highways during the night."

No wonder we hadn't been bothered by beach guards at the inlet. Or did we have the full story? "Are these two guard units the only Inminkyun in this area?" I asked.

"They are the only permanent units. The past few days, however, they have been sending out large patrols looking for our camp because of our raids."

This information was something unexpected. Chi had said nothing about it, but it was natural that it should happen. Realizing their vulnerability to organized patrol action, Yong, too, was at once concerned. "What plans do you have to move your people?" he asked the leader.

The leader showed his surprise at this question. "We have already moved," he said. "Our camp is now in these hills east of the inlet." He indicated a point about three miles away, which appeared much safer. Sanctuary could be found in other nearby hills to the south. "We brought a small raiding party back with us to meet with you and the Sorae people before we went on into Inchon to get supplies."

His tone indicated doubt, apparently concerned with how we would take this information. As far as my own plans were affected, his move couldn't have been more timely, and the fact that he had a raiding party here opened a course of action to us I had not considered feasible until the moment. I spoke aside briefly to Yong.

"According to what they say, tomorrow there will be only fifteen Reds in this area during the day, unless a search patrol comes down this way. If we were to take Doku Gan and Ok-tong—and with this group we could do it—we'd have Ok-tong, the highest point, to ourselves the whole day. From there, we could look right down into Inchon and Wolmi-do during the bombardment from only about two miles away."

Yong nodded instant agreement and plunged into the details with the leader. It would be necessary to move in as close as possible to the Ok-tong guard area before dawn and lie in hiding until the night contingent and relief party had departed for Inchon. Two men would be dispatched to Doku Gan, and another man to the main road junction at Inchon to watch for any search patrol heading our way. We would intercept the noon messenger. There were ten men in the Manhak raiding party; Yong, Chae, and I brought our force up to thirteen.

Although the element of surprise would be in our favor, this would be our first open firefight with Red troops. I regretted not having brought along a few extra grenades. They would be very helpful in this situation.

In the event the action went against us, Yong and I would split off from the rest of the party and make for Doku Gan, and the others would go about their business. We considered that we could observe the bombardment from the point and get away before reorganized troops could arrive.

The planning out of the way, the Manhak leader wakened his

men and briefed them. It was two hours before dawn when we struck off for Ok-tong. The old man and the woman would remain well in the rear. As we traveled along the winding trail atop the ridge for about a mile, the tree stands gradually thinned and finally gave way to nothing but tall, strawlike growth. We had been informed that the Ok-tong camp was on the windward side of the hill. Except for a couple of rough thatch shelters pitched over platforms raised on stilts, the guard area was as bald of vegetation as a billiard ball.

Looking down at the countryside as we progressed, I noticed only an occasional light from the fires in the cooking ovens of the salt-processing works. A number of lights still twinkled in Inchon, which seemed exceptionally close. Shortly, we started a gradual ascent and the Manhak leader advised us that the enemy camp lay about five hundred yards above us. The reduction in the amount of scuffling of shoes and feet as we ranged closer was noticeable. A halt was called while the leader, Yong, and I proceeded on up the hill to scout the camp itself before assigning positions.

We were on the main path leading to the camp and from it into the valley below. Not knowing what time the road patrol would be returning from its tour, we moved off the path and toward our respective sectors. The easiest way to spot a man at night is by means of his silhouette against the sky. In high places, such as this, where there are no background shadows to interrupt the vision, it is simply a matter of keeping low to the ground and sweeping the arc of sky as you advance. It was no difficult matter to spot the lookout at the far end of my sector and to avoid him, as I moved across the crest of the hill on my stomach like an ungainly iguana.

Immediately in front of me was the camp, and I studied it carefully. I would have to station three men in the vicinity and as close to the camp as possible with a reasonable degree of safety from discovery. It was too bad that we couldn't make the raid right now. Three men were sitting on their haunches around a small fire near the platforms, talking in low tones. Several others were sprawled out on mats on the ground. I wondered how many we could have caught asleep on those platforms.

Wishful thinking. The job would be a little tougher this time. There were no places this side of the crest that would afford cover, so I snaked back to the other side. The guard was still gazing off toward Inchon, probably thinking of the entertainment in the Chinese quarter.

Little bushes devoid of leaves were scattered about. With the tall brown grass growing around them, they were the logical places for our men to wait out the attack. Back at the rendezvous, we compared notes. Yong had found a couple of spots close in, approaching the camp from the bottom, whereas my men would come from the top. The leader's men would straddle the approach path, which would serve the additional purpose of cutting off any retreat— always a demoralizing factor.

We were not so much interested in taking prisoners as we were in getting the Reds out of the way with as little shooting as possible. Our only tactic, if it could be called that, was for our men on the path and at the top to open up first, figuring that this would make the Reds try to take shelter behind the two platforms. If they did this, they would be concentrated in two spots and wide open to the fire of Yong's group, which then would be directly behind them.

A second good reason was that if the top and bottom groups opened up at the same time, there would be the danger of crossfire. This high-level strategy out of the way, we beckoned our men and placed them. I took up a position within twenty feet of the pensive guard, figuring that if his post was also manned during the daytime, at least one man would be quickly out of the game.

By parting the grass in front and rising on my elbows, I could see the approach to the camp area. My first shot would signal the attack. I had insisted on this, for I was in nowise certain that my impatient compatriots would wait until the Reds returning to barracks at Inchon were out of range of the sounds of rifle fire.

Checking my clips and setting the forty-five on safety, I folded my arms under my face and started to consider some weighty problem, no doubt. I woke with a start. Cold perspiration bathed me at the shock of realization that I had fallen asleep. Why hadn't I taken a Benzedrine tablet? I had brought several along, anticipating my need.

I wondered if Yong had fallen asleep. The gods were still with us. No harm had been done, as dawn was just breaking in the eastern skies. I gulped down a Benzedrine hastily and wished Moon were here with a cup of coffee to wash it down. The guard was no longer at his post. I rose up intending to go check on the other men, but sank down again as I realized they'd probably shoot anyone approaching their positions.

It would be several hours yet before we could attack. It was a difficult thing to pass time under such conditions. Being able to do this without moving for hours and sometimes days on end was one of the most trying qualifications for reconnaissance work. Like a miser counting his silver, my mind automatically turned to evaluating the network of activity that we had set in motion during the past nine days.

What Kim had said was true. Bringing the Sorae San resistance group into the fold completed our coverage up to and including the capital city of Seoul and to the tactically important Kimpo airfield, between Seoul and Inchon. Information on all possible landing beaches was complete. Mining was another bright spot, and I felt that it would be unlikely that the Reds would attempt any further operations under the eyes of our patrols. The one weakness was that we couldn't observe possible night operations.

However, it would be a major effort for them to lay even one string of mines in the dark, and then it would almost have to be in shallow waters to avoid the strong current of the main channels. The navigation aids: Palmi-do would be working before the fleet came in. The Manhak San group was rapidly filling our lists with gun locations, troops, trenches, supply depots, and other good targets, some of which I hoped to see go up in steel and flame today. And now the Sorae group . . .

Our Air Force units would take care of their targets. Our foothold on Yonghung-do remained precarious and a subject of continuing concern in spite of our successes over the Taebu-do crowd. There seemed no way to stop their infiltrations on such a large island, just as the Reds didn't seem capable of stopping our landings and raids on other points around the harbor. Arriving at this point, I let my mind wander off into a consideration of the overall potential of behind-the-line operations in support of conventional tactics.

Use of native guerrillas had definite advantages in terms of reducing the requirement for logistical support, but major disadvantages, particularly in the Far East, when it came to exerting command direction. There is a great temptation on the part of the guerrilla leader to try to take over politically and then to bargain with his outside supporters for postwar power. This situation may become downright embarrassing to those trying to conclude a treaty that will ensure a lasting peace.

On the other hand, looking at Korea, I saw how relatively simple it would be to land companies and even battalions of troops well behind the lines, by ship or plane, with no intention of staying after they had effected their mission—such mission being to destroy sufficient enemy warmaking materials to make the enemy commander shunt off a large body of badly needed troops to chase the invaders out. This desired effect accomplished, our troops could be airlifted out by helicopter or use a predetermined avenue open to the sea, where they could be taken off. Crudely put, it would be a refinement of the panzer column technique of the Germans, designed to cut off vital material support to the front, thereby causing its collapse.

It was a fascinating subject and I studied it in its many details and ramifications, growing more enthusiastic in its potential by the minute. As my thoughts whirled on, aided and abetted in no small part by the effects of the Benzedrine, time passed rapidly. Take this present operation of General MacArthur's, I said to myself, by way of clinching the matter—it was nothing more than proof of what I had been theorizing. The grand concept was to land behind the lines in sufficient force to drive inland to the point where the enemy's main line of communication could be cut—Seoul. A less ambitious plan would have been to drive in with a lesser force to destroy everything possible before the enemy depleted his reserve or front-line strength to the extent necessary to drive the force out. I tried to visualize the demoralizing effect of ten or twenty large bodies of troops loose behind the lines. They could act as rallying points for both dissident and resistance groups of natives. . . .

The arrival of a six-man patrol interrupted my train of thought. Evidently, this was the time for reveille, as the arriving men went around waking the rest of the guard. I had no sooner settled back than other voices could be heard. This was the daytime duty guard, and counting them as they left the trail, the figure of thirteen men given by the Manhak leader proved correct.

The sun began outlining Manhak San, and I made a mental check of whether I had anything exposed that might reflect its rays.

I had left my Navy cap with its bright gold and silver shield with the woman to carry; binoculars were under my jacket. Reaching around me, I pulled the stiff grass toward me at an angle and cautiously transferred the grass underneath me to my legs and back. It was another good hour, occasioned by many mysterious delays, before the night guard departed.

The sun's rays quickly dried the dew that had gathered on my back. Flies commenced buzzing around my head, and the activity of small field spiders and ants in my clothes all heralded the heat of the sun and my mounting discomfort. A guard had resumed the post above me and had been joined by another. Facing obliquely away from where I lay, they watched the northern traffic. Soon I saw the off-duty party on the road below and watched them until they faded into the main highway junction at Inchon.

I could expect the cruisers to show in the channel about nine o'clock. The bombardment would commence at ten and last until twelve. There would be an hour while they maneuvered into position and anchored. That hour would be sufficient time for anything we had to do. In the meantime, to attack before nine o'clock would chance premature discovery through possible channels unknown to us, such as curious farmers. During the next few hours, I had no time for fanciful theorizing on grand strategy, being completely occupied with ants and problems of a personal nature related thereto.

At nine o'clock, I had my forty-five covering a vital spot on the near guard. The way they were sitting, I knew the force of the heavy slug at such close range would carom the victim into his companion. As I squeezed off the round, I had my usual qualms. Were the others still with me? Were they awake? The heavy pistol threw my arm up in spite of the supporting grip of my left hand on the wrist, the report practically startling me to my feet.

The one man was down and the other struggling violently to get free from the pinioning body. My second shot was almost drowned out by a fusillade of fire from our men on the left, who were now standing fully exposed on the crest of the ridge. I shouted for them to get down, but instead they charged forward into the camp area. Coming in from their right, I saw the enemy turn to face this radical element and threw myself to the ground as they fired. Out of the corner of my eye, I saw two of the men spin and fall. As deliberately as I could, I squeezed off the rest of the clip, but it was impossible to assess any damage.

Yong, seeing how the situation had gone, had wisely thrown the grand plan to the winds and come charging in with his submachine guns. The Reds went down like rag dolls. I didn't dare get up for fear of catching the withering crossfire as the Manhak leader charged in following Yong. It was over in less than a minute. Oddly enough, the only thing that remained pictured in my mind was Yong's expression as he led his small unit up the hill. I would never have believed that his handsome face could be transformed into such a mask of hatred and ferocity, and indeed I could not help but notice the positive effort of will he put forward to restrain the commission of atrocities. I am quite certain that my presence alone stayed his hand.

Glancing quickly over the scene, I could see nothing that would interfere with the next phase, so I went back over the crest and stripped to the skin. Ants. Little stinging ants. I shook and dry-scrubbed my jacket and trousers until my knuckles were sore. They were miserable little brutes. Back at my ant nest, I retrieved my binoculars and studied the Inchon highway. No unusual movement. We'd have to depend on our lookout man up there from now on.

Yong was having the enemy battle casualties covered from the sun by the thatch and mats. Two of our men had been killed outright and another two wounded. I started to inquire as to the reason the men had charged into the camp instead of picking the enemy off from cover, but gave it up when Yong said it was a useless task.

It was about nine-thirty when I spotted the cruisers in Flying Fish Channel, and for its effect I promptly turned my glasses over to the Manhak leader and the Sorae man and woman. Their quiet comments to each other as they viewed the men-o'-war through the glasses betokened their awe. Afterward, the glasses were handed around to the entire group and accepted gingerly as though they were some embodiment of black magic.

Deliberately, for the purpose of further impressing these future allies, I stated where the cruisers would anchor during the bombardment and gave the time they would open fire. Anyone less informed than Yong would have been quite convinced that the cruisers were acting under my direction and control.

The old man had brought along the maps, and these we spread out on the crest of the hill. Yong and I would work as a team in observing and plotting the positions of Red guns as they fired at aircraft, which I expected to appear momentarily. This was to be the first day of the softening-up. From now until D-day, our aircraft would plaster Wolmi-do and Inchon daily, attempting to demolish our accumulated list of targets and others as fast as we could send them in.

Precisely at ten, the USS *Toledo* and USS *Manchester,* with HMS *Kenya* and HMS *Jamaica,* opened up. Within a few minutes, several squadrons of aircraft were adding to the eruption of Inchon with five-hundred-pound bombs. Within the next hour, we had plotted and replotted about twenty enemy guns. Watching them closely, we could see that they weren't being knocked out. If we'd only had two-way communication with either the cruisers or planes, we could have zeroed them in on these targets.

It gave me a feeling of awe to sit up here and leisurely observe the scene below. Grandstand seats at a bombardment. We instructed the Manhak leader in this plotting procedure. Hereafter he would undertake to spot the guns and give us the information, keeping track of those destroyed and new batteries set up.

We were forced to abandon our position when a report came in that the search patrol was out again and headed in this general direction. As the Manhak leader had two wounded men, it would be wise to move away now. A short conference reassured the Sorae San man that his weapons would be at the inlet on tonight's high tide.

Formalities of departure were concluded with grave bows on both sides, and the three of us moved off down the path for Manhak and our sampan at the inlet.

12

YONGHUNG-DO'S LAST STAND

ONCE AGAIN we arrived back at the CP in time to observe another sunrise. I had no idea of the depth of feeling that now bound our three women to my lieutenants and Chae. They were standing on the scarp, their full white skirts flapping in the breeze—the first things we saw as we approached the beach. From the deep circles under their eyes, it wasn't difficult to deduce that they'd had little or no sleep that night.

I alone was surprised when Lim put Chae to bed in her cot, naked as a jaybird, and climbed in beside him with the same amount of clothing. Not that anything could come of it, for Chae shivered himself to sleep in a matter of seconds, long before Lim's bodily warmth could take effect.

The next four days constituted a hectic kaleidoscope of activity, with General Headquarters becoming more and more insistent and demanding. Yong had dropped in weight I don't know how much, but he was mere skin, bone, and hard sinew. Our small supply of Benzedrine diminished in direct relation to our weight. Kim looked like a caricature of a starved American Indian, his high cheekbones and moon face emphasized by the Marine fatigue hat that he insisted on wearing. Very seldom did we ever catch this Manchurian guerrilla in his bunk.

Lee reported in with the startling news that he had sunk a minelaying junk up in the northern approaches. Blown it sky high with the first shot. I was slightly put out to learn that he had taken no steps to determine whether the load of mines was destined for an existing mine field or a new one. However, this was unreasonable to expect of Lee, and I dropped it quickly. I was distinctly aware of the change in my normally easygoing nature. I was constantly catching myself up short in an unreasonable outburst. Yong and Kim grew quieter, if possible, and more fiercely intent. On the whole, it became an arduous task to restrain their native propensities. Only the redoubtable Chang remained steady—consistently efficient, cruel, and a prime source of satisfaction to the entire group of *kisaeng* girls whenever he chose to bring his junk with its prizes into anchorage.

Yang, one of our original CP guards who had been wounded in the junk battle, had finally died, despite the constant attendance of the doctor. And Song, another guard, was dead from an infiltrator attack on the east promontory—the fourth member of the CP guards to go. Day by day, the infiltrators from Taebu-do were again growing in strength. The Reds had abandoned their first tactic of awaiting a buildup for a general attack, and were now launching nightly attacks on isolated outposts.

Slowly, they were drawing around to our almost unassailable beach CP position. Song's death was proof of their strategy. It was apparent that they were in small groups and never stayed in the same place two nights in succession. Curfew and identification papers produced only rare success, and those caught were generally of no use to us by the time we took them from the villagers. For the rest, my opinion that a man well-camouflaged cannot be seen even from the distance of a few feet was borne out by the constant failure of mass search parties to turn up anything more than vagrant chickens or an escaped shoat. However, I was vindictive enough to wish the persistent Reds, wherever they were, the intimate company of ants.

Lee was continually being called out to intercept enemy barge traffic up by Chinnampo. We received word that all other fleet units had been called in and were concentrating for the big push, leaving this inshore job exclusively to Lee. He pulled his ship and crew through those last few days by skill and sheer nerve alone, and was in there pitching steel along with the overtowering cruisers and destroyers on D-day.

To avoid the danger of riots, we shipped the prisoners and others that Chang brought in down to Tokchok-do as fast as Kim could interrogate them. Kim cordially detested these mass-production methods and pleaded for more time. Under different circumstances, it would have been both possible and desirable, but here we had to keep things moving rapidly. Thoroughness was compromised for speed—a bad condition, but dictated by overriding security considerations.

On the thirteenth, another bombardment group steamed up Flying Fish Channel, and as before, I prayed fervently that our mine checks had been thorough. But on this morning, as the lead destroyers came opposite the southern tip of Taemuui-do, they sighted a string of mines. As I had warned our mine patrol out of the harbor waters while the fleet units were in, they hadn't had a chance to make the discovery of what had been the previous night's mining activity.

Our ship captains were justifiably cautious of any native craft approaching their vicinity in these hostile waters, and, indeed, had orders to sink all such craft. The mines were well out of the main ship channel and awash at low tide, so it was a relatively easy matter for the destroyers to knock them off. After this upsetting experience, we redoubled our patrol and kept one junk constantly on the move in all the channels. No other strings appeared to haunt my restless dreams.

By this time, Tokyo had laid on a most efficient procedure for blasting the targets we reported. A list of targets submitted tonight would be blasted the following day, and our guerrillas would have a report on the damage and still more targets the following night. We keenly felt the lack of radio communication with our people near Manhak and at Sorae. With it, we would have cut in half the time required to report a target to Tokyo. I determined that in any future mission of this nature, I would be certain to carry extra radios.

The invasion fleet had sortied from Japan and was en route to Inchon. By this time, confused Red spies that swarmed the Japanese ports had reported the fleet headed for seven different points. Daily, we scanned our information for evidence that the Inchon Reds were taking more than local precautions against a possible United Nations landing, but nothing appeared. At Seoul, everything was normal.

Chi brought in some excellent information on Wolmi-do. A previous report placing the Red strength on that island at not more than five hundred men was confirmed. Furthermore, a five-hundred-pound bomb had hit the Wolmi-do mess hall dead-center during the meal hour and had killed about one hundred of the garrison. Morale was at a low ebb. The Inchon garrison commander would not send replacements. Laborers were difficult to procure, and the defense work lagged.

In the meantime, Yong and I divided our days between the now hazardous task of waylaying Red junk traffic (they had deliberately blown up two of their junks when we came alongside, hoping to take us with them), and trying to neutralize the infiltrator groups running rampant on Yonghung-do. By the morning of the fourteenth, we had taken the radical step of withdrawing our outposts and set up a perimeter defense that included the ferry landing, the village, and the western promontory of our CP area.

Keeping a constant eye on the tide tables, it was evident that beginning with the night of the twelfth, the Reds could wade across from Taebu-do. Each succeeding day until the fifteenth, the water would drop still lower. Except for starlight, the nights would be totally dark. It was just a matter of time now until they made another concerted effort to dislodge or capture us, but we were gambling they would hold off until the fifteenth, feeling that when the fleet arrived, they would not only forget about us but would leave Taebu-do in a hurry.

The night of the thirteenth we spent patrolling the perimeter. It was obvious after an analysis of the many short skirmishes of the night that they were not yet ready to make an all-out effort to take the island. Kim assured us that they would hold off until reinforcements came over from Taebu-do, and hazarded a guess that the attack would be patterned somewhat after the last attempt. I called in Chang and his raiders as soon as it was light enough to locate them. Only two of his original craft were still in commission, supplemented by the pompom that, due to engine trouble, could hardly be considered safe after a particularly nerve-shaking experience the previous day.

We had made a run-up beyond Palmi-do to check on what the mine patrol had reported to be a string of floating mines. Approaching the objects as they dipped and gyrated to the choppy waves, it was impossible to determine what they were. Painted black with orange stripes and markings and fastened on a common thin cable, they appeared to be a string of buoys such as are used to mark a small boat basin. We queried our boatmen, who were familiar with such things at Inchon, but they could not remember anything like them.

We moved in alongside the lead object and studied it carefully. It was no type of mine within my experience, but it could have been the buoy section of an antenna mine. Checking the distance to the next object, I thought the interval entirely too short. The explosion of one mine would set off a chain reaction and blow the whole line.

Still, working under the adverse conditions of darkness and fast tidal currents, inexperienced hands could have made such an error. The things were in midchannel and in the most critical spot in the harbor. We secured a line to the lead object and headed for the shallows of Taemuui-do, hoping that the next instant we wouldn't join our ancestors. Between the faltering engine and tide, we barely made progress. Two hours later, we were able to let go. Assuredly, no unit of the invasion fleet would venture into such close waters. We promised ourselves that if we had an opportunity later, we'd find out what it was those buoys were marking.

As we let go, Min called our attention to three large junks sailing down on Yonghung-do from Taemuui-do—most inviting prizes. Intercepting them would be painfully slow. It would mean setting a course over the mudflats between the islands. The level of water over the flats was dropping one inch each minute. We had perhaps a little more than an hour to make our catch and get away or be stranded high and dry on the mud between the two Red-held islands.

Had we not removed the heavy machine gun from the pompom to bolster our defense perimeter, we could have concluded this matter in a hurry. All we had aboard now were a couple of grease guns and forty-fives. We'd have to close to within four hundred yards of the junks before we could even scare the occupants into believing we were seriously entertaining designs on their property.

The owner of the pompom stuck his head out of the engine-room hatch for a breath of air. Glancing around, he discovered we had changed course and were not heading for Yonghung-do. With that, he was on deck immediately, looking for Min, and, finding him, he commenced shouting wildly. His power and diversity of expression was something to behold as he informed Min in no un-certain terms what a crazy thing we were doing. He disapproved. He was going to shut down the engine. It was his boat, et cetera, et cetera, et cetera.

Min listened calmly, his face a complete blank. After the ha-rangue was over he rose, picked up a long bamboo pole, and shoved it into the water as far as he could. A ten-foot pole, it did not touch bottom. Without a word, Min offered the end of the pole for inspection. The owner was crestfallen. He shuffled back to the engine-room hatch and disappeared. Min resumed his seat on the gunnel.

There was about a mile interval between our quarries, who were hugging the coastline to take advantage of the eddies. A quartering wind filled their sails, giving them a lively appearance. Although not possessing the smooth, flowing lines of our modern racing yachts, with their graceful sails, the junks impressed me with their qualities of strength and endurance. In this area of typhoons and rugged shores, a craft combining such features was to a sailor beautiful in spite of itself.

Observing carefully the path of the lead junk, I could see that she would easily cut across well in front of us. Stepping to the pilot-house, I had Rhee open the bearing about ten degrees and settled down to watch. The bearing commenced closing again, and it was soon quite apparent that she would escape us, as she turned north-northeast between the islands. We wrote her off and held our course for the second. It was possible that she, too, would slip by us out of range.

The huge one-lunger diesel was continually threatening to quit, the worried owner sometimes catching it up on the final gasp. It was a case of ignorance being bliss. If I had taken the trouble to look into the jury-rigged complexities of the monster that was making the deck shudder under my feet, I am certain I should never have permitted anyone to risk his life in the craft—much less my own.

The bearing was slowly closing on the second junk. It was impossible to open again or we'd run aground on Chang's little hide-out island of Sinbul-do. "Yong," I said, "throw a few shots in her direction. Perhaps it will make her come around."

It didn't. As we passed Sinbul-do close aboard, the junk put her helm down and came about on a port tack to clear a final head-land. The wind could now do something for us, and did. As she cleared the headland too close and came under the lee shore, her sails ceased to draw. An unfavorable eddy swung her out into the channel within half a mile of us, before her sails again filled. Through my glasses, I could see the boatmen heaving away at the huge sculling oars, trying to regain their lost advantage. We tried a few more shots with no effect. They could not put back into the beach. Their only chance lay in heading straight up the channel on a parallel course with ours, and we were slowly overhauling them.

Our engine gave a final gulp and died. We were past Sinbul-do, and immediately were set down toward Yongyu-do on a four-knot current. Looking anxiously down into the hellhole engine room, I could see the old man working feverishly with his compressed air tank. Evidently, a line had clogged. Yong nudged me.

"The junk has dropped its sails, Mr. Clark," he said. "They're using the oars."

At the moment, I could not care less what the junk did. Unless that one cylinder started pumping again, we were going to cash in our chips just as surely as if it were our hearts that had stopped. I grabbed the bamboo pole and started sounding, as we were swept along with the current. It touched bottom easily the first try. Eight feet of water. The pompom needed five feet. Oddly enough, we were closing the junk, and at the same time the distance between the two islands.

Yong clutched my arm and pointed to starboard. Little splashes of water were tracing neat tracks to within a hundred yards of us. The Reds on Sammok-do were trying to reach us—and with machine guns. Fortunately, we were drawing away from them. A rasping cough came from the engine room, and the deck surged as the engine caught and died again. Another sounding showed seven feet of water. Unless something happened in the next few minutes, we would be aground and shortly high and dry.

Yong, undismayed, walked a line of submachine-gun fire over to the junk, which was now within extreme range and was rewarded for his effort by the appearance of a new series of splashes on our port side. Yongyu-do had opened on us, although still out of range. This not-unforeseen development was deadly serious, as we were rapidly being set down into range. The Reds doing the firing were easily visible on the beach in front of the village.

Another huge grunt from the engine room indicated that our grizzled engineer was still at work. As we came within range, we moved to the starboard side behind the protection of the pilothouse. Slugs began tearing splinters and tossing them around like hay in a storm. The junk had decided that she was finally in danger from us with Yong lacing her topside with slugs, and had put about, as Yong shouted threats and imprecations at her. She was our only hope for survival if the engine could not be fixed soon. Grabbing Min, we dashed forward and heaved the anchor over the side to forestall the imminent danger of grounding.

Yong talked the junk in alongside to port, in a Chinese landing, effectively cutting off the fire from Yongyu-do. We were in fair circumstance now until the tide ran out beneath us. The pole indicated another six inches—six minutes. "Min," I said, "take a couple of men on board the junk and get her ready to sail at once. If we have to abandon the pompom, maybe she'll get us away." I had no idea of how much water she was drawing. For all I knew, she might be sitting on mud this minute.

The deck bounded to a new thrust of the giant piston. Then, after what seemed hours, another, and another. The engine was going again, but ahead. Throwing open the pilothouse door, I told Rhee to back her down and put her rudder amidships. Then I shouted to Min to take over the helm on the junk and pilot us out of this trap. At first it appeared that we weren't going to move, but the junk took a slight roll to leeward and I could feel our keel lift and start sliding along on the mud.

Climbing the bulwark of the captured junk, I had to duck down immediately to avoid the slugs that were still pouring in. I quickly snaked across the deck and under the shelter of the starboard bulwark, then aft to where Min was steering by means of a line secured to the tiller, which he worked lying flat on deck, now and then taking a quick look at the course he was steering.

"You know the channel in here, old warrior?" I asked hopefully, and was rewarded with a grunt and a vacuous smile. I drew what reassurance I could from this garrulous outburst and started bob-bing up and down in turn as I tried to follow our course out. We were soon beyond range, and Min turned the junk crew to hoisting sails. Jumping back into the pompom, we cast loose and turned around to find the third and final object of our chase in irons off the headland.

It was a simple matter to take her. The two Red policemen aboard were completely cowed by our preliminary softening-up volleys. We headed home with our prizes, not without regret. The pirate, Chang, would give us a good lecture on tactics when we re-turned. If he had anything to say about a lack of discretion, I could counter at length with many equally foolhardy ventures he had blithely entered on. The honorable engineer was topside again—this time inspecting with some concern the shattered port side of his boat. I'd have to get the village carpenters to give him a hand. . . .

That was on the twelfth.

This was the fourteenth, our last day. By this time tomorrow, we hoped to be walking the streets of Inchon, contacting our guerril-las and pushing our effort on to the north. We had strong hopes that we'd be able to hold Yonghung-do against the Reds. It was al-most noon, and at the height of the final pre-invasion bombard-ment, that the Red infiltrators began demonstrating something of their intentions. A mud-begrimed messenger limped in from the ferry landing. "The Inminkyun have cut us off from the village at the swamp. We don't know how many there are. Fifteen, twenty, maybe more. The section leader asks for aid," he stated simply.

"How did you get here?" Yong asked.

"I swam out into the channel and let the tide carry me up past the Inminkyun, then over the hills," he replied. We realized that the rest couldn't do this unless they abandoned their weapons. Those weapons we would need desperately if it came to a showdown later on. The thing to do now was to break up the block at the swamp, get our men out, and walk across later. It was bad, but there was no help for it.

"Get ten men from the village guard, Yong. Bring as many grease guns as you can and pass out a few grenades. Chae and I will meet you on the hill this side of the swamp."

Yong was off at a trot. Chae was at my elbow, eagerly awaiting orders. "Take a few grenades, Chae, and get Ahn's grease gun and a couple of clips for me." Lim was staring fixedly at us from the tent, eyes wide and unblinking. She looked pathetically small and inadequate. Was she invoking her Eastern or Western gods in favor of her man? Probably both. I had the feeling that when it came to Chae, Lim took no chances of ignoring help from any omnipotent source.

I was glad that my wife, Enid, was under the impression I was on a routine jaunt to Hokkaido or Maizuru. Women should not be subjected to such trying experiences. Chae ignored Lim completely. I dropped a couple of grenades in the voluminous pockets of my marine trousers and slung on my glasses and the grease gun. We cut across the rice paddies for the swamp. Walking along at a steady pace, I reviewed in my mind's eye the terrain at the swamp. The trail leading to the ferry landing bisected a low hill on the northern side and the swamp and paddy area on the south.

The messenger had not known where the Reds' strong point was established. It was likely that it was in the swamp, which would provide excellent cover and a ready means of escape should pressure become too heavy—a first principle in such operations. However, the swamp did not make a good vantage point for observing the trail approaches. The tall, thick swamp grass would limit vision to the immediate sector in front of the observer. It was reasonable to assume, then, that the Reds had one or more men staked out on the hill to the left of the trail. It was unlikely that they would concentrate the main force there—much too easy for us to trap them away from their cover.

We'd have to use caution in approaching the hill. Come in on the rise from a neutral angle. We couldn't waste any time. If my reasoning was correct, we'd have to clue in Yong before he put in an appearance. I lengthened my stride until Chae, with his short legs, was almost trotting.

Clearing a valley, I cut off the trail and climbed a small rise to where we could see our objective about a mile distant. My glasses disclosed nothing at this range. Sticking to the ridge path, I circled around to the east and then cut south, making the final approach through the bush and scraggly tree stands. Down a final small depression and I was on my stomach, snaking up the last few hundred yards. I left Chae behind with my cumbersome equipment and to warn Yong if anything went wrong with this little recon job.

This snaking business I found hard on my ankles, elbows, and thigh and shoulder muscles, and as much as I pressed myself to the ground, I felt as though my rear end was making like a hula dancer's and just as conspicuous. At the top of the hill, nobody was in evidence. From cover, I glanced up and down the trail. The view was unobstructed. Then I realized that it would be just as good from a position down the slope facing the trail. Why would lookouts be up here when they could do the job from a point much closer to their comrades?

I took time out to undo my trousers and shake out the accumulated grass and stuff scooped up in my progress. Continuing on, I thought it very foolish of the Reds not to cover this approach. But then, maybe they couldn't afford the luxury of complete security.

Over the crest, I halted again and carefully scanned the slope beneath. In full view also was the swamp and the narrow trail skirting it. I couldn't see a thing that looked remotely human.

I'd have to resort to a little deception. An old ruse, but not completely outworn. I jerked a few pebbles toward the trail on the left and watched carefully for any movement. I didn't hear the pebbles light, nor did I see anything move. Perhaps a bigger one. I jerked a stone over and was rewarded almost at once. Not more than ten yards down the slope, the grass moved suddenly. Nothing else, but there was no breeze to cause the disturbance.

I thought I saw the swamp grass part in several places but could not be certain. Eyes sometimes see what you want them to see. I returned to Chae.

"Chae, run back and bring Yong and his men up here. When he arrives, ask him to take his men to this side of the top of the hill. I'll be there waiting." It was a matter of minutes until Yong arrived, and I explained the situation to him.

"There must be another block down the trail on this side, or the ferry men could have come through over this hill. More Reds probably on the other side of that next rise. I don't understand their strategy in splitting forces, unless they have men staked out along the swamp from here all the way up there. It'd take fifteen or twenty men at least."

"The messenger said there were about that many, Mr. Clark. Don't know how they estimated the number, though, looking at it from here," Yong said.

"Looks like we'll need all the help we can get. Suppose we do it this way. You cut through past that next rise. Wade on out if you have to, but get to the ferry guard. Bring them in on a frontal attack, but make it a feint—don't want any casualties we can avoid. After you open up, we'll take them from the channel side. Should do the trick. They'll probably get into the swamp right away, but at least we'll get our people through before they can do anything else."

"I'll attack straight up the path, then," Yong said. "Make them think it's just another attempt to get through."

"Good. Don't get between the rise and the swamp. If they have men on the rise, leave them a clear path to the swamp so they can retreat. I want to avoid bringing this thing to a showdown until tomorrow morning, if at all possible."

Yong nodded understanding and was gone.

I picked two men and stationed them to cover the lookout and the area below. They were to pick off the lookout with a grenade and then pin down the others by spraying the swamp grass with bullets. Firing from up the line would be the action signal.

By the time I saw Yong's party moving up the wide flat delta area toward the swamp, my men were in position to attack anything that moved on the rise, from either the flank or the rear. Yong approached slowly, deploying his seven men across the area with wide intervals between them. Six others were well in the rear, carrying the heavy machine guns and ammunition. Yong stopped the line within several hundred yards and stalked forward alone at a crouch. He disappeared from sight around the rise.

That was just like Yong when I wasn't with him. He was using himself for bait. I wouldn't forgive myself if he was hurt. Should have gone myself. A single shot cracked from the other side of the knoll, followed immediately by a ragged fusillade. We would be in the line of fire from Yong's men if we came in from the rear, so we charged around the left flank and up the slight slope. I saw nothing at all until a muzzle flash from almost underfoot showed their men to be well camouflaged in the grass.

A short burst with the grease gun knocked down the blurred and descriptionless figure that attempted to rise. My men were flanking me on both sides, screaming and yelling like demons, and firing literally at everything. An accurate volley sent several of them sprawling, and I shouted for the others to get down. Those near hit the ground with me, but two others kept on going until they were brought down. I cursed them and myself for their undisciplined savagery, and jerked out my grenades.

I couldn't see any targets, but the force of the explosion would tear the courage loose from hardier men than I unless afforded the protection of a foxhole. As the others followed suit, the ground ahead of us was turned into a churning maelstrom of fire, smoke, and heaving dirt. Through it all, I saw the enemy get to his feet and turn tail toward the swamp. After them again, I noted they weren't in uniform and estimated that about ten finally made it into the thick reeds on the other side of the trail.

Yong was waving and shouting his men through behind us as we covered the swamp. Suddenly, one of mine folded up and went down. The shot had come from behind us—toward Yong's men. One or more of the Reds had stayed behind. Yong had heard it and had the spot pinpointed. Two of his men ran at a trot for a small scrub growth. Another crack from the scrub and they hit the ground. There was nothing for about a minute, and then a dark object lobbed through the air. The scrub went skyward with earth and whoever had chosen to die.

There were no further casualties as we abandoned the ferry landing to the Reds. The operation had cost us one dead and four wounded. The Reds had lost three dead and two wounded. The advantage had been ours; the casualties should have been far less. Was I justified in permitting these untrained and undisciplined, yet brave and even heroic, men to engage regular troops of the Reds?

It was a travesty that these people had to die violently while Kim Il Sung, the instigator of the whole rotten mess, remained smug and secure. How to reconcile all this death and destruction without trying to eliminate this monster?

Kim had ready what was destined to be our final report for General Headquarters. As usual, he had some choice remarks to go along with it. The Red police and soldiers were very poor sources for information. It wasn't that they didn't want to tell all they knew, they were just plain afraid to do so. Their indoctrination had included lectures on the long arm of the Reds. It extended into our prisoner-of-war camps, and if they talked, or otherwise betrayed their Red overlords, they would be sought out and punished even though in our custody. It meant simply that they were more afraid of their own people than they were of us and would take their chances accordingly.

First setting up a temporary defense line that extended from the left flank of the village to the shores of a narrow inlet off Yonghung Channel, we called the various leaders to the CP to review our situation and plan the next stage of defense. It was decided that the perimeter should not go beyond the present line extending from the inlet through the village to the west promontory. This line would permit us to maintain a watch from the eastern tip of the small peninsula to its southern side by the inlet.

The peninsula shores were rocky and dangerous for any landing en masse. We could expect to hold this line until the village itself was overrun. A lookout stationed there would be able to observe any junk movement from Taebu-do, provided there were stars tonight. The defense line would be about a mile long: far too tenuous to maintain against an equal force with the advantage of surprise.

"We'll set up a defense in depth, Yong, terminating at the west promontory—our final escape route. The first line will be manned mainly for the purpose of discovering the Reds' intentions and will fall back to the second line as soon as any pressure is applied. The second line will include only the rice paddies, the beach, and the west promontory. For defense, it is excellent. The Reds will have to cross about six hundred yards of open paddies to get to us. We can set up machine guns for enfilading fire both from the beach and the hill leading to the promontory. This will mean abandoning the village if they go after it first—which I think unlikely, unless they get reinforcements from Taebu-do."

"What about the people if we abandon the village, *Taicho-san?*" asked the headman, with concern.

"I'll come to that point, *Shicho-san.*"

"Chang, how many people do you think you can get into those junks we've captured?" I asked.

"*So desu ne.* [Well, let me see.]" He deliberated the reply, then turned to Min. "*Min-san,* you have been with these junks. What number would you say, old warrior?" Chang asked.

"There are seventeen in condition to sail, *Taicho-san.* By crowding, each should take about thirty people," Min said. That would give a capacity of five hundred ten. There were more than a thousand islanders.

"Kim, will you work out with the headman the selection of those people who should leave with the junks? The Reds will be looking for the ones who have helped us in any way. Be sure that all of those are on the list to leave. Particularly our three girls."

"What about the *kisaeng* girls, Mr. Clark?" Yong said worriedly.

"Better include them, Kim. The prisoners Chang brought in today, however, can stay behind. They'll be in no danger if they explain to the Reds what happened to them. Have the whole lot ready to board the junks at sunset. I don't want to drown half of them getting them aboard in the dark. We should know by sunset if the Reds mean business."

"I suppose they should go to Tokchok-do, *Kuraku-san*?" Kim asked.

"Yes, Kim, but be sure they have instructions not to use either Flying Fish or the East Channel. There's a middle passage they can take. You know of the passage, Min-san?"

"*Hai,*" he replied. "If *Kim-san* wishes, Chang and I will instruct the junk captains," he offered, and Kim accepted, happy to have this seafaring detail off his hands. I was concerned for fear these junks would run afoul of our fleet in the channels.

This important matter taken care of, we returned to our defense problem. "Once the Reds locate our strong points," I said, "and that won't be difficult, they'll likely move around to take our hill position. If they do that, then these men must fall back on the promontory. With that position gone, our CP will be outflanked and we will also have to fall back so that the promontory will be our third and final line. We'll try to hold there until dawn, when the Reds will see our invasion fleet and, I hope, will be anxious to get back to their own island and the mainland. However, if we can't hold on, we'll take to the junks Chang will keep in reserve. Do you agree with this plan?" I asked.

They did. Being no military tactician, I held no great confidence in my concept of such matters and could only hope that the plan would work. The two main things we had to keep in mind were getting the islanders away if it became necessary and putting the Palmi-do light in operation at 0030 tomorrow morning.

The conference broke up and we set out to implement the plan. It was close to six o'clock and sunset when we were satisfied with our preparations. Snipers were already busy, but they were at a disadvantage, having to fire uphill into the village. The fire served a useful purpose in putting even the most doubting islander on guard, and those who were to remain behind chose protected positions in the more heavily constructed houses. It also served to help the headman and Kim get their charges on the way to the promontory. Even so, only about three hundred could be persuaded of their danger and the necessity for leaving.

There was no sign of an attack by sunset, but to be on the safe side, I ordered the junks loaded. A night on board would be uncomfortable, but not as nerve-racking as it would be in the village. Rhee was standing by with the pompom for a quick trip to Palmi-do with our gear aboard, ready to move out temporarily or permanently.

The evening dragged on while we checked and rechecked our positions and weapons. With the coming of dark, the snipers had knocked off and were in all likelihood snaking up the hill to the village and taking up advanced spots for the big push. Nothing was moving within the perimeter now. If something should move, it would bring a hail of lead unless it was prompt in answering the challenge. I had stationed myself at the CP; Yong was on the hill. The quiet covered the area with a mask of innocence. The events that were breeding under its guise would erupt and consume this entire area in the fires of battle.

It was difficult to believe, yet at this moment the invasion fleet was rendezvousing off Flying Fish Channel. A sharp challenge broke the stillness, followed by an undertoned reply. Ahn brought in a messenger from the peninsula.

"A group of junks is moving from Taebu-do around to the south side of the island, *Taicho-san*," he reported.

"How many? Could you count them?"

"*Iie*. It is too dark, but at least four or five."

The tide had been ebbing for almost two hours, but it had been one of the two highest tides of the month. If they were well under way, they would be able to land at the south cove. It would take them a good hour to get there and another hour to move their troops within striking distance. I sent the messenger on to inform Yong and Kim, and added that I thought we could expect an attack around ten.

Paikyun came around with a bowl of cold fish and rice, saying that Moon had sent it down for us from the promontory. It was delicious; my stomach recalled that it hadn't been fed since early morning. Flipping the last traces of it into my mouth with my fingers, I found myself toying with the question of just who had brought it from Moon and looked around for Chae. He lay on the grass behind his machine gun, but there was another body alongside his—too close to be a man's.

I clucked at him. He detached himself and came over. "Is that Lim, Chae?" I asked.

"*Hai, so desu, Taicho-san* [Yes, it is so, Leader]," he replied.

"Better get her back to the promontory, Chae," I said. "Things are going to start moving here in a little while." He assented, and shortly the wraithlike Lim departed.

It was about ten-thirty when the sound of firing came from beyond the village and was immediately followed by a stillness more poignant than before. If that was the Reds, we could expect our perimeter outposts to join us. Within a few minutes, several scattered challenges rang out and our men came in. The village was abandoned. The Reds had sent in strong recon parties from both sides and were now cutting across the peninsula. If our lookout down there had anything else to report, he was going to have to get it through Red lines now.

"Ahn," I called quietly. He came up at once.

"The Reds are crossing the peninsula. I want you to inform our lookouts at the end of the peninsula that they've been cut off and to watch themselves when they send messages through. At eleven-thirty, they're to return here."

Ahn repeated the message and left. I didn't think there would be more junks coming over, but the Reds might try to wade across later.

I used my glasses to survey the flat, dry paddies extending out in front almost to the village, which was a dark patch to the right. They'd be coming in soon. Maybe only one, maybe fifty. A short burst of machine-gun fire from Yong's position startled me, and I searched the area carefully for the target I had missed. No, I couldn't see a thing moving out there. Maybe just a trigger-happy gunner.

Another twenty minutes went slowly by. I could picture all kinds of stealthy moving going on out there, and hoped that they hadn't developed a camouflage that blended with the rice paddies. I didn't relish the thought of a sudden cascade of grenades raining down around us. I wondered if the engineer would be able to get that monstrosity of his started when the time came. The pompom hadn't turned out to be as useful as we had anticipated.

My musings were interrupted by Ahn's return. "Another group of junks is in the channel headed for the east promontory, *Taicho-san*," he said. "I saw them. There are seven."

"You mean they're headed north, toward Inchon, Ahn?" I asked, and he confirmed it. Could be they were Taebu-do troops on their way to reinforce the Inchon garrison. More likely, it was the second of a two-pronged attack on Yonghung-do—and that was bad. In the dark, it would be difficult to stop them from landing at our backs while we were engaged in the paddies. It was good tactics on their part. It would make our CP position untenable.

"Tell Yong and Kim what you have seen, Ahn, and then return here," I said. Let them in on the bad news, too, so they'd be prepared. Lee and his gunboat had left yesterday morning. He wouldn't be returning until tomorrow, when he'd steam in with the fleet. Probably a guide ship. Surely could use him now. I studied the waters off the eastern promontory, my eyes doing their best to build junks out of pliable darkness. They'd be coming around there unless they were going in to Inchon.

I reflected nervously that if they did go on north, it could mean the invasion secret was known. Within a few short hours, the garrison commander could call in another thousand troops—more from Seoul. No, they had to come in here, they must . . .

"*Taicho-san*, something moving out there," said Chae. I turned my glasses to where he pointed. Nothing. Nothing at all. Then part of the paddy field grew legs, dashed forward a few yards, and melted away again. I called Paikyun. "Run over to Yong-san and tell him about seven Reds are crossing the paddy heading for his position. They are right over there."

I handed him my glasses. He saw them and sprinted away. I would have taken them under fire, but didn't want to expose my position until there was a general attack. This was obviously a scouting party feeling out our positions.

They were halfway across. Paikyun was back. Yong had them in view and was waiting until he felt he could get them all. More optimistic than I. In this deceptive darkness, I wouldn't expect to get more than half. Muzzle flashes ruined whatever darkness accommodation your eyes had gained.

When Yong turned loose, it would be the signal for the big push across the paddies by the Reds. They would know then, they thought, where the resistance was located. I strained my eyes in the direction from which the scouting party had appeared.

"Chae," I whispered hoarsely, "tell the gun crews to keep their eyes away from Yong's position. Tell them to watch over there where the other Reds are waiting."

Yong finally opened up, and within seconds a black line moved away from the foot of the hill to the left and advanced rapidly across the paddies in front of us toward the hill on the right, where Yong was cutting loose with everything he had. They were spread out; individuals could not be distinguished, but there were a good hundred or more.

I let them get well within the sweep of our two light and two heavy machine guns, then turned the gun crews loose. The noise was deafening against the sound backdrop of the small tree stand we were in. I moved back so as to be able to observe the effects of the fire without being blinded by the flashes. The entire line was down and practically invisible. They'd probably taken shelter be-hind the low banks that separated the paddies. I called to Chae to cease fire. Yong's group had stopped, and complete silence crept over the field.

No, not quite. There were moans coming from out there. They had it made if they had the guts to keep going. We couldn't stop them this way—it could only be hand-to-hand, and we didn't have that many men. Well . . . The other junks . . .

I strode hurriedly to the beach and searched the waters to the east. They were there. Clear of the promontory. Another ten min-utes and they would be landing. I would have to give them some kind of reception.

"Chae, take one of the heavy machine guns and set it up on the beach. Do what damage you can to those junks and the troops as they land." He had it set up and firing in five minutes. The Reds in the paddies, probably realizing that reinforcements were at hand, took new courage and sprang forward again. Again, our two posi-tions poured a crossfire into them.

I was surprised to see the large flashes of grenades going off around them. Yong must have sent a man or two down into the paddies. I robbed the machine-gun crews and did the same, telling them not to go more than twenty paces beyond our position or they'd be cut down by our own fire.

Soon, there was no movement in the field, and I sent Ahn to Yong, telling him we were moving back to the promontory. I'd stay with one gun as long as I could and then abandon it. Quickly, the men dismantled their pieces, loaded the ammunition, and shoved off with orders to report to Kim and a message for Min to get under way for Tokchok-do with his charges. The junks were disgorging their loads about five hundred yards up the beach. It was impossible to determine the effectiveness of our fire at this distance. I wished we had tracers.

I stopped the fire. We would wait until they came to us and then perhaps we could do some real damage. The Reds in the paddies were quiet now. Our fire must have had some effect. But then why should they move again until their comrades could give them an assist?

A clucking came from the brush in front of us and the passwords were exchanged. It was the lookout from the peninsula with his messenger. Eleven-thirty already? I looked at my watch. Quarter to twelve. He had a final report to make. Just as they were leaving, they had noticed movement along the beach across the channel. A few minutes later, figures had started out into the channel, and soon many were wading across toward the ferry landing. This gesture wasn't needed to convince me that the Reds intended to have Yonghung-do—and tonight.

Up the beach, the Reds deployed and moved slowly down the sand toward us. We held our fire and laid out a few grenades. I wished they would hurry. Time was getting short, and we would soon be due at Palmi-do. After what seemed ages, they were within a hundred yards and from their actions, very uncertain. I watched closely for scouts. We were well-hidden in a small depression with shrubbery all around. They'd have to step on us to find us.

There was a movement on our right. Probably a scout. We let him pass. Another passed even closer. Then a compact mass of men came within our sights on the scarp and the beach below. "Give it to them, Chae," I whispered, and as he opened up, I started chucking grenades as fast as I could. It was short. They went down like tenpins, and those that didn't scurried for cover under the scarp.

It was all we could do. I placed a grenade on the breech of the gun and we raced away through our familiar camp area. We hadn't gone twenty yards when we heard a high-pitched scream behind us that brought us to a stunned halt. Lim. That was Lim. We both recognized her voice, even in terror. Back we went now, crouching and beating toward the beach from where the scream had come.

We snaked over the scarp. The beach was free of Reds. They'd taken to the high ground in pursuit of us, but a white patch half hung over the scarp ahead. Chae was there before me. It was Lim. Blood covered her face and bare breasts. Her small shoulder jacket had been jerked off in tossing her aside. The side of her head had been caved in by a single blow, probably from a rifle.

"Come, Chae, we must get out of here," I said as gently as possible, but with urgency.

"No, *Taicho-san*, leave me. She must be taken care of. I won't leave her to the Red dogs. I'm going with her." His voice was coarse with passion and hatred.

"You can do nothing, Chae," I said, misunderstanding the implication. "Come. If you wish, we'll take her with us," and I moved forward to pick her up. He brushed me aside and gave me a shove that threw me down the beach. Before I could recover my feet, a jagged explosion rent the air and felled me again. Chae had blown himself to bits with a grenade.

I picked myself up, cursing at the things love made people do, and headed for the mudflat. It was the only way to the promontory now. Slubbing along in a blind rage through the mud, I couldn't shake Lim and Chae from my mind. Lim must have returned again after we'd sent her back. Love—I didn't know she could be that devoted. Now I knew. Of all the lousy luck!

By the time I arrived at the promontory, the Reds were pouring one-twenty mortar fire and everything else they had into the rocks and crags of our defense and were searching out our junks. I was just short of getting blown to pieces by our own people before I could shout the password.

I issued orders to abandon the place at once while Chang covered the rear with the guns on his two raiders. At last we had everybody aboard, and we slipped into a sampan and sculled out to the pompom. Rhee had the old diesel roaring, sparks shooting from the stack ten feet into the air. An excellent beacon for the Red gunners, but the anchor was housed and we were under way immediately. A few stray slugs found their way to us but caused no damage. Rhee set a course for Palmi-do. Off our port quarter, we could see Chang safely away toward the middle passage.

Yonghung-do was in Red hands again, and they had Chae and little Lim, and many, many others known less well to me, but equally brave and determined that Korea should be at last reunited.

Rhee called to me from the pilothouse. "A junk up ahead of us, *Taicho-san*," he said.

I couldn't believe it. Nothing else should happen now. We had only minutes to get to that lighthouse, but he was right. A huge junk, by the dark bulk of it. No masts. "Hail her, Yong," I said.

He did. No response. We came closer. It was a junk barge. A full sixty feet long and twenty feet in the beam. What the devil? At a time like this. I could only think of it being a floating mine set loose on the ebb tide to carry down the channel and blow up the first ship coming through. A fantastic thought, but it was a danger to any ship in the channel, whether it blew up or not, and would certainly upset any skipper who saw it coming down on him in the dark.

"Go alongside it, Rhee," I said. We could take no chances, light or no light.

Yong and I swarmed up the side and turned a flashlight into its cavernous hold. Empty. I gave an uncontrollable sigh of relief. Probably a derelict, broken loose from its moorings at Inchon. There was a towing chock, and I shouted down for a line and made it secure. Then we hopped back aboard the pompom. "Tow her to a current you know will set her on the beach east of the channels," I said to Rhee, and he changed course.

It was 0030 of the fifteenth when we landed on Palmi-do. The light should be in operation right now. We'd promised it. The fleet, twenty miles down the channel, would be starting through without a light, thinking we had failed. We started running and were caught up short by a machine-gun burst at our feet and hit the ground instinctively.

I wasn't thinking straight anymore. What the devil was happening here? Yong was shouting in Korean. He was angry by the tone of his voice—sore clean through. Dully, I remembered our own guard here. Of course, it was our own boys. They hadn't been notified. I had forgotten it. Yong grabbed my arm and we were running again toward the steep path up the hill.

By the time we arrived at the top, my heart was beating like a trip-hammer and I could barely hoist myself up the steel-runged ladder to the light. It was 0050 when we adjusted the vector shade to throw the light down Flying Fish Channel. I felt defeated. Completely defeated. Everything had gone wrong at the last. Good planning would have avoided all this. I opened the small hatch that led out onto the narrow catwalk outside the light and went out.

"Yong," I called back, "will you please have one of the men stay awake and get us up when the first ship comes into sight?" With that, I passed out.

It seemed only seconds later that Yong was shaking me out of the stupor into which I had fallen. He pointed to the waters more than two hundred feet below us, and I raised myself on one elbow and looked over the side of the catwalk.

It was the invasion force. Silently, ghostly, six dark shapes, lean and hungry from this vantage point, were gliding by beneath us. It was like a dream, or a nightmare. I knew those ships. Had served in them. How could they move without noise? But they did. If it weren't for my eyes, I wouldn't believe them to be there.

Slowly, they slid out of sight around the eastern tip of Palmi-do, and their places were taken by others and still others. Finally, the huge shapes of the cruisers loomed up and took their stations. This was the day. This was it. Had we given them enough information? Had it been accurate? A sudden shudder coursed through me. . . . Doubts began to assail me from all sides.

EPILOGUE

GENE CLARK QUICKLY realized that his doubts were a product of his almost total exhaustion. As the sun rose, the United Nations invasion fleet—230 ships from seven navies, plus swarms of LSTs and smaller craft—gathered in the waters around Palmi-do. As Clark and his two Korean partners watched, cruisers, destroyers, and aircraft from two carriers began battering the fortress island of Wolmi-do, the invasion's first objective.

Through his binoculars, Clark spotted USS *Mount McKinley,* which he knew was CHROMITE's flagship. He decided to get aboard her as soon as possible and request help for Yonghung-do. With Yong and Kim, he boarded their flagship—the pompom with the antiquated diesel motor—and headed for the big communications ship. As they approached, Clark climbed on top of the flagship's cabin and waved his hat.

Instead of a warm greeting, he got a roar from a megaphone: "Stand off!" The *McKinley*'s captain was afraid his ship was about to be attacked by some sort of suicide squad. Clark ordered Rhee, the flagship's captain, to cut the engine while an LCVP commanded by an ensign was lowered from the *McKinley*. He cautiously circled Clark's old boat, aiming a submachine gun at him.

"Who the hell are you?" he called.

"I'm Lieutenant Eugene Clark of the United States Navy," Clark shouted back. "Put that gun down before you hurt somebody."

The ensign told the *McKinley*'s captain there was a mysterious navy lieutenant aboard the peculiar-looking Korean scow.

"How do you know?" the captain asked.

"He's got a naval officer's cap on his head."

Clark was permitted to come aboard—and eventually got his Korean partners to safety as well. But all he could do was wave goodbye to Rhee and the owner of the flagship. Clark never saw them again.

Carefully adjusting their timetable to the radical tides, a battalion of the 1st Marine Division's Fifth Regiment stormed Wolmi-do and its smaller companion island of Sowolmi-do at 6:33 A.M. on September 15, capturing both with amazingly light casualties. Not a single Marine was killed; only seventeen were wounded. The machine-gun nests that had lined the shore when Clark and Yong explored it were smoking rubble thanks to the air and sea bombardment. The bigger guns that had ranged on Captain Lee in the PC-703 were also impotent wrecks by the time the Marines hit Wolmi's beaches.

Just after sunset, with the returning tides, the Marines charged into Inchon Harbor. Two battalions of the Fifth Marine regiment headed for the seawall in downtown Inchon, while three battalions of the First Marine Regiment hit the suburban area Clark and Yong had spotted as a likely landing site. A reporter in one of the downtown landing craft said the seawall looked "as high as the RCA building." But thanks to Clark, the Marines knew exactly what they were doing. Their LCVPs had ladders sticking up in their bows ("looking like the antennae of bugs," the same imaginative, and no doubt terrified, reporter thought).

The LCVPs slammed into the wall with their engines wide open, holding them in place against the concrete while Marines scrambled up the ladders. Meanwhile, the Marines on Wolmi poured fire into the buildings beyond the seawall, suppressing any pockets of North Korean resistance. Anticipating the radical tides once more, the high command ordered ten LSTs loaded with ammunition and supplies to remain in the mud at the seawall when the tide ran out, giving the invasion force the logistic backup it needed to sustain the beachhead.

Aboard the *McKinley*, Clark realized he could not alter the invasion's timetable. But on D-day plus one, thanks to his pleas, a battalion of Marines was detached from the main attack to seize Taebu-do and Yonghung-do. The leathernecks blasted their way across both islands, amply revenging Lim, Chae, and the others who had died to help make Inchon possible. Clark was distressed to learn that the Communists had murdered more than fifty people who had helped him but who had refused to take his urgent advice to flee aboard Chang's junks.

Thanks to these loyal Koreans' sacrifices and Clark's information, the invasion of Inchon was a spectacular success. By September 25, the 1st Marine Division was in the outskirts of Seoul, the South Korean capital. Meanwhile, in the Pusan perimeter, General Walton Walker went over to the attack and smashed gaping holes in Kim Il Sung's shaken divisions. With their supply lines cut, the North Korean army disintegrated. Many surrendered; others fled north, a disorganized mob.

Soon, General Douglas MacArthur flew to Seoul to join President Syngman Rhee in proclaiming the restoration of the Republic of South Korea. For his "conspicuous gallantry and intrepidity" in obtaining "vital intelligence information," the Navy awarded Lieutenant Eugene Franklin Clark the Silver Star. The Far Eastern Command added the Legion of Merit for "exceptionally meritorious conduct."

Eugene Clark's adventures in Korea were not over. When the United Nations decided to unify the country and ordered General MacArthur to invade North Korea and advance to the Yalu River boundary with China, Clark was asked to make an island-hopping foray up North Korea's west coast. With a group of 150 South Korean guerillas, including Lieutenant Youn Joung, he headed north to find out where the enemy was laying mines that drifted down the coast into the Inchon area. He also had orders to secure islands that the Navy could use to rescue pilots who had to ditch planes damaged by antiaircraft fire.

Capturing several islands after fierce firefights, Clark interrogated captives and sent agents ashore. Soon he was radioing back useful information about North Korean mining operations. By the end of October, Clark and his band were seizing islands in the mouth of the Yalu River. There, his Korean agents reported an alarming discovery. Large numbers of Chinese Communist troops were crossing the Yalu into Korea. Clark immediately flashed this earthshaking news to headquarters in Tokyo.

The American high command, mesmerized by the success of Inchon, ignored it—with disastrous consequences. Soon confronted by a million Chinese "volunteers," the badly outnumbered UN Army was forced to retreat to South Korea. There, under a new commander, General Matthew Ridgway, they drove the Red Chinese back across the thirty-eighth parallel into North Korea.

For his daring incursion to the Yalu, Gene Clark won the Oak Leaf Cluster in lieu of another Silver Star. Although he vowed he was through with operating behind enemy lines, early in 1951, Clark was persuaded into one more adventure. He escorted Brigadier General Crawford Sams, one of the U.S. Army's top doctors, ashore by night near Communist-held Wonsan to investigate a reported outbreak of bubonic plague. Killing sentries commando-style, Clark's team penetrated a small Chinese Communist hospital, and Dr. Sams soon concluded the disease was a particularly virulent brand of smallpox. The UN command was saved the daunting task of vaccinating their entire army against the plague. For this exploit, Gene Clark won the Navy Cross.

Meanwhile, the war in Korea became a stalemate that was ended by negotiation with the Communist Chinese and Koreans in 1953. Kim Il Sung's attempt to export Communism at the point of a gun thus ended in humiliating failure. An independent prosperous South Korea rapidly became an example of what free enterprise could achieve in Asia, while North Korea remained a stagnant Communist backwater under its monstrous leader.

In 1966, Gene Clark retired from the Navy with the rank of commander and lived quietly in California and Nevada with his wife Enid until his death in 1998, at the age of eight-six. To the end of his long life, he found it deeply satisfying to know that the light of freedom he had ignited on that September morning on Palmi-do was still shining among a brave people he had learned to respect and admire.

Eugene Clark served in the Navy during World War II, and after the war, among other assignments, was attached to General Douglas MacArthur's G-2 (intelligence) staff in Tokyo. He was there when the Korean War began, and was approached for the Inchon mission. For his role in the invasion, he won the Silver Star, and the Far Eastern Command added the Legion of Merit for "exceptionally meritorious conduct." Later missions resulted in an Oak Leaf Cluster and the Navy Cross. Clark died in 1998, after retiring from the Navy in 1966 with the rank of commander.

Thomas Fleming is the author of forty books, including *The New Dealers' War, Duel, Liberty! The American Revolution*, and the bestselling novel *Officers' Wives*. He lives in New York City.